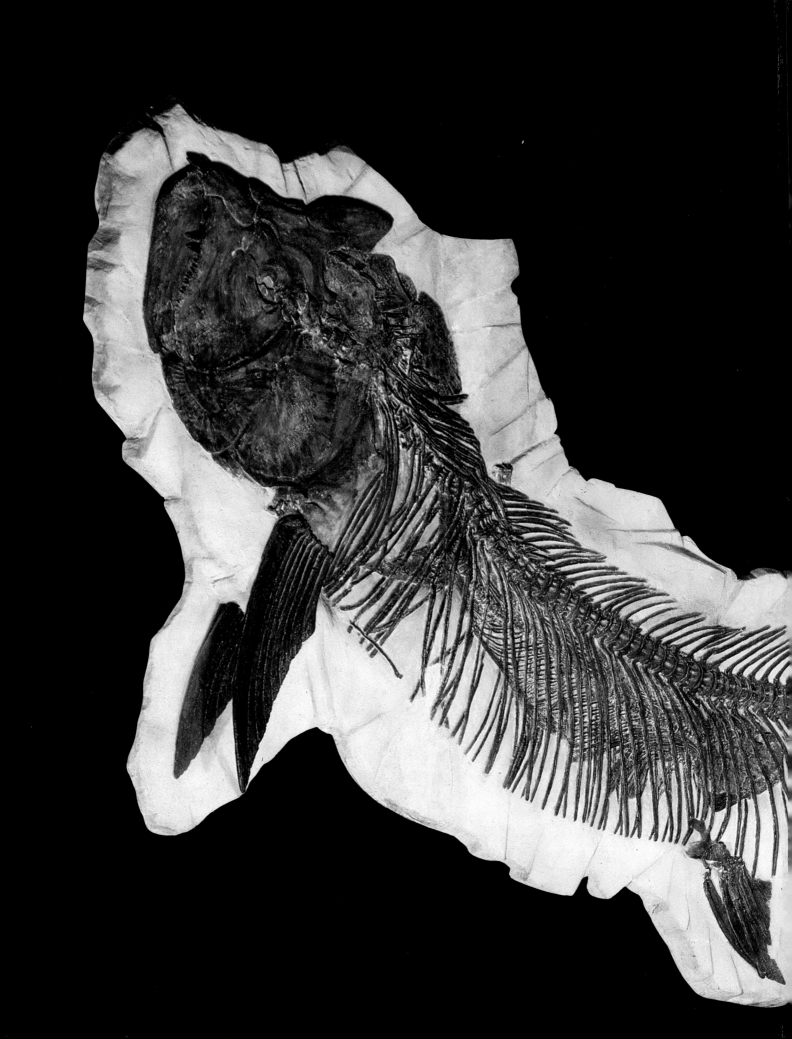

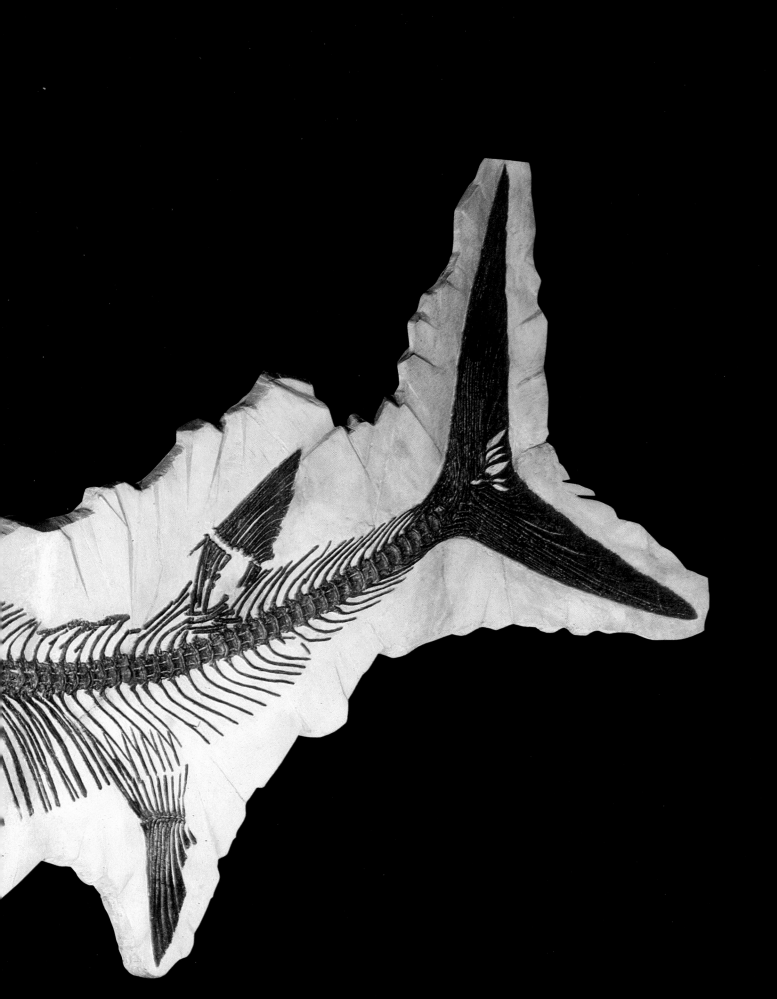

THREAD

The Smithsonian
Looks at Evolution

OF LIFE

By Roger Lewin

Smithsonian Books
Washington, D.C.

Distributed by
W.W. Norton & Company
New York, N.Y.

Page 1, king penguins congregate on bleak South Atlantic isle; 2-3, swallowed almost whole some 65-80 million years ago, four-foot Ananogmius *lies within body cavity of* Xiphactinus; *4-5, cineraria in bloom; above, frogs and toads hint at extraordinary diversity to be found in class Amphibia alone; 10-11, sea hare releases ink from openings in its mantle; 12, three-horned chameleon in sleeping posture.*

The Smithsonian Institution
Secretary S. Dillon Ripley
Assistant Secretary, Public Service
  Julian T. Euell
Director, Smithsonian Institution Press
  Felix C. Lowe

Smithsonian Books
Director Glen B. Ruh
Senior Editor Alexis Doster III
Editors Joe Goodwin, Patricia Gallagher
Assistant Editor Amy Donovan
Picture Editor Nancy Strader
Assistant Picture Editor Patricia Upchurch
Picture Research Frances C. Rowsell
Copy Editor Bettie Loux Donley
Editorial Research Elizabeth L. Parker
Assistant Researchers Heidi Hughes,
  Jeffrey T. Yorke
Production Consultant Irv Garfield
Production Assistant June G. Armstrong
Business Administrator Janet Woodward
Business Assistant Therese Gates
Marketing Coordinator Margaret K. Mooney
Marketing Consultant William H. Kelty
Design Direction Komai, Watermark Design

First Edition
5   4   3   2   1

Printed and Bound in U.S.A.

Library of Congress Cataloging in Publication Data

Lewin, Roger.
  Thread of life.

  Includes index.
  1. Evolution. I. Smithsonian Institution.
II. Title.
QH366.2.L48 1982   575   82-16834
ISBN 0-89599-010-5

CONTENTS

INTRODUCTION

Charles Darwin died 100 years ago this year, and yet the science of evolutionary biology is more robust, more vigorous, and more stimulating than ever before. These truly are exciting times for scholars and for anyone interested in the beauty and wonder of life on Earth.

Evolutionary biology used to be the sole province of naturalists and fossil hunters, but now a vast range of scientific disciplines is involved in a common pursuit—an understanding of the origin and nature of the living world. Some people recoil from such a goal, thinking that knowledge of nature will somehow diminish its beauty, its wonder. This surely is faint-hearted, as knowledge itself is a precious gift to Mankind, and an insight into the intricacies of organisms and their history enhances, rather than detracts from, our respect for and delight in what we see.

The range of scientific disciplines now engaged on the broad front of research in evolutionary biology, joined most recently and in spectacularly promising fashion by molecular biology, demonstrates how pervasive is the domain of evolution. Few sciences remain untouched by it, and for biology it is a ramifying and governing principle. One remarkable conclusion from the great volume of diverse research activity of recent times is that the core of evolutionary biology, as shaped by Darwin's own ideas, has been shown to be sound again and again.

Science progresses by the constant sharpening of ideas one against the other, while diligent observation provides a means of structuring those ideas. And the more fertile a science is, the more audible will be the clash of opposing views. Unfortunately, the vigorous debate currently experienced in the world of evolutionary biology has been wrongly interpreted by some as an indication that evolutionary ideas are invalid. Nothing could be further from the truth.

Any book about science, but particularly one about evolution, can only be an interim statement, an up-to-the-minute story of the unfolding of ideas and knowledge. The general corpus of evidence attests to the fact of evolution; of that there can be no doubt. And the broad lines of explanation are firmly established in numerous respects too. But there is still much to be determined. The intellectual journey initiated by Darwin promises now and for generations to come a rich reward of discoveries, some of which will confirm and extend what we already suspect, while others will surprise and astonish us. What follows in this book, therefore, is not a description of a final destination, but is in many ways a signpost to future discovery.

Ernst Mayr

Ernst Mayr
Museum of Comparative Zoology
Harvard University
August 1982

DIVERSITY, CONTINUITY, AND CHANGE

TIME AND THE ROCKS

Part of the fossil record yielded up by the walls of the Grand Canyon, ancient vertebrate footprints busily track across rock from Supai formation.

Today's world is populated with at least three million species of living things. Most are insects, a large proportion are plants, some 8,600 are birds, and only 4,000 are mammals. The organisms around us are, however, merely the most recent manifestation of life forms whose lineages stretch far back through the Earth's long history. Indeed, 99 percent of all species that have ever lived are now extinct. Just as 10 million years ago most contemporary species had yet to appear, so in 10 million years' time most of today's actors will have been replaced by a new cast. To be sure, many of the new species will occupy niches—ecological communities—similar to today's, but they may look different and do things differently, too. Time and change: these are the themes of life.

And where better to grasp in one panoramic sweep the reality of time and change but on the rim of the Grand Canyon, the world's greatest geological gash? If you stand atop the famous Mather Point and peer down to the Colorado River a precipitous mile below, you are effectively looking back through almost two billion years of Earth's history. Layer upon layer of sediment was deposited here through the passing eons, eventually building up a vast layer cake of time. You can see the stack of strata before you in the canyon walls, carved into baroque patterns by the persistently gnawing agents of erosion.

Entombed in these strata are the petrified remains of creatures that thrived in the past but are now extinct; they are the cast of time and change. The record of the past is, however, incomplete in

Journeying through space and time, travelers snake their way up the Grand Canyon's Kaibab Trail, past layers of rock containing fossils that represent some two billion years of Earth's history. Overleaf, panoramic view of the Grand Canyon from Desert View captures the immensity of this vast mile-deep gorge, carved through ancient sediments by the Colorado River over the past six to ten million years. Page 15, Mene rhombeus, a beautifully preserved 50-million-year-old fossil fish from Bolca, Italy.

18

many places: at times geological conditions simply weren't appropriate for the accumulation of sediments. It is as if you are looking at a book missing some of its pages. Nevertheless, the story revealed by the Colorado River as it sliced through these ancient sediments is striking. A journey beginning in the floor of the canyon and making its way to the rim revisits in a day an odyssey of life's unfolding that passed in two billion years.

In some of the oldest canyon rocks there are glimpses of bacteria and ancient colonies of blue-green algae, a simple form of life that nonetheless was one of the most important on Earth until almost 600 million years ago. Some of the oldest fossils in the canyon are to be found in the massive Tonto Platform that dominates much of the eastern part of Grand Canyon. A mule track crosses these ancient rocks, and the lucky traveler might chance to see a fossilized trilobite, a small, delicately armored creature that scurried over the shallow sea floor some 500 million years ago. Trilobites were arthropods, the group of spineless animals to which today's crabs, insects, spiders, scorpions, millipedes, and other "jointed-limb" creatures belong. They flourished in the oceans for several hundred million years until all their number fell into extinction some 200 million years ago.

The deposits of the Tonto Platform, particularly the Bright Angel shale, contain remains of other marine life of the era. They were, as a group, diverse but relatively simple, and all lacked backbones. It is only higher up in the canyon wall—about an hour on the back of a mule, but some hundreds of millions of years later in history—that animals with backbones enter the scene. Here in the great Redwall limestones are countless entombed skeletons of strange-looking fish, together with the inevitable trilobites and many other marine invertebrates. This 500-foot layer of red-stained limestone records the history of shallow-sea life over some 25 million years.

Still higher in the sequence, in the terra cotta-colored rocks of the Supai formation, are the first signs of land animals—tracks that look for all the world as if they have just been made by a small, short-legged, low-slung animal. These tracks date back to perhaps 300 million years ago. The first reptile fossils in the area come from the soft silt deposits of the 200-million-year-old Chinle forma-

Fragments of 190-million-year-old logs in Arizona's Petrified Forest National Park glow with pearly colors; mineral-laden water in once-marshy burial grounds seeped into the wood, replacing organic material with semi-precious stone.

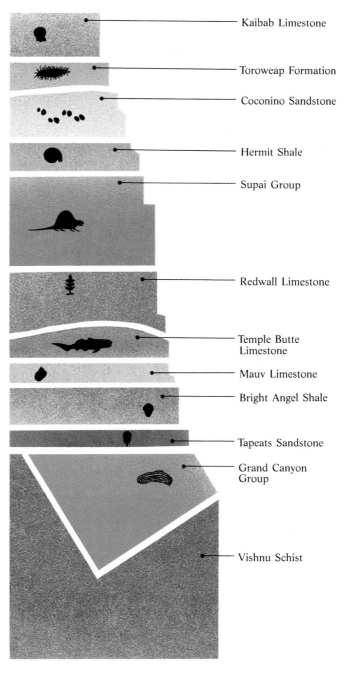

A Slice Through the Grand Canyon

- Kaibab Limestone
- Toroweap Formation
- Coconino Sandstone
- Hermit Shale
- Supai Group
- Redwall Limestone
- Temple Butte Limestone
- Mauv Limestone
- Bright Angel Shale
- Tapeats Sandstone
- Grand Canyon Group
- Vishnu Schist

Smithsonian paleobiologist Porter Kier examines a modern sea urchin, an echinoderm whose ancestors appeared some 500 million years ago.

Studying and cataloging fossils from collections around the world, Kier finds dramatic evidence of evolutionary change in some species of sea urchins. Left, a 140-million-year-old fossil sea urchin with spines preserved.

tion, the extensive erosion of which has resulted in the exotic terrain of the nearby Painted Desert. More advanced fish fossils are to be unearthed in the Grand Canyon too, along with plants preserved in the layer cake of time. Ferns and other primitive forms are to be found in the older rocks laid down around 300 million years ago. Time and change: the progression continues.

Though the story of life's history runs coherently through many hundreds of millions of years, the more recent history of the Grand Canyon, including the age of the dinosaurs and the rise of the mammals, is not recorded. Either erosion has removed the layers, or sedimentation simply wasn't taking place at that time in the region through which the Grand Canyon now slices. Nevertheless, the story revealed in the walls of the canyon is powerful testimony to the steady coherence of time and change. Nowhere do you find fossils out of place: you don't see amphibians among the earliest trilobites in the Bright Angel shale, you don't come across traces of reptiles side by side with the first amphibians, and you never see fossils of mammals with those of the earliest reptiles.

"This strict segregation or progression of fossils is found in rocks throughout the world," says Smithsonian scientist Porter Kier. "Every time you go to look at fossil-bearing deposits you are testing that observation. If someone were to find a mammal fossil in rocks of 500 million years ago, that would throw everything that evolutionary biologists now believe up into the air," he says. "So far, nobody has. Nobody has found a fossil that is out of place in the sediments, anywhere."

A paleobiologist at the National Museum of Natural History, Kier is a proficient sailor and skin diver. He is also an expert on sea urchins, both the living varieties and the ones whose fossils stretch

Diving in warm waters off Belize in Central America, Kier collects modern sea urchins for study and comparison with ancient forms while monitoring the reef's echinoderm population and distribution.

back several hundred million years into biological history. Some years ago, he decided he would collect data on as many fossil species as he could find from about 220 million years ago toward the present. "Some of the information was available in scientific papers and books," he recalls, "but for the rest I had to go to museums all over the world to make my own drawings of the shapes and body patterns of the different species." Kier's aim was to lay out identification cards for each of roughly 300 sea urchin species according to their age in the geological record. "No one had done this sort of thing before, so I didn't know what to expect."

What Kier saw was the emergence of a whole new way of "making a living" as a sea urchin. Before 170 million years ago, all sea urchins grazed on the rich food resources that abounded on the surface of the sea floor. After that time there arose, in addition, a large group of species that spent their

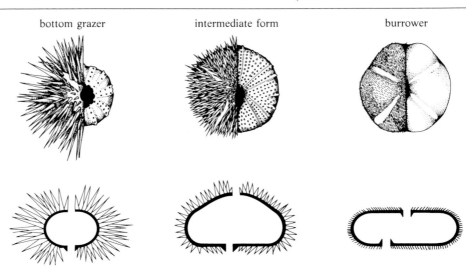

Modification in sea urchin body structure and spines marks emergence of sediment burrowers among animals that existed for millions of years as bottom grazers.

bottom grazer   intermediate form   burrower

Smithsonian lepidopterist John Burns checks on some of the approximately four million specimens—chiefly moths and butterflies—in the Lepidoptera collection at the National Museum of Natural History, above. Colorful array of beetles, left, hints at the diversity to be found in the Institution's—and the world's—myriad specimens.

time burrowing in the fertile sediments on the sea floor. The grazers were regularly shaped domes covered with long spines. The burrowers were elongated with short spines. Scientists, of course, knew that a group of irregularly shaped burrowing sea urchins had arisen at this time in history. But until Kier's investigation, no one had seen how the features of the ancestral species had changed in a step-by-step fashion to give rise to an entirely different type of animal.

The grazing species have a large tooth-lined mouth on the bottom surface and a small anus directly on top of the dome. Such an arrangement, while perfectly suited to a grazing way of life, is poorly adapted for burrowing in fine sediments. Not only would the long spines impede progress in burrowing, but the arrangement of mouth and anus would be inefficient in dealing with sediment feeding. "What happened," explains Kier, "was that the spines shrank, the body flattened somewhat and became elongated, the mouth lost its teeth and shifted to the front end, and the anus shifted toward the rear." This new arrangement works well in a burrower that has to pass sediments through its body, sort out nutrients, and dispose of large quantities of excreta.

Surrounded by his array of sea urchin portraits, Kier was hit by the kind of insight that all scientists hope for but few experience. "I saw a great swath of evolutionary change," he says. "A whole suite of characters had undergone a rapid and co-ordinated shift about 170 million years ago. It was dramatic. It was one of the great days in my life.

"This is a tremendously exciting story of evolution," says Kier, "because you can see how the changes built up and how it was all related to the demands of a new way of living." At least as important as the remarkable documentation of this complex and unexpected array of changes was the recognition of the rate at which it all happened. "The shift occurred in just a couple of million years. I was astonished when I realized this. It was so fast for such enormous changes."

Kier's investigations give him a perspective of time and change, of a dynamic in life's history. For him and for others who study the countless fossils that are scattered through the Earth's geological strata, life manifests a compelling diversity through time. The shift from a time in which the seas had only bottom-feeding sea urchins to a later period when both bottom feeders and burrowers existed represents a pattern of change that is written large and often in the rock-bound archives of past life.

Most of us are aware only of the diversity of living things around us now. But what a diversity it is. Even the most urbanized city dweller is forced to be aware of nature, if only in the form of the myriad creatures that might infest his home as "pests." But a wider view of the natural world readily absorbs an irresistible impression of the multitude of forms. As ecologist Paul Colinvaux has written: "There is really nothing else so odd about life as its variety."

Virtually every part of every land is occupied by life in some form. The seashore, for instance, is a kaleidoscope of life—plant and animal, large and small. It is, as anyone knows who has sat long enough and quietly observed, also a battleground. Eat and be eaten: it is the dynamic of the seashore equation. Just offshore might be a coral reef, the richest community of organisms living anywhere in the ocean. "The interaction of growth and erosion

gives the reef an open and cavernous fabric that in an ecological sense is almost infinitely stratified and subdivided," writes Norman Newell, a paleontologist at the American Museum of Natural History in New York. The reef is a complex web of life in which each individual seeks to survive and reproduce. Yet the survival of some depends inescapably on the premature death of others.

On land the tropical rain forest is the closest equivalent to the teeming life of the coral reef. Its infinitely stratified niches sustain an almost infinite variety of organisms, from the fruit-eating monkeys in the treetops to the armies of termites on the forest floor. The forest's fecund environment is obvious enough, as is the more modest productivity of the grassland savanna. But even the seemingly unpromising upper one-inch layer of soil over an acre near any city will yield perhaps a million crawling, squirming, running creatures and

Dozens of epiphytes—air plants—reach for the sun on a single tree limb in Costa Rican rain forest. Such forests nurture a vast variety of life in their vertically stratified niches. Fecund and stable, the coral reef, above right, is another finely balanced assemblage of life in competition.

Death at the boundary of sea and land: a ghost crab catches a newly hatched green sea turtle during its frantic dash to the sea.

upwards of two million spores and seeds. If variety is life's oddest feature, then its abundance must run a close second. Each step—from large forms such as humans, antelopes, and lions, to smaller ones such as rabbits, rats, and mice, to still smaller beetles, ants, and termites, and finally to microscopic bacteria and algae—takes one down a pyramid of escalating numbers. The diversity of species and the number of individuals in each species leap at each size interval. There are, for instance, a million insects on this Earth for every living human.

Life's variety of form is matched by its versatility in adapting to varied environments. From the extraordinary denizens of the ocean depths to the stunted plants high in the mountains, life manifests itself in some form. A plant called tillandsia survives in the arid and otherwise lifeless sands of the coastal desert of Peru, sustaining itself on wisps of fog, virtually the only source of moisture.

Animals and plants have equipped themselves to combat the demands of some of the most extreme environments on Earth. Some Antarctic fish, for instance, have a natural antifreeze running through their veins, enabling them to thrive where others would perish. Some plants possess such extraordinary biochemistry that they are able to tolerate and flourish in the toxic habitat of mineral tailings. But the organisms most skilled at living where life would seem to be impossible are bacteria and algae. Colonies of algae make a collective living under thick ice in Antarctic lakes. And primitive bacteria thrive in the hot sulphurous pools of Yellowstone National Park. Their ability to adapt in many ways carries echoes of earlier times in Earth's history when conditions were very different from today's.

Reproduction is a key preoccupation of all organisms. Failure to reproduce obviously means no progeny, and an epidemic of such failures can doom a species to extinction. Once again, the ways of going about the business of reproduction are legion. It is not simply that some creatures lay eggs while others give birth to live young, or that some plants have spores and others seeds—it is something more basic than that. For instance, a salmon may lay 28 million eggs in one season, a figure that is topped fourfold by the even more profligate oyster. The result of this prodigality, both for salmon and oyster, is that reproducing individuals just replace themselves in the population, and no more. Which is just as well, because if all the potential offspring of an oyster escaped being eaten and developed successfully to maturity, and all their progeny were to be equally blessed for a mere five generations, an oyster mountain would accumulate that would be eight times as large as the Earth.

The opposite extreme in reproductive strategy is to have just one or two offspring which are then carefully nurtured through the hazards of infancy. Parental care thus gives the maximum possibility of offspring surviving to adulthood. The most extreme example of this design is ourselves. Among the myriad forms of life, all stages in between these two strategies are to be found somewhere.

Far from being just another option in the spectrum of reproductive profligacy, parental care has important corollaries. Most obvious is the opportu-

Tiny footprints in the sands of southwestern Africa's Namib Desert: the dune beetle and other unidentified insects survive one of Earth's harshest environments.

nity to learn in the secure confines of a social unit. A vervet monkey infant must learn, for instance, which foods are good to eat and which should be avoided, and when and where such foods are available throughout the year. Learning has, of course, been taken to stratospheric heights in humans, whose life is pretty much artificially created and therefore must be learned; this is called culture. On the other hand, a salmon fry has no opportunity to learn from its parents, and so the possibilities in a salmon's life are closely constrained. In order to be able to exercise options, you have to be able to learn what the possibilities are.

So, life's diversity extends through physical form, to the tactics of reproduction, to behavior. But just as one might marvel at the variety of it all, the things that make each species separate from another, so is the coherence of it awe-inspiring. There is a coherence in the relationship between organisms at two levels. First, in their interdepend-

Six-foot red-tipped tubeworms, below, thrive in the sunless habitat of extreme depths 8,000 feet down in the Galapagos Rift, off Ecuador. The food chain in the rift area depends entirely on minerals streaming from hot-water vents in the sea bottom, rather than on photosynthesis.

Sparring male ibex, above, exhibit agility and sure-footedness that make them at home in rugged mountain ranges of Asia, southern Europe, and northeast Africa.

Amaumau ferns, left, invade land newly created by a lava flow in Hawaii Volcanoes National Park.

Reproductive strategies range from intensive care of young to no parental care at all. Snow monkeys both tend and teach their usually single offspring; untended strands of toad eggs, right, produce many tadpoles, few of which will survive to maturity. Opposite, ostrich adults patrol flanks as fledglings stroll across African savanna.

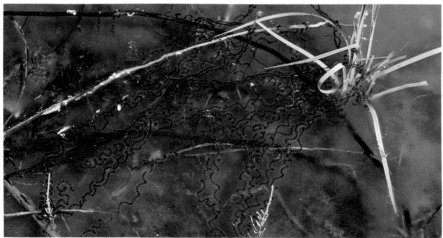

ence. Colinvaux writes of this: "The ordered array of trees in a temperate forest, the understory bushes in their proper places, the carpet of flowers that blooms in the spring before the trees have spread their leaves, the saplings awaiting their turn in the canopy, the animals eating leaves, spreading pollen, and hoarding nuts, the fiercer animals hunting the first lot down and checking their depredations, the soil underfoot where decomposing remnants of life are stirred by other animals and made to give back their raw materials to be used again by the forest—how well this ecosystem works!"

How well indeed. There is an order and a harmony in nature that has for centuries drawn the respect and admiration of naturalists. Each species has its niche, for which it is appropriately equipped in structure and habits. And each niche is inseparable from all others around it. It is the business of biology to explain the origin of nature's order and harmony. How is it that a termite colony operates with such clipped precision in constructing its grand architecture and in pursuing its complex social interactions? How is it that the lion and the antelope coexist in balanced relationship? How did the human hand achieve its dexterity, the eagle's eye its keen sight, the porpoise its sleek hydrodynamic shape? Such are the questions faced by evolutionary biology.

The second level of coherence in the relationship between organisms is in their biological heritage. Anyone can look around the living world and mentally assign the creatures he sees to various groups: those that have backbones and those that don't, for instance; those that swim in the sea rather than fly in the air—and so on. Biologists have a system called taxonomy for classifying living organisms, depending on an array of specific char-

acteristics the organisms display. The classification goes from the very general to the very specific, like the reverse of an address on an envelope.

A *kingdom* is the largest classification group, and for a long time biologists were content to assign living organisms to either the plant kingdom or the animal kingdom. However, there were problem organisms that refused to fit neatly into one category or the other, particularly among single-celled organisms. Now a new five-kingdom system is gaining favor, and it has the benefit of reflecting both evolutionary history and complexity as we see it in the world.

The first and lowliest kingdom is the Monera, into which go all bacteria and blue-green algae. Although some of these organisms possess pigments to trap the sun's energy (as plants do) while others do not, all share the same simple cellular structure. The next kingdom, the Protoctista, is also populated by single-celled organisms, but their cellular structure is more advanced, with a greater diversity and complexity of structure than those of the Monera. The third step up this ladder of increasing complexity brings us to multicellular organisms, of which there are three kingdoms: Fungi, and our old friends Plantae and Animalia.

As Stephen Jay Gould of Harvard's Museum of Comparative Zoology points out, the rise in basic complexity as one passes through these three levels is accompanied by a rise in diversity of types within kingdoms. "Increasing complexity of design begets more opportunity for variation upon it," he comments.

Immediately below the level of the kingdom in the business of classification is the *phylum*. This describes the organism's basic architecture or plan: for instance, all animals with backbones form a phylum. But all this quickly rises to levels of esoterica of interest only to taxonomic specialists. A quick run through the classification pedigree of our closest relative, the chimpanzee, will illustrate the general system.

Chimps are, of course, animals and so belong in the kingdom Animalia. Their backbones qualify them for membership in the phylum Chordata. As they suckle their young, are warm-blooded, and have hair, they are described as mammals, the *class* Mammalia. Chimps share the *order* Primates with other apes, monkeys, lemurs and their like, and humans: we all have flexible fingers, good vision, and relatively large brains. At the level of the *family,* chimps part company with the lemurs and their type, the monkeys and lesser apes. They share the family Pongidae with the gibbons, orangutans, and gorillas. The *genus* and *species* that formally describes the intelligent and mischievous animal with which most of us are familiar at the zoo is *Pan troglodytes.* (We humans, incidentally, share our family, Hominidae, with no other. Our genus and species is *Homo sapiens,* meaning wise man.)

This classificatory panorama of life gives the strong impression of relatedness of form and descent within groups. All modern primates, for instance, derive from a single ancestral primate. In recent years biologists' assumptions about relatedness within and between groups based on physical appearance have been dramatically underscored by a penetrating perspective from the molecular level. First of all, geneticists began to study the structure of animals' proteins, and it turned out that those species that appeared by their physical characteristics to be closely related also had closely similar protein structures. And the structure of proteins in distantly related species reflected that distance at the molecular level, all of which was highly gratifying to evolutionary biologists. Now, using information from certain genes (the basic unit of genetic information), it is possible to trace the relatedness of a group of animals without ever seeing them in the flesh, simply by performing the requisite laboratory tests on, say, bone marrow from each of the species involved.

From these molecular clues to links with other species, and from all of the other evidence of evolution, both fossilized and alive, scientists of many disciplines have pieced together a record of a billions-of-years-old process of trial and error, of success and failure, of adaptation and diversification, and above all, of continuity and change— the thread of life. Though many pieces are missing, the record is remarkably consistent, and the rare inconsistencies—exceptions to the expected—

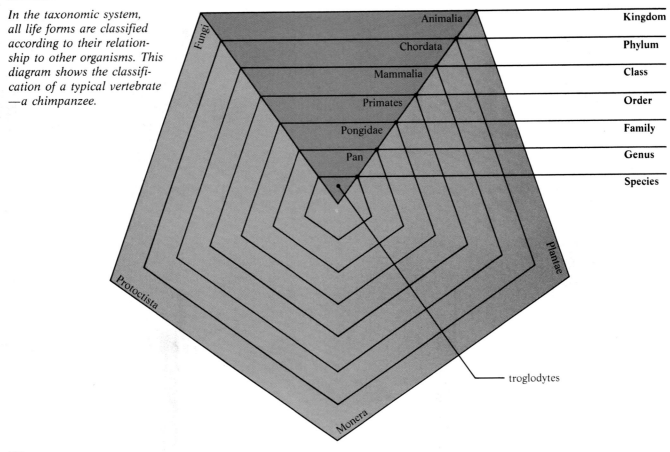

In the taxonomic system, all life forms are classified according to their relationship to other organisms. This diagram shows the classification of a typical vertebrate —a chimpanzee.

Kingdom	Animalia
Phylum	Chordata
Class	Mammalia
Order	Primates
Family	Pongidae
Genus	Pan
Species	troglodytes

Fungi · Protoctista · Monera · Plantae

tend to be more exciting than troubling.

Niles Eldredge, curator of invertebrates at the American Museum of Natural History, New York, and a prominent evolutionary biologist, recently thought he had come across an exception that would have brought the whole geological timetable of Central America tumbling to the ground. He received a letter from Alfonso Segura Paguaga, a geologist living in Costa Rica. Paguaga had in his collection a trilobite of a type that had lived some 400 million years ago. As Eldredge is a world authority on these creatures, Paguaga contacted him in New York. The puzzle was that in Costa Rica there are no rock exposures anywhere near 400 million years old. "I was flabbergasted," wrote Eldredge of his feelings when he eventually saw the fossil. "There before me lay a typical example of *Metacryphaeus tuberculatus*—a very common trilobite, indeed, but one known only from southern Peru and Bolivia." How could this be explained? "A radically new view of shifting fragments of continental plates colliding to form portions of Central America started to take shape in my mind," explained Eldredge. A find as unusual as this would demand an unusual explanation, a throwing out of previously held notions.

While Eldredge was trying to reconstruct sci-ence around this incongruous piece of evidence, he asked Paguaga to find out exactly where the rogue fossil had been found. Paguaga had been given it by a small boy and had not picked it out of solid sediments himself. It turned out, after some heroic detective work, that an old Indian had sold the fossil to an American just before he left Bolivia to go to live in Costa Rica. Not long after the American arrived in Costa Rica he had a minor car accident, and the fossil was lost. Along came the small boy who saw the fossil, picked it up, and later gave it to Paguaga, because he knew Paguaga was interested in such things.

"Of the thousands of Andean fossils in my office," said Eldredge, "none has taken a more circuitous route from the mountains of Bolivia to our labs in New York." Eldredge would have liked nothing more than to have been able to shake up his colleagues. All scientists would. But it was not to be. "The true stuff of sciences remains the sure and steady checking of ideas against worldly realities," he wrote of the episode. That peripatetic trilobite eventually was seen to fit in neatly with the worldwide repeated pattern of time and change in the fossil record. Life's pervasive harmony had not been violated, and the foundations of evolutionary biology remained unshaken.

Baby chimpanzee watches intently as mother uses tool to probe tree for termites. Chimps and man share the order Primates.

DARWIN AND THE *ORIGIN*

A scarlet-clawed Sally Light-foot crab feeds on algae along the volcanic shoreline of a Galapagos island.

Charles Darwin was 22 when he boarded H.M.S. *Beagle* at Devonport, southern England, on December 27, 1831. Ahead of him lay a five-year circumnavigation of the world. This upper-middle-class Englishman, a recent graduate in theology, Euclid, and the classics from Cambridge University, had every intention of complying with his father's wishes and becoming a minister on his return. His role on the voyage would be twofold: as gentleman companion to the ship's captain, Robert FitzRoy, a man of a powerful, obdurate, and irascible personality who traced his ancestry back to Charles II; and as naturalist, such a pastime being common among clergymen of that era.

At the end of the *Beagle*'s long voyage, FitzRoy had completed his Admiralty-assigned task of charting some of the commercially important but little-known waters of the southern continents, a task he pursued with relentless and sometimes irrational commitment. Darwin, meanwhile, had overcome the torment of seasickness, illness, and hardship in remote corners of the globe, and had patiently ridden out the buffeting of his autocratic captain's unpredictable and fiery temper. The five-year adventure had also seeded important doubts in the young naturalist's mind, doubts about the true nature of the physical and biological world around him.

Darwin never went into the church. Instead, a consuming curiosity drove him to explore natural phenomena such as the formation of coral reefs, the intricate and puzzling structure of orchid flowers, and the variety of emotional expression in humans and animals. He strove to become familiar with and to understand the whole of nature.

When, on November 24, 1859, Darwin published his most famous book, *On The Origin of Species by Means of Natural Selection*, the world

Reconstruction of H.M.S. Beagle *sails off Tierra del Fuego, retracing for BBC television the famous voyage during which Charles Darwin amassed evidence of evolution.*

learned of the fruits of more than two decades of deliberation. Darwin described overwhelming evidence in support of what many scientists of the age suspected but which conventional wisdom had not yet embraced: that over long periods of time species of animals and plants may change, eventually to give rise to new species. More important than demonstrating the fact of evolution, however, the *Origin* also offered a mechanism by which change comes about—natural selection.

Darwin described his book as being "one long argument." As it turned out, the argument contained in *Origin* proved to be one of tremendous persuasive power, for it stands as a landmark among the profound intellectual revolutions of the Christian era.

Darwin was attacked by those whose conceptions of Mankind's relationship to nature—whether spiritual or secular—were threatened by his ideas. But Darwin saw nothing implicit in natural selection that could be regarded as belittling humanity. Instead, as he wrote in the closing paragraph of the *Origin*, he saw a ". . . grandeur in this view of life."

The world into which Darwin was born in 1809 was one in which the mainstream of intellectual tradition conceived of living things as fixed, unchanging, unchangeable products of Creation. And the world that was their home was a relatively recent product of Creation, too.

The notion of the evolution—or the transmutation—of species was, however, not new with Charles Darwin. His own grandfather, Erasmus Darwin, had written extensively in prose and poetry of transmutation. In many ways he had touched on almost all the important ideas that were to form the complex fabric of the subject. He was a well known and respected figure, a great intellectual stimulus to other thinkers. One twist of irony that fate seems so fond of perpetrating is that, triggered by Erasmus' writings, Thomas Malthus developed his classic *Essay on Population*, a work which was to be so vital in setting Charles on the track of his mechanism for evolution, that of natural selection.

It is clear that talk of evolution was very much in the air, even as early as the birth of Charles Darwin. The Darwinian revolution had a long and vigorously smoldering fuse.

The framework of the natural sciences in Darwin's Victorian era had been erected initially very much according to the teachings of Christian dogma. Working with information adduced from

Portrait of Charles Darwin shows him soon after his marriage to his cousin, Emma Wedgwood, on January 29, 1839, some two years after his return from the voyage of the Beagle.

the Old Testament, James Ussher, Archbishop of Armagh, Ireland, had calculated in the 17th century that the precise date of the Creation was 4004 B.C., a date that put a maximum age of the Earth at a little under 6,000 years. Ussher's pronouncement held good for a time, but with the increasing interest in geology, a popular pursuit among men of the church, evidence gradually accumulated that sat uncomfortably with this traditional view. The stratified nature of rocks seemed to speak of events of a bygone age that perhaps no longer applied. And the discovery of the petrified remains of creatures that no longer existed demanded a different, more complex explanation. The diluvial theory was advanced, accounting for fossils as the victims of Noah's Flood.

As more and more fossils were unearthed, so the diluvial theory in its turn came under pressure. It became evident that the rocks contained not one population of animals that had apparently been wiped out, but successive groups, each clearly related to the next through time, but each distinctly different. The outstanding French geologist, naturalist, paleontologist, and member of the Academie des Sciences, Baron Georges Cuvier, came to the rescue of orthodox Christianity by developing the catastrophe theory, which postulated successive creations separated by cataclysmic annihilations. Catastrophism held that the great physical features of the world—the mountain ranges, the valleys, the vast plains and the deep oceans—were sculpted in instantaneous paroxymal events. The Earth had passed through repeated bouts of unimaginable violence powered by forces unknown in the present, but now all was calm, the end of a grand progressive plan having been reached with the emergence of Mankind.

By the time that catastrophism was at its height, the cumulative effect of the clergymen's geological hammers had seriously eroded the foundation of Ussher's age of the Earth. The French naturalist Comte de Buffon published in 1749 a revised estimate of about 70,000 years for the Earth's antiquity, and in private he entertained figures almost 10 times as great. Half a dozen years later Immanuel Kant wrote in terms of many millions of years in his *Cosmogony*. Thus, there was time enough for the successive waves of destruction and creation that catastrophism envisioned.

The Earth's geological history is the backdrop against which life's drama is played out, and as long as this was thought to be a succession of cataclysms there was simply no conceptual room for biological change through evolutionary processes. The replacement of the catastrophe theory by a theory of geological processes that would eventually accommodate evolutionary change was a slow transformation, beginning as it did in the last quarter of the 18th century and culminating at the end of the first quarter of the 19th. The acceptance of the new theory, known as uniformitarianism, was an essential precursor to the success of any evolutionary theory.

Uniformitarianism was conceived and nurtured by James Hutton (1726–1797), an imaginative and resolute Scottish doctor and naturalist. Hutton was a member of a small group of thinkers, the Oyster Club, which included Joseph Black, the chemist, and notably Adam Smith, the economist whose writings on social and economic theory were later to have a profound effect on Charles Darwin, giving him ideas that he would transfer to the biological arena. Hutton took his colleagues to see the rocks along the Scottish coast. Each successive rock formation, argued Hutton, appeared to have its origins in yet older formations.

Hutton's view was that the physical process we see around us today—scouring waves, wind and rain, and the occasional subterranean rumblings—are the self-same process that shaped the world in the past. No cataclysmic buckling of the Earth's crust, no boiling seas and gigantic tidal waves, no unimaginable forces of unmeasurable power. Simply the long accumulation of small changes over vast tracts of time.

The scientific world, it seemed, was not yet ready for Hutton's ideas, for within a decade of his death in 1797 the prevailing wisdom was being led by Robert Jameson, whose teachings were much more in line with the classic biblical timescale. However, the march of the Industrial Revolution, with its ever-growing appetite for new and more minerals and its need for roads and canals, raised activity in the geological sciences to a new pitch. Eventually the acceptance of Hutton's ideas was inescapable.

As with all great scientific advances, the final triumph of uniformitarianism depended on presentation of the ideas in cogent form at the right time. For this new view of the world's history, the credit rests with Sir Charles Lyell, a Scottish lawyer turned geologist who was born in the year of Hutton's death. His *Principles of Geology* in three volumes—the first of which was published in 1830—was to lay the foundations for much of the modern science of geology.

Lyell is justly remembered for presenting the case for gradual geological change so forcefully that it quickly gained wide acceptance. It is less well remembered, however, that the *Principles* contained the proposition that conditions on the Earth have been fundamentally the same since its formation, that observed change is part of a great cycle. Given sufficient time, the cycle begins again and passes through the same phases. Ironically, although uniformitarianism laid the basis for the eventual acceptance of evolution as proposed by Darwin, this second aspect of his work led Lyell to reject the notion of biological evolution until relatively late in his life.

One of Darwin's friends, Hewett Watson, asked, "How could Sir Charles Lyell . . . for thirty years read, write, and think on the subject of species and their succession, and yet constantly look down the wrong road?" It was only in 1862 after an intense effort on Darwin's part and a visit to the

Canary Islands that Lyell finally was convinced.

When Darwin boarded H.M.S. *Beagle* at the end of 1831, one of his prized possessions packed in with his limited luggage was the first volume of Lyell's *Principles*. And he ensured that the subsequent volumes would be sent to him during the voyage. It was Lyell that Darwin was reading as the *Beagle*'s odyssey brought him face to face with some of the great geological wonders of the world. It was through Lyell's eyes that Darwin saw the world in a way that no one had ever seen it before.

Another book greatly treasured by Darwin was *Natural Theology*, a work to which he had been introduced while studying at Cambridge. Written by William Paley, and first published in 1802, *Natural Theology* was for a century a major and influential work in an intellectual tradition that went by the same name.

Natural theology was a formidable bridge between religion and science. Indeed, many naturalists considered it their foremost task to gather evidence of God's existence. "Our task is . . . complete as soon as we have proved His existence," wrote the leading American naturalist, Swiss-born Louis Agassiz, in 1857.

Natural theologians delighted in the beauty and intricacy of nature. The beauty was surely put there by God for man's pleasure. And the intricacy and perfection of organisms and their structures could have no interpretation other than proof of purpose at the hands of God the Creator. Indeed, Paley began his book with his favorite subject, the eye, arguing that the eye is so perfect that chance can have played no part in its existence.

So it was, then, that when Darwin set out on the voyage of the *Beagle* he took with him a solid grounding in the Reverend Paley's arguments, and the newly published book by Lyell. For almost five years he would seek and probe and think. He would collect, describe, and ponder. Nothing would be too small or too inaccessible to be observed and catalogued. He was, as his uncle had once remarked, "a man of enlarged curiosity."

The voyage, however, furnished him no "Eureka," no blinding flash of insight. Instead, a simple doubt began to creep into his mind. Perhaps species are not fixed and unchanging after all. It was the possible fact of evolution that began to stir in Darwin's mind while he was on the *Beagle*. Confirmation of that fact, and the development of a theory that would explain it, had to await his return to England. In a letter he wrote five years before his death, Darwin recalled that, "When I

was on board the *Beagle* I believed in the permanence of species, but as far as I can remember, vague doubts occasionally flitted across my mind. . . . But I did not become convinced that species were mutable until, I think, two or three years [after my return home]."

Darwin's good fortune in seeing such a wide variety of terrain, environments, and inhabitants (plant and animal) during his journey around the southern continents was tremendously important in his subsequent synthesis of their cumulative meaning. In the unfolding of the evolutionary story, the romantic and mysterious Galapagos Islands played a central role.

Animals seek refuge from oncoming deluge in Edward Hicks's 1864 painting, Noah's Ark. *An attempt to explain the fossilized remains of extinct animals and plants, the diluvial theory of a divinely decreed flood remained prevalent in Darwin's time.*

The *Beagle* sailed in sight of this scattered group of young volcanic islands on September 15, 1835. Located south of the Equator some 650 miles due west of Ecuador, the Galapagos archipelago is, in Darwin's words, "a little world within itself." Darwin drew several important lessons from the islands and their inhabitants, some at the time, some later. He marveled at the profusion of life (albeit, a very peculiar slice of life) thriving on the islands, despite the fact that they are small and geologically recent. He was moved to write in his journal, "Hence, both in space and time, we seem to be brought somewhere near to that great fact—that mystery of mysteries—the first appearance of new beings on this Earth. . . ."

Darwin was particularly struck by the fact that, although many of the creatures he saw on the islands were species new to him, there was a strong resemblance to what he had seen on the South American continent. "It was most striking to be surrounded by new birds, new reptiles, new shells, new insects, new plants, and yet by innumerable trifling details of structure, and even by the tones of voice and plumage of birds, to have the temperate plains of Patagonia, or the hot dry deserts of Northern Chile, vividly brought before my eyes." Why, he asked himself, was life here created in the South American mold? And why, he questioned, should the inhabitants of the Cape Verde Islands (off the coast of west Africa) bear "the impress of Africa" while the two sets of islands are physically more like each other than either is to its neighboring continent?

According to Darwin's journal, ". . . the most remarkable feature in the natural history of this archipelago [is] that the different islands to a considerable extent are inhabited by a different set of beings." Birds, lizards, tortoises, plants, and sea shells—all vary island by island: many variations on a small number of themes distributed as if each island is most favorable for one form rather than another. This variability "strikes me with wonder," wrote Darwin.

"Reviewing the facts here given," Darwin concludes his account of the visit to the Galapagos Islands, ". . . one is astonished at the amount of creative force, if such an expression may be used, displayed on these small, barren, and rocky islands. . . ." Darwin's sense of wonder and puzzlement is clear in his words. Later he recorded how important his observations on the islands had been to the development of his theory. "In July [1837] opened first notebook on Transmutation of Spe-

...the different islands to a considerable extent are inhabited by a different set of beings. My attention was first called to this fact by the Vice Governor, Mr. Lawson declaring that the tortoises differed from the different islands and that he could with certainty tell from which island any one was brought

Galapagos Islands

Marine fossils from the Andes

Tierra del Fuego

I would not have believed how entire the difference between savage and civilized man is... their language does not deserve to be called articulate... I believe if the world were searched, no lower grade of man could be found.

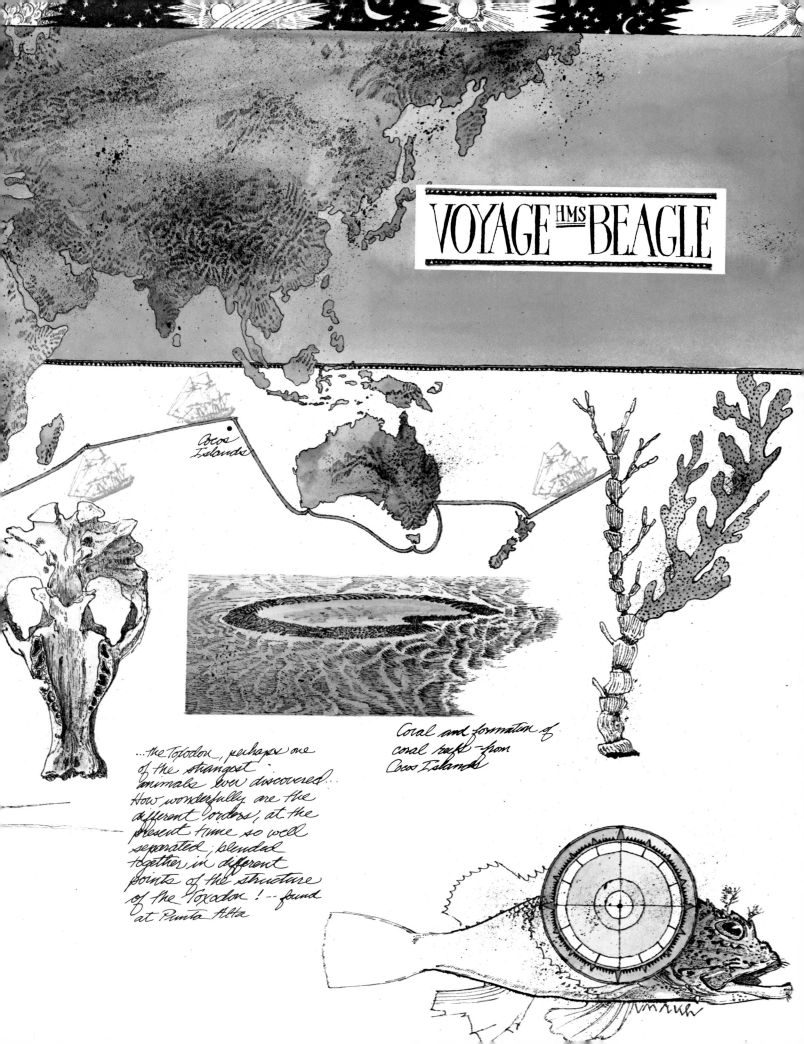

VOYAGE ᴴᴹˢ BEAGLE

Cocos
Islands

Coral and formation of
coral reef — from
Cocos Islands

...the Toxodon, perhaps one
of the strangest
animals ever discovered...
How wonderfully are the
different orders, at the
present time so well
separated, blended
together in different
points of the structure
of the Toxodon! — found
at Punta Alta

The unique, immensely diverse life of the Galapagos Islands captivated Darwin, challenging him to ponder the myriad modifications that had evolved among species. Although sea lions, above, circulate freely among islands and thus face little pressure to vary locally, less mobile giant tortoises, such as the one at right, are adapted to a particular habitat and vary from island to island.

cies. Had been greatly struck from about the previous March on character of South American fossils and species on Galapagos Archipelago. These facts (especially latter), origin of all my views."

The South American fossils had impressed Darwin for several reasons, most important of which was their striking similarity to the living creatures on the continent. Surely this spoke of some kind of continuity? "This wonderful relationship between the dead and the living," he wrote in his journal, "will, I do not doubt, hereafter throw more light on the appearance of organic beings on our earth and their disappearance from it than any other class of facts."

Back in England, in October 1836, he wrote a short letter to FitzRoy conveying his great joy at being back with his sisters and father amid the green fields of his homeland. Darwin was now 27. During his voyage he had amassed a huge collection of rocks, fossils, and preserved insects, animals, and plants. Now began the process of cataloging and describing them. In this task he was aided by Sir Richard Owen, who later became an implacable enemy of Darwin's theory of evolution, and John Gould, who would recognize the importance of the Galapagos finches. The description of the collections was published as the official *Zoology of the Voyage of the Beagle*, under Darwin's

Spiny, flat-lobed Opuntia echios *var.* gigantia—*a subspecies found only in the Galapagos—grows in extremely dry, porous volcanic soil beyond the ocean's spray zone. Its succulent flesh is an important food source for animals as diverse as giant tortoises and a species of Galapagos finch. Right, one of 13 species of Galapagos finches; their highly varied and modified beaks much intrigued Darwin, who hypothesized their descent from a single South American species.*

editorship. Meanwhile, in the remarkably short space of six months he penned his *Journal of Researches*, one of the greatest travel and natural history books of all time. In the following 10 years he produced three important scientific works: *The Structure and Distribution of Coral Reefs* (1842), *Volcanic Islands* (1844), and *Geological Observations on South America* (1846). He also devoted eight years to four volumes on the taxonomy and natural history of barnacles.

During this time he decided that, on balance, it would be best if he were married. So married he became, to his cousin Emma Wedgwood, on January 29, 1839. Five days before his wedding Darwin

was elected a Fellow of the Royal Society of London, Britain's highest scientific honor. In 1838 he had become Secretary of the Geological Society, a three-year appointment that was to establish his reputation in geology.

Darwin's output was impressive. His intellect was sharp and comprehensive. And yet the work for which he is best known, *Origin of Species*, did not appear until his 50th year, in 1859. It wasn't that his ideas were unformed until that time. He became convinced of the fact of evolution shortly after his return from the *Beagle* voyage; and he hit upon the mechanism for evolutionary change—natural selection—in the fall of 1838. For more than

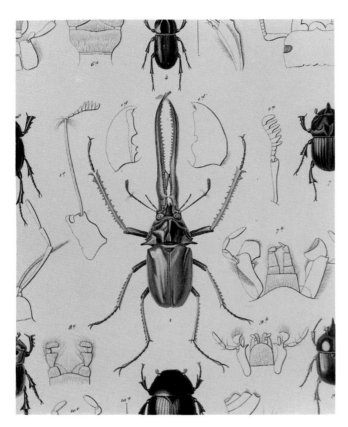

Above, long-pincered Chiasognathus granti, *one of the beetles Darwin observed during his two-year stay in Argentina. Darwin's personal collection of beetles is exhibited at Down House in Kent, where he moved with his wife and children in 1842 and lived until his death in 1882. The house is today preserved as a memorial to the great naturalist. Opposite, a view of Darwin's study, in which he wrote* Origin of Species *and many other books.*

20 years he amassed evidence. So, why the delay?

In 1842 the Darwin family moved from their London home to an elegant Georgian house in the small village of Downe in Kent. The once dynamic young man rapidly turned himself into something of a recluse, frequently shunning social and business encounters. Some explain his transformation of character as the manifestation of a chronic tropical disease contracted on his voyage on the *Beagle.* Others argue that his symptoms were those of neurosis, the sickbed and solitude being an escape from unwanted encounters. Darwin knew that his ideas on evolution would be controversial, as they challenged both the scientific and religious establishment as one. He intensely disliked disputation. "I do so hate controversy," he wrote to a colleague late in his life. Perhaps the long delay in publication of the *Origin* was simply a massive procrastination in the face of certain public outcry and condemnation.

Just less than a year after returning from the voyage on the *Beagle,* Darwin first embarked seriously on documenting his work on evolution—or transmutation of species as he originally called it. In July 1837 he opened a notebook on the subject, drawing together the reasons why he was coming to believe that species did, in fact, change through time. In October the following year Darwin read "for amusement," as he records in his autobiography, Thomas Malthus's *Essay on the Principle of Population.* It was to be a landmark event, at least in the way it is described in the autobiography.

During the summer of 1838 Darwin had been exploring philosophy; he had been examining the writings of Adam Smith on social systems and economics; and he had been seeking quantitative leads in the work of the Belgian statistician, Adolphe Quetelet. It is the true mark of genius that from such diversity of these and other ideas, Darwin was able eventually to extract a golden thread, a proposal that, in the words of Ernst Mayr, is "one of the most novel and most daring new conceptualizations in the history of ideas."

Darwin knew that every animal is different from all other members of its species, even if sometimes the differences may appear to be small. He knew too that such differences were often passed on from one generation to the next: they were heritable. And, most important, he knew that by judicious breeding, certain characteristics could be enhanced and others diminished. It was a stroke of luck that Darwin was intensely interested in animal breeding, ranging from horses to pigeons, and had

therefore observed these phenomena at first hand. It was a combination of his reading in the social, economic, and statistical sciences and his observations on animal domestication that led to his great insight.

From his reading he knew that every species has the potential to produce more offspring than will eventually survive. So, there must be a struggle for survival. What determines which individuals shall live and which shall perish? Because all individuals are different from all others, some will be better equipped than others, either in physical or behavioral attributes, to exploit the prevailing environment. It is these individuals that will preferentially survive, and they will pass their special attributes on to their offspring. "This preservation of favorable variations and the rejection of injurious variations, I call Natural Selection," Darwin wrote. Incidentally, the phrase "survival of the fittest," with which Darwin's name is now so closely associated, was at the suggestion of philosopher Herbert Spencer, who earlier had brought the word "evolution" into popular use.

When Darwin turned to Malthus's essay, it was not for the first time that he read the minister-economist's influential ideas on the limits on growth of populations. On this occasion, however, all the pieces of the puzzle were in his mind.

Darwin now had his theory of a mechanism by which evolution could take place. His task would be to amass sufficient evidence to convince others.

In May 1842 Darwin drafted a brief sketch of the evidence for evolution and the mechanism by which it comes about. Two years later he extended this version to an essay of some 230 pages. He wrote at the time to his friend and colleague Joseph Hooker, ". . . I am almost convinced . . . that species are not (it is like confessing a murder) immutable." Darwin was more circumspect in what he confessed to Lyell, for whom he had great respect and admiration—and, it must be said, awe. He admitted to Lyell his doubt about the fixity of species, but then carefully avoided the subject on which the two so profoundly disagreed. Darwin's strong feelings about the great geologist may well have been another factor contributing to the *Origin*'s long delay.

With the 1844 essay complete, Darwin put his active engagement on evolution to one side and immersed himself in his work on barnacles and other matters until 1854. Returning almost reluctantly to the topic, Darwin continued the process of accumulating evidence in favor—or perhaps it is

Darwin's theory of evolution was first presented on July 1, 1858, in the assembly room of London's Linnean Society, above. His subsequent writings proved highly controversial and sparked such attacks as caricature, below left.

Type." Darwin read the essay, which Wallace thought might be of some interest to him, and was stunned. "I never saw a more striking coincidence;" he immediately wrote to Lyell, "if Wallace had my manuscript sketch written out in 1842, he could not have made a better short abstract! Even his terms now stand as heads of my chapters."

In every major essence, Wallace had created a theory of evolution by natural selection just like Darwin's. In later years Wallace recalled how his insight had come to him during a fit of malarial fever, from which he frequently suffered. In Wallace's own words:

During one of these fits, while again considering the problem of the origin of species, something led me to think of Malthus's *Essay on the Principle of Population* (which I had read about ten years before), and the "positive checks"—war, disease, famine, accidents, etc.—which he adduced as keeping all savage populations nearly stationary. It then occurred to me that these checks must also act upon animals, and keep down their numbers; and as they increase so much faster than man does, while their numbers are always very nearly or quite stationary, it was clear that these checks in their case must be far more powerful, since a number equal to the whole increase must be cut off by them every year. While vaguely thinking about how this would affect any species, there suddenly flashed upon me the idea of *the survival of the fittest*—that the individuals removed by these checks must be, on the whole, *inferior* to those that survived. Then, considering the *variations* continually occurring in every fresh generation of animals or plants, and the changes of climate, of food, of enemies always in progress, the whole method of specific modification became clear to me, and in the two hours of my fit I had thought out the main points of the theory. That same evening I sketched out the draft of a paper; in the two succeeding evenings I wrote it out, and sent it by the next post to Mr. Darwin.

Both men had come to the same conclusion through the insight provided by Malthus's essay. They differed, however, in that the lessons on domestication were important for Darwin, while for Wallace they were not.

Darwin was distraught that he had been anticipated. He also fretted that he might act in a way that would seem to others to be unfair to Wallace. Soon, however, Darwin persuaded himself that the priority of the idea was truly his, and he allowed his friends Hooker and Lyell to organize a joint presentation of Wallace's paper with extracts from his 1844 essay and part of a letter he had written to Asa Gray, the great American botanist. The order of the presentations, to the Linnaean Society on July 1, 1858, was to be Darwin's contribution fol-

more apt to say, in defense—of his theory. In 1856 Lyell advised him to outline his work in detail, a prospect Darwin did not anticipate with equanimity. However, Lyell recognized the great importance of the work and, with Hooker, urged Darwin to publish it, lest he be forestalled by someone else.

"Natural Selection" was to be the title of the magnum opus on which Darwin immediately set to work. It would have been at least 2,500 pages long, or three quarters of a million words. But it was never published. Lyell's warning came true.

On June 18, 1858, Darwin received a letter from a young British naturalist, Alfred Russel Wallace, who at the time was on a small island in the Malay Archipelago. Attached to the letter was a short essay entitled "On the Tendancy [sic] of Varieties to depart indefinitely from the Original

lowed by Wallace's, with arrangements made by Lyell and Hooker. Wallace was not consulted about the program—his distant and isolated location would have made a rapid presentation impossible even if Lyell and Hooker had sought his agreement.

Though some of Wallace's disciples have grieved at what they perceive as his mistreatment, Wallace himself always graciously acknowledged Darwin's priority. It is true that what for Darwin had been the good part of a life's work had been but a moment's inspiration for Wallace. Most important, though, was that Darwin was able to support his claims with an enormous mass of persuasive evidence. Elegant though the notion of natural selection is, a simple presentation of the theory might not have captured the attention that was to be accorded to the *Origin*.

With the presentation of the papers to the Linnaean Society successfully accomplished, Darwin immediately settled down to what he insisted was not a major book but an essay, to be entitled, "An Abstract of an Essay on the Origin of Species and Varieties through Natural Selection." The publisher persuaded Darwin to drop the term

"abstract" and adopt the title now so famous. The *Origin* was published on November 24, 1859, all 1,250 copies being sold on the very first day.

Inevitably, Darwin worried about the book's reception. But in particular he wanted the approval of Thomas Henry Huxley, a young yet accomplished anatomist, great orator, and enthusiastic popularizer of science to the masses. "If I can convert Huxley I shall be content," Darwin wrote to Wallace shortly before the *Origin* was published. Darwin was more than content with the praise he received from Huxley in a letter dated November 23. Huxley expressed deep admiration for the cogency of the argument. But the letter must have sent a shiver down Darwin's spine, because while offering his support, Huxley appended a warning: "I trust you will not allow yourself to be in any way disgusted or annoyed by the considerable abuse and misrepresentation which, unless I greatly mistake, is in store for you."

Huxley did not mistake. Indignation and abuse were expressed in plenty. Critics raged. Cartoonists penned acerbic caricatures. Darwin's brainchild was scorned as the "monkey theory," an unsubtle and inaccurate reference to the implica-

48

The most famous public confrontation over Darwin's theory of evolution took place in 1860 between Bishop Samuel Wilberforce of Oxford, left, and Thomas Henry Huxley, both depicted here in Vanity Fair. Taunted by Wilberforce as to whether it was through his grandmother or grandfather that he claimed descent from a monkey, Huxley disdained the bishop's ridicule and won resounding acclaim. Opposite, title page of a first-edition Origin of Species, surrounded by some books that greatly influenced Darwin, including Charles Lyell's Principles of Geology.

tion that humans are related to the apes. But the weight of Darwin's argument was such that within a decade acceptance of the fact of evolution was firmly established as the new intellectual tradition.

Huxley was as good as his word. He, more than anyone, proselytized on Darwin's behalf, while Darwin remained safely out of reach at his house in Downe. The most famous public confrontation on the new theory took place at the Oxford meeting of the British Association for the Advancement of Science the year following the Origin's publication. Bishop Samuel Wilberforce, who had been heavily coached before the meeting by Sir Richard Owen, taunted Huxley with the question of whether it was through his grandfather or his grandmother that he claimed descent from a monkey. Although the exact words were not recorded, Huxley's reply, according to his grandson Sir Julian Huxley, was something like this: "If I had to choose between a poor ape for an ancestor and a man highly endowed by nature and of great influence, who used those gifts to introduce ridicule into a scientific discussion and to discredit humble seekers of the truth, I would affirm my preference for the ape." Huxley's brilliant attack

on prejudice as a substitute for science won tumultuous acclaim, and the bishop's argument was lost.

Darwin's "one long argument" in the Origin had replaced the notion of progression and improvement through successive creations, by the simple concept of change, a constant adaptation to local conditions. From time to time species become extinct and new species arise from existing ones. The new species are not "higher" in any sense than extinct ones, just suitably adapted to prevailing conditions. In one lyrical passage in the Origin Darwin described the result in the following way: "As buds give rise by growth to fresh buds, and these, if vigorous, branch out and overtop on all sides many a feebler branch, so by generation I believe it has been with the great Tree of Life, which fills with its dead and broken branches the crust of the earth, and covers the surface with its ever branching and beautiful ramifications."

The tone of the book is a disarming mixture of defensiveness and assertion, confidence and a ready admission of difficulties with the theory. "Nothing at first can appear more difficult to believe than that the more complex organs and instincts should have been perfected, not by means

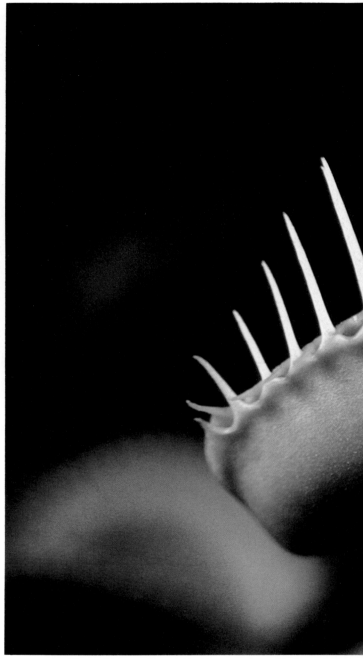

superior to, though analagous with human reason, but by the accumulation of innumerable slight variations, each good for the individual possessor," admits Darwin. But then he says, "this difficulty, though appearing to our imagination insuperably great, cannot be considered real if we admit the following propositions, namely,—that gradations in the perfection of any organ or instinct, which we may consider, either do now exist or could have existed, each good of its kind,—that all organs and instincts are, in ever so slight a degree, variable,—and, lastly, that there is a struggle for existence leading to the preservation of each profitable deviation of structure or instinct. The truth of these propositions cannot, I think, be disputed."

Darwin repeatedly addresses the issue of time, the essential prerequisite for evolution. "It cannot be objected that there has not been time sufficient for any amount of organic change," he writes in his conclusion. Perceptively, he adds, "the lapse of time has been so great as to be utterly inappreciable by the human intellect." Darwin also stresses again and again the "extreme imperfection of the fossil record," as an explanation of the relatively sketchy picture of the past that may be inferred from fossil evidence. Indeed, he devoted an entire chapter to the subject.

For a book of such weight and influence in the development of western intellectual tradition, it

After completion of the Origin, *Darwin immersed himself in the study of plants, conducting numerous experiments that led to the publication of six books on botanical subjects. Two of his major studies involved climbing plants such as the wild cucumber, above left, and the carnivorous Venus's-flytrap, shown above devouring a frog.*

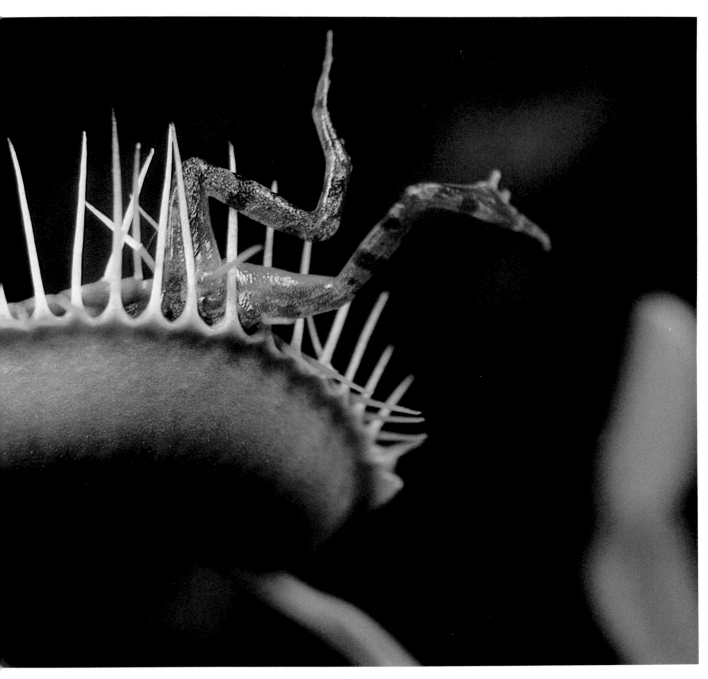

In its native Himalayas,
Paphiopedilum venustum
*displays wax-like flowers.
Darwin studied and
included similar orchids in
his work,* The Various Contrivances by Which Orchids
Are Fertilized by Insects.

seems somewhat incongruous that a number of early pages should be devoted to the breeding of pigeons. Darwin was indeed a pigeon fancier, but description of these intensely bred creatures was part of his powerful argument from animal domestication. Indeed, Darwin lamented that naturalists neglected the lessons to be learned from variation under domestication. But it is intriguing to note that many who did draw inspiration from observations of animal and plant breeding before Darwin came so close to—without quite reaching—a theory of evolution by natural selection. Artificial selection was a fertile source of instruction to be carried over to the natural world. Darwin put the argument in these words: "Why, if man can by patience select variations most useful to himself, should nature fail in selecting variations useful, under changing conditions of life, to her living products?" He concludes that there is "no limit to this power, in slowly and beautifully adapting each form to the most complex relations of life."

As would be expected from Darwin's experience and observations while on the *Beagle*, he emphasizes in the *Origin* the profound implications of the similarities between extinct and living animals in any one area of the globe. And one can imagine the flood of recollections that were embodied in the following passage: "We see the full meaning of the wonderful fact, which must have struck every traveler, namely, that on the same continent, under the most diverse conditions, under heat and cold, on mountain and lowland, on deserts and marshes, most of the inhabitants within each great class are plainly related; for they will generally be descendants of the same progenitors and early colonists." This, and the relatedness Darwin saw between inhabitants on remote islands with those on the neighboring continent, was firm evidence for his "descent with modification," the phrase Darwin used until adopting Spencer's simpler "evolution."

Descent with modification sees relatedness between species in space. But more important, it points to relatedness in time, stretching back ultimately to the beginning of life. "All organic beings that have ever lived on this Earth," concluded Darwin, "have descended from some one primordial form, into which life was first breathed." This notion of common descent of all life is an important message of the *Origin* that is often forgotten.

Two major criticisms of the *Origin* arose in Darwin's time, both of which worried him intensely. The first concerned the physical source of variations. Darwin knew that variation occurred and that in general it was heritable. But he had no idea of how the phenomenon might be explained. The second came in the form of calculations by the great Victorian physicist Lord Kelvin (1824–1907) that indicated that the world was too young for Darwinian evolution to have occurred.

As matters transpired, both these substantial challenges vanished with the march of scientific knowledge: the first, with the discovery—or rather, rediscovery—of the genetic basis of inheritance at the turn of the century; and the second, with the discovery that in his calculations Lord Kelvin had failed to take account of the important effects of radioactivity on the temperature of the Earth—he couldn't, because the phenomenon was unknown when he first made the calculations. (Even when the omission was realized by others, Kelvin himself obstinately stuck to his original figures, isolated from the opinion of all his colleagues until his death.)

For Darwin the publication of the *Origin* was the end of one period of intense anticipation and the beginning of another of intense productivity. While Herbert Spencer and others were busily recruiting the theory of natural selection to describe and model Victorian society under the phrase "Social Darwinism," about which Darwin was bemused and wary, Darwin was engaged on works such as *On the Various Contrivances by Which British and Foreign Orchids Are Fertilized by Insects*, *The Variation of Animals and Plants Under Domestication*, *The Expression of the Emotions in Man and Animals*, and many others. Most important of these was a book published in 1871, entitled *The Descent of Man, and Selection in Relation to Sex*.

Some years earlier Huxley had ventured into this potentially inflammatory area with his book *Man's Place in Nature*. In it he wrote, "The question of questions for mankind—the problem which underlies all others, and is more deeply interesting than any other—is the ascertainment of the place which Man occupies in nature and of his relations to the universe of things." Huxley's answer to this great question was that Mankind is a natural part of the natural world, that humans are related to the apes—not descended from them as was popularly misconceived, but sharing a common ancestry.

Darwin believed the same when he wrote his contribution on the subject. Indeed, he had held this view for a very long time, but had not ventured to state it publicly. "During many years I collected notes on the origin or descent of man, without any intention of publishing on the subject," he wrote in the introduction to *The Descent of Man*, "but rather with the determination not to publish, as I thought that I should thus only add to the preju-

dices against my views." Times had changed by 1871, opinions had shifted, and Darwin felt it safe to express in detail his thoughts on Man's relations to the universe of things.

It was a bold essay, touching on both physical and mental attributes of Mankind. He was entirely comfortable with the notion of a shared ancestry with the apes, and this, remember, was at a time when almost no fossil human ancestors had been found. Darwin made a remarkable prediction concerning Man's birthplace in his book: "In each great region of the world the living mammals are closely related to the extinct species of the same region. It is, therefore, probable that Africa was formerly inhabited by extinct apes closely allied to the gorilla and chimpanzee; and as these two species are now man's nearest allies, it is somewhat more probable that our early progenitors lived on the African continent than elsewhere." Virtually every discovery made since Darwin's prediction in the field of human origins has served to make it more probable than not that he was right.

Darwin died on April 19, 1882. The world he left had been transformed in his lifetime by the tremendous material advances of the Industrial Revolution. But the intellectual revolution that bears his name had wrought an even bigger transformation. "The greatest impact of the Darwinian revolution . . . was that it finally completed the liberation from superstition and fear that began in the physical sciences a few centuries before," wrote George Gaylord Simpson. "Man, too, is a natural phenomenon."

Trees still arch gracefully over Darwin's beloved Sand Walk, or "thinking path," around which he strolled twice daily for both physical and mental exercise.

THE FORCE AND SHAPE OF EVOLUTION

Five fossil mollusks from Kenya's Lake Turkana region document the gradual evolution, left to right, of a new species, a phenomenon that occurred here repeatedly during an ancient period of isolation.

Lake Turkana is a magical place, its jade green waters stretching in a 150-mile dog's leg in Kenya's northern territories. Famous for its enormous Nile crocodiles and succulent tilapia and perch, the lake supports a richness and variety of life seemingly at odds with its harsh, sun-baked surroundings. Herds of zebra and antelope thrive on the eastern shore; scores of species of birds make the area an ornithologist's paradise. Life has flourished in and around the lake during its four-million-year history. The dark sandstone deposits surrounding it yield fossilized remains that mark the fluctuating fortunes of those many different creatures that have lived there.

Most dramatic of the fossils found near Lake Turkana are those that tell the history of our earliest human ancestors, a story still being pieced together by Richard Leakey and his colleagues. But the dust-dry deposits are rich in other fossils, as any visitor to the area comes to appreciate quickly. The eastern shore is truly a treasure house of secrets from life's past. Ironically, one of its least conspicuous and least imposing fossils has recently been recognized as the bearer of a major evolutionary tale.

In the mid-1970s Peter Williamson, a British paleontologist, collected fossil mollusks from the area. Relatives of these simple clams and snails still live in the lake. Williamson's task was to help reconstruct the time frame during which these and other animals had been buried by river and lake sediments. It was a worthy, though not particularly earthshaking, project—the stuff of which much scientific progress is made. As things turned out, the individual mollusk fossils were less useful for dating than had been hoped. "But, when I examined them carefully back in the laboratory," recalls Williamson, "I began to realize that the collection as a whole documented something totally unexpected, something much more important than was originally intended: the evolution of new species."

The geology of the Lake Turkana basin is extremely unstable. Sudden earth movements and

*Mist rises from waters of Lake
Turkana, above. Throughout its four-
million-year history, Lake Turkana has
nurtured an astounding variety of life,
including giant Nile perch, left, this
one the catch of an El Molo tribesman.*

55

volcanic eruptions punctuate the passage of time; these upheavals, together with changing climates, have caused the waters of the lake to rise and fall periodically, sometimes by hundreds of feet. Williamson had collected fossil shells from deposits laid down during one of these rapid regressions in lake level. "The organisms in the lake came under tremendous environmental stress during this period," he says. "At the same time, the low water level meant that the lake was no longer in contact with many other large bodies of water in which these mollusks lived." Turkana mollusks became isolated for a few tens of thousands of years.

"The result of this isolation was that the mollusk population was free to vary," explains Williamson. "In the end clearly identifiable new species became established and settled down in a form distinctly different from the parent species." The same phenomenon occurred in 13 species of mollusks in the lake. "The most important thing," stresses Williamson, "is that through a few meters of sediment you can see all the intermediate forms between the original and the new species." The transition took somewhere between 5,000 and 50,000 years, ". . . in relative terms, an instant in geological time, given that these species have otherwise remained unchanged for millions of years."

When Williamson published his work at the end of 1981 it caused great interest and excitement among evolutionary biologists. The rapid nature of much change and the capricious way in which geological deposits accumulate conspire to minimize the chances of documenting the origin of new species. Williamson's observation—helped along as it was by the kind of good fortune that many important discoveries require—is therefore momentous. It doesn't change the way many evolutionary biologists view the natural world, but it gives the kind of confirmation that they earnestly seek.

Evolutionary theory has two major tasks: it must explain how new species arise, as well as why species appear to be suited to the demands of their environment and daily lives. When Darwin published *The Origin of Species* he quickly convinced most scientists to accept the fact of evolution, but his explanation of the mechanism of evolutionary change—natural selection—was to be challenged by rival theories until the 1930s.

One school of thought—the *selectionists*—were more Darwinian than Darwin himself. They emphasized the power of selection to the virtual exclusion of all other factors that might contribute to evolutionary change. Selectionists attributed to

natural selection a power for shaping perfection in the living world comparable with the God-given perfection that was part of natural theology.

A second school promoted an idea that had been popular since the beginning of the 19th century, that of the *inheritance of acquired characteristics.* This was a part—just a small part—of what French naturalist the Chevalier de Lamarck had suggested in 1809, and it was an idea with which Darwin had considerable sympathy. The theory was particularly attractive because it equated evolutionary change with the changing needs of individuals. For example, an individual giraffe seems to "need" a longer neck to browse on the highest leaves in a tree. Genetic variation therefore arises preferentially in this direction, and very soon long necks are common in a population: the trait is passed from generation to generation.

However, later research indicated that there is no effective way for genetic variation to arise to meet the needs "perceived" by individual organisms. This eventually led to the eclipse of the theory, as did the recognition that the genetic material of germ cells (which give rise to eggs and sperm) and cells in the rest of the body are effectively separate—there is no way for genetic changes arising in, say, neck superstructure to be transmitted from those cells to the germ cells and then on to the next generation.

A third concept, the *mutation* theory, arose after the rediscovery in 1900 of genetics. According to this school, the direction of evolutionary change was determined principally by genetic

changes—mutations—that caused large shifts in physical or behavioral characteristics. If the modifications were large enough and were beneficial, new species might eventually result. An important figure in this school, geneticist Richard Goldschmidt, coined the term "hopeful monsters" to describe mutated individuals. It was a term that was quickly caricatured by opponents of the theory, who made it seem that Goldschmidt and his supporters were proposing the instant origin of species, always supposing that the monster's hopes were fulfilled.

By the 1930s the extreme positions were no longer tenable, and a melding of ideas was brought about under the term the *modern synthesis.* It is in large part a combination of selection theory and mutation theory, and it has dominated evolutionary biology until recently, when a new generation of dissenters has emerged.

Many people who are unhappy with the idea of evolution complain that it amounts to progress ruled solely by chance. How can a structure as complex as the eye arise—by chance? How can there be so much order in the world—by chance? Is the human mind the product of mere chance?

The answer is that evolution by natural selection is *not* evolution by chance. To be sure, the origin of variations, about which Darwin wrote so much, is a phenomenon of chance. Random mutation—that is, reassortment of genetic characters by chance—leads to random variation. The second stage of the process—selection—is, however, decidedly nonrandom. Selection favors organisms

Concealed by its tawny camouflage coat, stealthy lioness, above, crouches in ambush by a herd of zebras and single springbok. Bald eagle, left, clutches a fish in specialized talons that puncture its prey's vital organs.

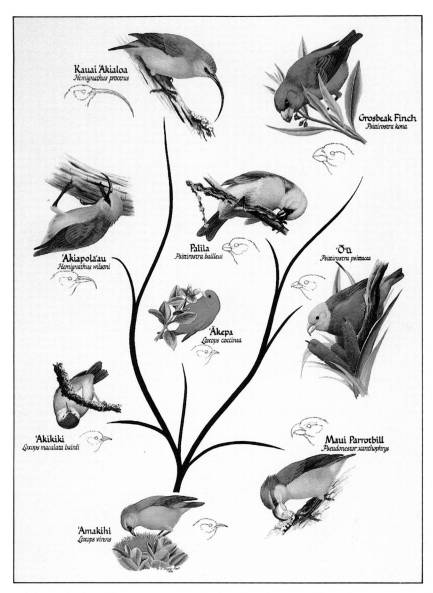

Kauai 'Akialoa
Hemignathus procerus

Grosbeak Finch
Psittirostra kona

'Akiapola'au
Hemignathus wilsoni

Palila
Psittirostra bailleui

'O'u
Psittirostra psittacea

'Akepa
Loxops coccinea

'Akikiki
Loxops maculata bairdi

Maui Parrotbill
Pseudonestor xanthophrys

'Amakihi
Loxops virens

Colorful Hawaiian finches exhibit their bills—adaptations to the varied ecological niches within the islands. This single family—which may once have numbered as many as 43 species—has evolved nearly every type of bill that exists elsewhere in the world.

with variations in structure or behavior that enable their owners to exploit their environment more effectively. An individual that, through genetic variation, has digestive enzymes capable of breaking down cellulose more thoroughly, or runs faster in pursuit of prey, or evades a potential predator through more convincing camouflage, is likely to do better in the struggle for existence. As the beneficial features have emerged through genetic variation, they are heritable, and some of the individual's offspring will carry them.

As noted earlier, Darwin drew the simple analogy between an animal breeder enhancing certain valued characteristics through selective breeding and the demands and opportunities of particular environments favoring particular features in wild populations through natural selection. The outcome is emphatically not random, even though an essential stage in the process (variation) is. The

key to natural selection is that it is creative. It is not simply the elimination of the unfit. Natural selection builds adaptation through the continued differential success of certain characteristics as against others. If, however, conditions alter dramatically, then the selective force is different and other features may be favored.

The chance to document natural selection in action occurs but rarely. An opportunity to do so fell—by chance—to two Canadian biologists, Peter Grant and Peter Boag, while they were collecting data on a population of finches in the Galapagos Islands in the mid-1970s. "We were studying the medium ground finches on Daphne Major," explains Boag. "The island is a low volcanic cone jutting out of the Pacific to the north of the large island of Santa Cruz. The crater in the middle of Daphne Major is steep, and the floor is covered with white sand. It's hot, dry, and dusty."

The medium ground finches living all over the island, inside and outside the crater, share the island with the comical blue-footed boobies, which nest on the white sandy floor. Vegetation is low, rugged, and sparse. The island lies in the rain shadow of its larger neighbor, all of which makes Daphne Major one of the least hospitable spots in the archipelago.

When Boag and Grant started collecting data on the island's finches in 1975, conditions for the birds were about as favorable as they could be. Rainfall had been good and food was adequate. In 1977, however, only an inch of rain fell on the island. The annual grasses and other small plants, from which the finches normally derived a reliable supply of seeds, died from the drought. "Instead of the small seeds that the birds usually fed on," says Boag, "there was only a much reduced supply of larger, tougher seeds from a small scrubby plant that had been introduced to the islands by the first European visitors some 300 to 400 years ago."

Boag was distressed by the result of the drought. "Many of the birds were dying and it looked as if we were going to lose our data," he recalls. "But when we started to look at the information we'd collected, we realized that something interesting had happened. The birds that were surviving were the bigger ones, the ones with larger beaks." Because larger finches can eat larger seeds, these individuals appeared best able to use the larger, tougher seeds that were available during this lean time. "The evolutionary response is real," says Boag, "but we can't be absolutely certain that the change we see is directly tied to the size of the seeds available. However, it does look to be a good example of natural selection."

This study does not show the birth of a new species. It is a snapshot of natural selection in action. But imagine a small population of birds under this same selection pressure for a very long time, over many generations. Eventually the individuals that would thrive there would have adapted to the harsh conditions, perhaps by devel-oping even larger beaks, and probably other characteristics too. With long enough separation from other populations of medium ground finches, the bigger-billed variety might eventually become a new species. They would no longer be able to breed with their "parent" species.

Adaptation to different life-styles appears to have been responsible for the 14 different species of finches that now live among the Galapagos Islands. They all wear the same rather dull livery as their ancestral species which, sometime during the past two million years, colonized the archipelago from South America. Through the two-stage process of natural selection, populations of individuals adapted to different habitats, to different demands of the environment. New species were established, marked principally by the size and shape of the bill, which is, of course, linked to the type of food the birds eat. Their separate adaptations also involved the loss of ability to interbreed. What had once been one species branched to give rise to many. This type of evolutionary history is known as *adaptive radiation*.

Once Darwin had been alerted to the unusual features of the Galapagos finches, they fitted in very well with his developing ideas on the mutability of species. However, had his voyage taken him farther north to the Hawaiian Islands, he would have chanced on an even more spectacular example of adaptive radiation, once again of finches. Storrs Olson and Helen James of the Smithsonian's National Museum of Natural History are currently studying these birds, and already it is clear that the story of evolutionary history in Hawaii is much more dramatic than with the Galapagos finches.

"The Hawaiian islands were colonized at some point in the last five million years," says Olson, "and since that time there has been a tremendous radiation of new species." The original species probably came from the North American mainland, or perhaps Asia, and was probably similar to finches we know today. "Until recent times there were as many as 43 different species of

Bearing a second set of teeth, pharyngeal jaws of cichlid fishes are shown in red in this top view of a typical cichlid. Jaws in the back of the throat enable fish to occupy highly specialized niches.

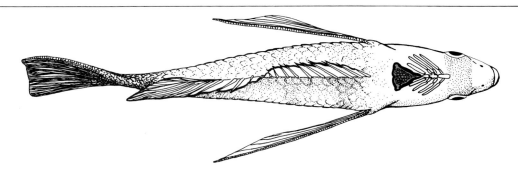

Hawaiian finches," he says, "although many have since become extinct through removal of forests and other changes in the island habitats."

The adaptive radiation of the Hawaiian finches was impressive. They filled a number of ecological niches, exploiting foods from fruit to insects, and from seeds to nectar. There are several species that use their long curved bills to extract nectar from flowers; so similar to continental honeycreepers are they that until now they have been referred by the same name. Bill forms that have evolved elsewhere in the world in widely different groups of birds can be found in this single radiation of finches. One Hawaiian finch has even developed a bill very like a parrot's, with its independently movable lower jaw. Another species, however, sports a totally novel bill. The upper part sweeps down in a long curve, while the lower part is relatively short. The bird tilts its head backwards, uses its lower jaw to rap a tree branch, and then catches emerging insects and grubs with its pointed upper bill.

"The impressive thing about these birds," says Olson, "is the rapidity with which the evolution must have happened. It seems to me very likely that, under the right circumstances, a new species could arise in just a few thousand years."

Perhaps the most striking adaptive radiation of all is to be found in some of the African lakes, particularly Lake Victoria. The lake is a relative youngster, having formed some three quarters of a million years ago. And yet there are almost 200 species of cichlid fish—small freshwater forms—thriving there. This group has evolved very rapidly from one of the handful of cichlid species that live in the rivers of Africa.

During its formation, Lake Victoria went through a stage when its rising waters were in effect a series of large "ponds" connected by narrow waterways. The incipient lakes offered all of the different types of river fish an opportunity to flourish, and the ponding effect provided a multitude of separate niches. The cichlids moved into them, adapting and specializing.

Cichlids have a second pair of jaws—called pharyngeal jaws—as does the whole group to which cichlids belong. The structure and musculature of the cichlids' pharyngeal jaws, however, allows a good deal more manipulative facility than is possible in most other groups of fish. This apparently gave the cichlids a competitive edge over other species.

The subsequent explosive radiation has produced a bewildering range of feeding habits. Insects, mollusks, algae, large plants, and small fish—each is a food favored by one cichlid species or another, and each food source represents a series of adaptations that, among other things, has involved radical modification of the pharyngeal jaws. One cichlid species has exploited the habit of another species, that of brooding young in the female's mouth. The predator grips the unfortunate mother by the jaws, and releases her only after she has disgorged her young directly into the attacker's mouth. Another follows schools of a different cichlid species, occasionally biting a fish in front of it by the tail. The predator cichlid then proceeds to scrape off and eat the scales of the struggling captive using its pharyngeal jaws. This strategy is aided by the predator's close resemblance to its chosen prey.

The story of Lake Victoria is repeated in several other African lakes, and it is convincing evidence of the creative evolutionary force of adaptive radiation. The cichlids are strikingly colored, and this almost certainly is important in the rapid differentiation of species, as the colors and patterns are vital in attraction and courtship displays between males and females of the same species.

Powerful though selection might be, it can work only with the material at hand: that is, genetic variation. Look around you at your relatives and friends. You are all members of the species *Homo sapiens*, and yet you recognize distinct differences between one person and another, differences that are strongly inherited within families. Every individual member of a species has the genetic material—genes packaged within chromosomes—that is special to that species. But, as you note when you look at people around you, humans exhibit a good deal of individual variation. Each of us has only a representative sample of all the human genes on Earth. We are variations on a theme.

This genetic variation, which yields endless combinations through the mixing medium of sexual reproduction, is the first and most immediate source of variation that is available to natural selection. The combinations may be numerically endless, but the physical end products are pretty much restricted to what we all recognize as being within the norm. Variation that is limited to the shuffling of existing genes will not usually give rise to substantial changes although, as experience with domesticated animals shows (especially in the worst excesses of dog breeding), severe artificial selection can produce marked shifts in form.

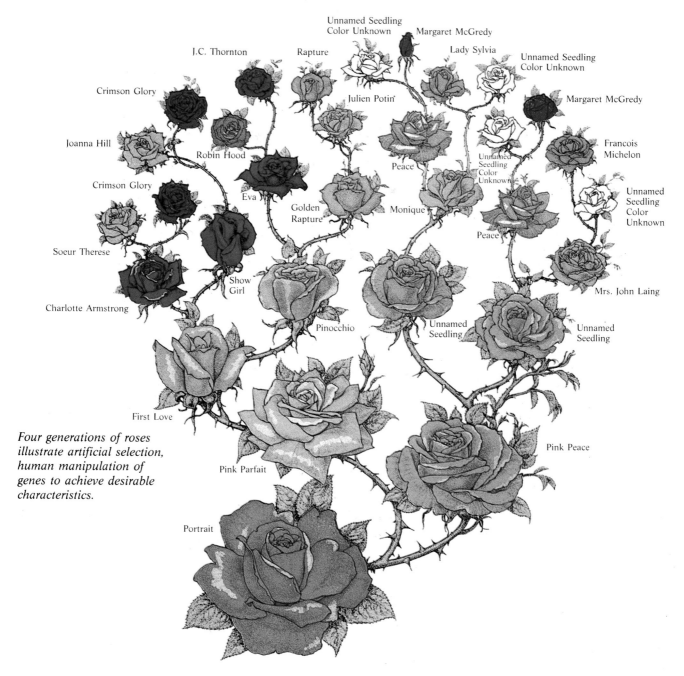

Unnamed Seedling
Color Unknown

Margaret McGredy

J.C. Thornton

Rapture

Lady Sylvia

Unnamed Seedling
Color Unknown

Crimson Glory

Julien Potin

Margaret McGredy

Joanna Hill

Robin Hood

Peace

Francois
Michelon

Crimson Glory

Eva

Unnamed
Seedling
Color
Unknown

Unnamed
Seedling
Color
Unknown

Golden
Rapture

Monique

Soeur Therese

Peace

Mrs. John Laing

Charlotte Armstrong

Show
Girl

Pinocchio

Unnamed
Seedling

Unnamed
Seedling

First Love

*Four generations of roses
illustrate artificial selection,
human manipulation of
genes to achieve desirable
characteristics.*

Pink Peace

Pink Parfait

Portrait

Greater potential change, however, comes from mutations in the genetic material itself. Here the possibilities are roughly twofold, with greatly differing consequences. Mutations may occur in the gene code for building blocks in the body. Or they may affect the genetic instructions for how these building blocks will be assembled. A single example, close to home, will make the point.

When the structures of human proteins are compared in detail with those of a chimpanzee (our closest living relative), little difference can be found. Perhaps one part in a hundred can be shown to differ. And yet, in spite of distinct physical similarities between humans and chimpanzees, the differences are immediately obvious. Clearly, the differences are produced by the way the building blocks are put together, rather than by the building blocks themselves. It is the arrangement of these almost identical building blocks that produces chimp-like shape and behavior on the one hand or human-like shape and behavior on the other. This discovery, by Allan Wilson of Berkeley, has led him to suggest that much important evolutionary change can be traced to what he calls *regulatory mutations*.

Where might such regulatory mutations have greatest effect? The answer is, in that near-miraculous sequence of events that leads from an unformed ball of cells to an identifiable individual: the process of embryological development.

In the 19th century, German natural philosopher Ernst Haeckel propounded his "biogenetic law," popularly expressed in the tongue twister, ontogeny recapitulates phylogeny. In other words, the embryonic development of the individual retraces the evolutionary steps of its ancestral group. For instance, every terrestrial vertebrate embryo for the past 300 million years has developed at some point a set of gill arches and blood vessels appropriate for it, just as its marine ancestors did in adult life. And in embryonic burrowing sea urchins there is a transient appearance of the jaw apparatus typical of their ancient nonburrowing predecessors. Such reminders of the past history of a group of organisms are, incidentally, about as good evidence of evolution as one could wish for. They reveal the ways in which the evolutionary process often puts old structures to new and unexpected uses. As paleontologist Stephen Jay Gould has said of this embryonic odyssey through the past: "This complex and circuitous pathway works well enough in building a human baby, but no engineer starting from scratch would have ordained such a design."

Haeckel's biogenetic law implies that evolution is typically accomplished by a speeding up of development, so that what was an adult stage in the parent species becomes a phase through which the embryo of the new species passes, eventually to reach a novel adult form. It is true that such a process has accompanied some evolutionary change. But it is equally true that new species arise by the opposite process, a slowing down of development. No better example exists than, once again, the human and the chimpanzee.

Humans did not evolve from chimpanzees, but we do share a common ape-like ancestor which probably lived some five million years ago. How might the human form emerge from an ape ancestor by slowing down the developmental clock? Adult humans have a bulbous cranium, just as

embryonic apes and monkeys do, while mature apes and monkeys have a low forehead and narrow skull. The mature human's vertical face, small brow ridges, and small jaws and teeth are typical of embryonic apes but atypical of adults. Our heads are balanced atop our backbones, with the opening for the spinal cord placed in the base of the skull—just as it is in embryonic apes. But in adult apes, the spinal opening has shifted toward the rear of the skull. Our big toe is straight, strong, and nonopposable, again the arrangement found in embryonic apes but not in adults. The growth in the number of our brain cells is switched off much later in development than happens in apes, and so

An example of neoteny, or retardation of development, the adult Mexican salamander axolotl *retains larval gills.*

we have bigger brains. Neoteny, as the retardation of development is known, was clearly an important factor in human evolution. And there are many other, similar examples in the living world.

Alteration of the timing of development—both retardation and acceleration—through regu-

The 50-year evolution of Mickey Mouse provides another example of neoteny, as the famous Disney character—through such changes as larger relative head size and larger eyes—becomes increasingly juvenile in appearance.

Free-swimming sea squirt larva displays tiny notochord, or primitive spinal cord; cord disappears as animal matures and attaches itself to sea floor, below. Many scientists believe that vertebrates evolved by neoteny from such a tadpole-like larval stage.

latory mutations is probably one of the most direct ways by which evolutionary change is effected.

Recollect once again, though, that each of us, along with all our terrestrial vertebrate cousins, has had a brief acquaintance with the fish-like state of our ancestors. Such persistence of history in our embryonic development tells us that dramatic shifts in the complex pattern of changes that constitute embryonic development are not easily accomplished. While small changes here or there may occur, the overall sequence clearly cannot be modified extensively. Small changes in some aspect of development can, however, result in important differences in the adult stage.

This points to the important conclusion that natural selection works under constraints, in this case, the constraint of history. Stephen Jay Gould tells the story of a colleague who assured him that "land vertebrates had four legs *because* this number represented optimal design for locomotion of a bilaterally symmetrical, elongate body under gravitational conditions. Scarcely believing my ears, I reminded him that the ancestral fish had four fins, the homologues of our arms and legs, for reasons quite unrelated to their later invasion of land. . . . Four legs may be optimal, but we have them by conservative inheritance, not selected design."

The belief that every organ and organism is

HOMOLOGY AND ANALOGY

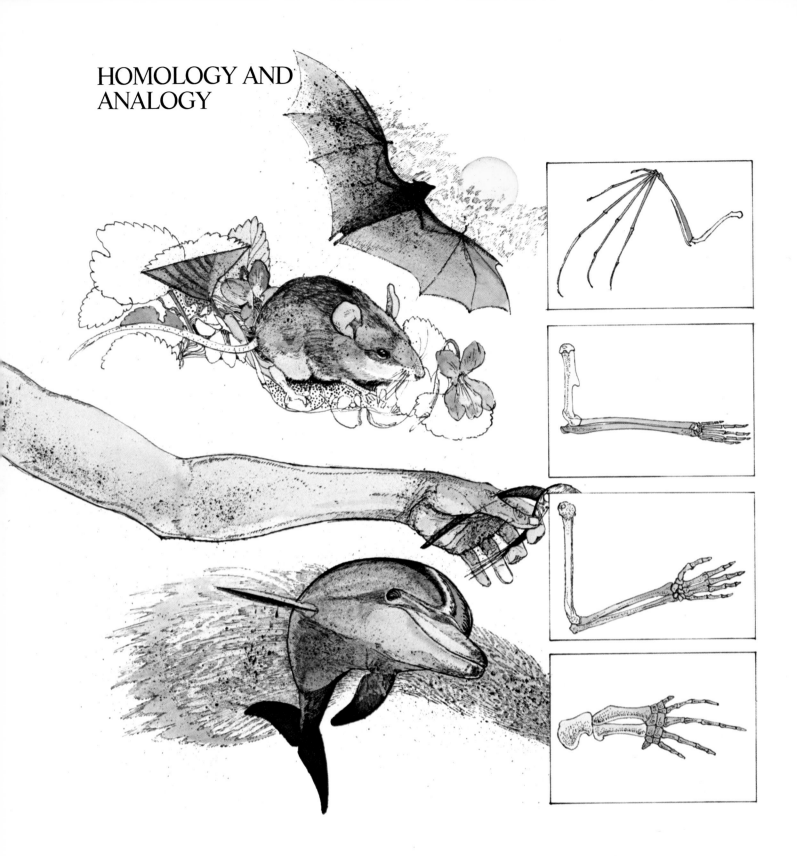

Homology: a bat's wing, a mouse's forelimb, a human's arm, and a dolphin's flipper are said to be *homologous* because they are structurally similar although they perform different functions and are modified accordingly. Each forelimb has about the same number of bones arranged in the

same way. This structural concurrence points to a four-limbed vertebrate ancestor shared by all four species. The earliest land-dwelling vertebrates possessed forelimbs very much like a primitive version of the limbs shown here, with the same bones in the same general arrangement.

Analogy: while the bat's wing and the bird's wing are homologous because they evolved from the same early terrestrial vertebrate limbs, they are *analogous* to the butterfly's wing and the flying fish's fin. Analogous structures are those that perform similar functions—in this case flight—but have

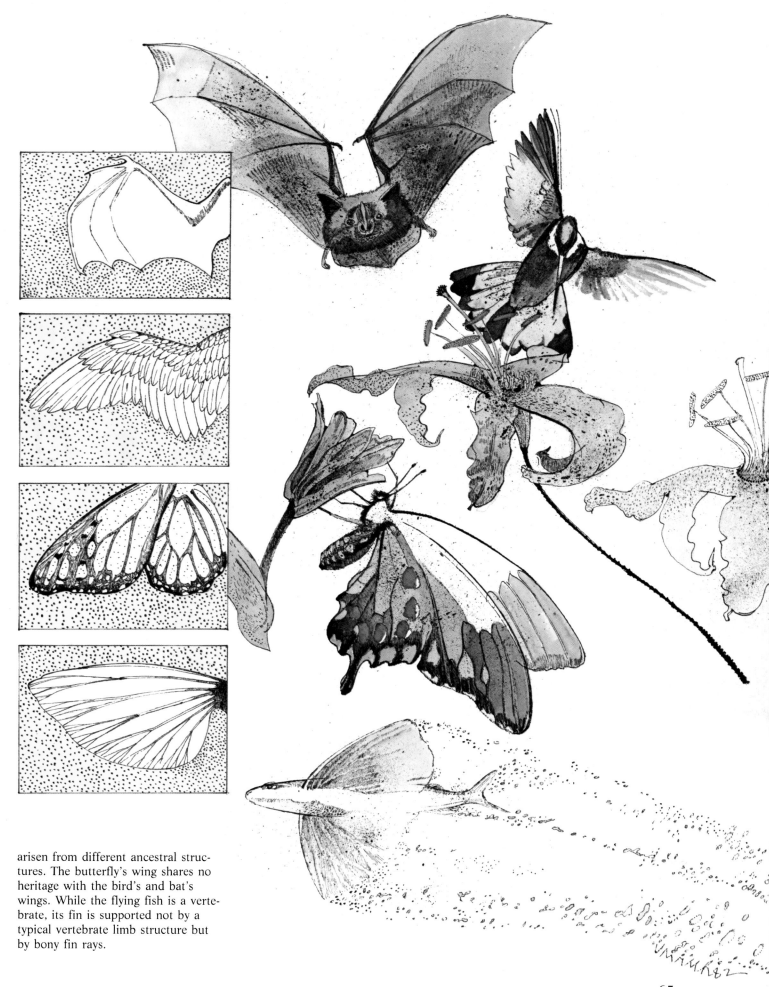

arisen from different ancestral structures. The butterfly's wing shares no heritage with the bird's and bat's wings. While the flying fish is a vertebrate, its fin is supported not by a typical vertebrate limb structure but by bony fin rays.

Simple pinhole eye of the chambered nautilus, above, is one of more than 30 different patterns of sight organs evolved by various branches of the animal kingdom. Nautilus's open-pit eye lacks a lens, yet has served its kind well for 500 million years.

Compound eye of arthropods is most highly developed in crustaceans such as the hermit land crab, above, and insects. Close-up of a fly's eye, left, reveals the intricate mosaic of multiple lenses—essentially separate eyes— which comprise this type of eye.

the product of natural selection for optimal adaptation clearly ignores the constraints imposed by the nature of the raw material with which selection works. Evolution, as French Nobel Prize-winning molecular biologist François Jacob has remarked, works like a tinkerer: " . . . a tinkerer who does not know exactly what he is going to produce but uses whatever he finds around him . . . to produce some kind of workable object." Evolution cannot be seen as an engineer who can come up with optimal solutions to every problem; otherwise there would surely be animals rolling around on wheels.

Darwin delighted in signs of tinkering in the makeup of organisms, for they added strong support for his theory. "The framework of bones being the same in the hand of a man, wing of a bat, fin of the porpoise, and leg of the horse . . . at once explain themselves on the theory of descent with slow and slight successive modifications," he wrote in the *Origin*. Biologists describe these structures, different though they are in function, as homologous, because they are constructed from the same basic form. The human arm, the bat's wing, the porpoise's fin, the horse's leg—all are

related in evolution through common descent.

The opposite of homology is analogy, when structures do the same job but bear no direct evolutionary relationship to each other. The wings of butterflies and birds represent an example of analogy. So does the swimming equipment of the ichthyosaur (an extinct reptile that returned to a life in the seas) and true fish. The fins and tail of the aquatic reptile were nearly identical in appearance to those of bony fishes, but they were built from different structures. The engineering demands of swimming helped to fashion structures that were suited to underwater propulsion. Sometimes there are just a few engineering solutions to particular problems and so, if it is physically feasible, natural selection will favor the variations that conform closest to those optimal designs.

Just as Darwin marveled at signs of history in an organism, because they supported his theory, he was disconcerted by what he perceived as the challenge of "organs of extreme perfection." The vertebrate eye—British priest and theologian William Paley's favorite argument in support of supernatural intervention in nature's perfection and har-

Lens and retina of the image-forming eye found in vertebrates and some invertebrates allow such complex functions as binocular vision, color sensitivity, and focusing. Gull, above, has evolved superb eyesight, a prerequisite of flight. Eye of the Tokay gecko, left, affords the precise vision needed to catch insects.

mony—bothered Darwin a good deal, but in the end he was able to accommodate it within the theory of descent. "If it could be demonstrated that any complex organ existed, which could not possibly have been formed by numerous, successive, slight modifications, my theory would absolutely break down," he wrote in the *Origin*. "But I can find no such case," he concluded. Not even the eye.

"Eyes appeared a great many times in the course of evolution," remarks François Jacob, "based on at least three principles—pinhole, lens, and multiple tubes. Lens eyes, like ours, appeared both in mollusks and vertebrates. Nothing looks so much like our eye as the octopus eye. Both work in almost exactly the same way. Yet they did not evolve in the same way. Whereas in vertebrates the retina's photoreceptor cells point away from the light, in mollusks they point toward light. Among all solutions found to the problem of photoreceptors, these two are similar but not identical. In each case, natural selection did what it could with the materials at its disposal."

Ernst Mayr and an Austrian zoologist, Luitfried v. Salvini-Plawen, once calculated that eyes have evolved at least 38 times in animals. "Some are very simple, just a photoreceptor cell," says Mayr, "and some are very complex, with lens focusing and color sensitivity, like ours. There is no problem in accepting the gradual evolution of highly complex eyes step by step from simple eyes."

The gradual increase in complexity of a photoreceptor until one day it is as awe-inspiring as the human eye is indeed an acceptable evolutionary process. The organisms stretched out along this evolutionary path presumably made full use of the eye at each stage of its development. But how does one explain the evolution of a structure that is useful only when it is fully evolved? The mammalian jaw, for instance, allows much more flexibility in the way food can be processed than does the reptilian jaw from which it evolved. And yet this flexibility cannot have become apparent until the mammalian structure had completely formed. Natural selection cannot induce changes that in the future will bring benefits. The benefits have to be immediate. So how did the mammalian jaw evolve?

"Unlike mammals, which have just one bone in their lower jaw, reptiles have a number which

present day

evolutionary time (20 million years)

Gradualism

Punctuation

measure of species difference

Does evolutionary change proceed gradually or in sudden bursts? Here both alternatives are applied to two similar hypothetical examples of evolution in which over a period of 20 million years one "parent" species gives rise to four extant species, with four relatives going extinct. Gradual- *ism, left, sees evolutionary change proceeding steadily through time, whereas in punctuation, right, most change is concentrated in relatively rapid bursts. Both modes are important in evolutionary history, but the question is which of the two is the more frequent?*

are either held together by sutures or connective tissue," explains A.W. Crompton of Harvard. "Within the mammal-like reptiles, and particularly in the line that eventually gave rise to mammals, there apparently was selection for improved hearing. Sound was conducted to the inner ear from an eardrum, supported by the lower jaw, via the bones forming the jaw joint. To improve their sound-conducting qualities, these bones were progressively reduced in size." As a consequence, the jaw joint became relatively weaker, and the musculature of the jaw also changed so that the reduced jaw joint would not be overstressed. "The final stages of the change involved a complete separation of the two small reptilian jaw joint bones from the lower jaw to form part of the middle ear, and the establishment of a new joint between the now-enlarged single lower jaw bone and the skull. This new jaw joint was much stronger than that in the advanced mammal-like reptiles. In addition, it

made it possible for the animal to bite alternately on one side and the other, and to produce a grinding motion by moving the lower teeth across the uppers." The stage was then set for the evolution of many types of teeth that could process food more effectively than was previously possible.

"The evolution of the mammalian jaw appears to have been the side product of the evolution of better hearing," says Crompton.

A similar explanation can be advanced for the evolution of feathers. Feathers are an essential part of a bird's flying equipment. But of what use is a half-evolved feather that is too rudimentary to help lift a bird into the air? Or a fully formed feather on a creature not otherwise constructed for flight?

Birds probably evolved from small feathered dinosaurs, similar to the fossil bird-like form called *Archaeopteryx* (meaning ancient bird). According to John Ostrom of Yale, *Archaeopteryx* had feathers, but probably could not fly very effectively. So what might the feathers have been used for? At least two plausible explanations have been offered. First, for a small, active dinosaur, thermal insulation would have been extremely beneficial, and feathers, no matter how rudimentary, would have served well as insulation. A second possibility is that *Archaeopteryx* used them as a kind of web in which to scoop up small prey, such as insects. The point, however, is that no matter what function feathers first evolved to fill, once present they would be available for selection for flight.

The idea that a structure evolves under one set of selection pressures and, when fully formed, is modified for a totally different function, has been given the unfortunate term *preadaptation*. It's unfortunate because, says Stephen Jay Gould, "The term implies that species adapt in advance to impending events in their evolutionary history, when exactly the opposite meaning is intended." Natural selection is a force for the present, not a predictor of the future.

Darwin always viewed the appearance of new structures in evolution as the result of the accumulation of many small steps. In fact, as was implied earlier, small changes in the timing of the developmental clock can bring about large physical changes quite rapidly. Although it is highly improbable that important evolutionary innovations arise by single leaps, their origins may plausibly be the result of a relatively rapid transition through a few thousand generations under appropriate selection.

A series of such changes taking place in a small population isolated from the main population of a species, cut off perhaps by an arid valley, a mountain range, or a large river, could rapidly give rise to a new species. Once established, the new species might remain geographically separate from the ancestral species. It might, however, move back into the ancestral range and live side by side with the original species if their life-styles were now sufficiently different and competition not too severe. Or, having recolonized the ancestral range, the new species may outcompete the parent species and push it to extinction. This process, in which a new species "buds" off from an existing species, is known technically as *speciation*, whether or not the parental species eventually survives to exist alongside its "progeny."

New species may also arise when an entire species gradually changes through time under the influence of some sort of selection pressure. After a number of generations, the descendants change sufficiently so that if compared with their original ancestors they would be judged to be different species, even though they never coexisted.

Evolutionary biologists differ over explanations of the tempo and mode of evolutionary change. Some—those who adhere to the theory of punctuated equilibrium—argue that new species emerge relatively suddenly, then remain largely unchanged until they become extinct. Others—the gradualists—agree with Darwin's deeply held belief that species arise through a long and gradual series of steps and exist in a more or less constant process of slow change. Constantly bewailing the imperfect state of the fossil record, he argued that the lack of fossil evidence of gradual change in species was due to missing pages in that record. In this Darwin may have been too cautious. For, as Stephen Jay Gould says, "If rapid speciation is the principal mode of evolutionary change, then what we see in the fossil record is exactly what we do see: the gaps are real, not due to imperfection."

The average life-span of a terrestrial animal species is some 5 to 10 million years, during which time there is generally very little change in the physical form of the species. In this context, a speciation event that takes place in a small, isolated population of individuals over perhaps 50,000 years represents just one-half to one percent of the probable life-span of the species. This, relatively speaking, is a rapid event. "As a consequence," says Gould, "the world is packaged, for the most part, into relatively discrete and unambiguous species. If species changed slowly and gradually into other species as an intrinsic part of their history, the world of nature . . . would be dominated by groups in transition, imperfectly separated from related groups."

Turning now to the fossil record as a whole, what does it tell us of the pattern of life through evolutionary history? Probably the most common notions about the history of life are that it has followed a path of progressive improvement and progressive increase in the diversity of forms. Both impressions are false.

First, it should be said that the usual fate of a species is extinction. The overwhelming majority of the two million or so species now alive are relatively recent newcomers to the planet. Perhaps most are not as new to the planet as the 100,000 years or so that modern humans have been around, but in general, species' tenure is to be measured in a few million, rather than tens of millions, of years.

A steady balance between speciation and

In his 1951 book, The Horse, paleontologist George Gaylord Simpson used this phylogenetic chart to show the many starts and stops along the evolutionary path of the horse.

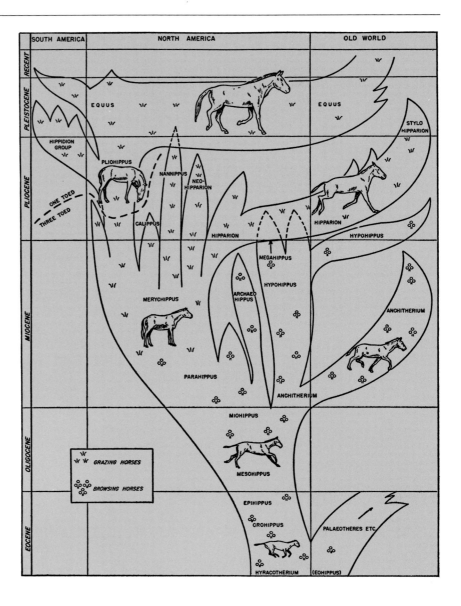

extinction would have produced a smooth evolutionary history, a steady turnover of species. In fact, life's history has been distinctly episodic, with major extinctions and radiations punctuating the passage of time. The Earth formed some 4.6 billion years ago, and within a billion years or so primitive life was established in the shape of single-celled organisms. Then, for almost three billion years life's history was very much a variation on a theme, with no really dramatic departures. Around 600 million years ago multicellular organisms appeared, and within a few tens of millions of years all the basic designs for complex life forms had been established. Since then life has again and again consisted of variations on a theme.

There are more complex organs and organisms now than there were soon after the explosive beginnings of multicellular life, but that is a matter of history, not the outcome of some determining force that pushes life to better and better accomplishment. "The limb of a mammal cannot be considered an improvement over the fin of a fish," comments George Gaylord Simpson, "because neither performs more effectively the functions of the other or adds to the functions of the other."

There is a tremendous human desire for neat, unequivocal description of the world in which we live. This, says Simpson, "explains the long and necessarily futile search for simple, absolute, deterministic laws of evolution." There are no such laws. "The fossil record is consistent with historical causation that is in continuous flux, nonrepetitive, and therefore essentially nonpredictive. It is not consistent with absolute, repetitive, and predictive determinism."

The Earth is about halfway through its probable life-span, as most astronomers believe that the sun is due to explode in about five billion years. "There is nothing in the fossil record that suggests that the origin of complex life from the early single-celled ancestors was inevitable," says Gould. "It's not unreasonable to say that the world might well have passed into extinction with only the blue-green algae as witnesses. As it happened, complex organisms did arise. But we mustn't believe there was anything inevitable about it."

Throughout the relatively brief time during which multicellular organisms have existed on Earth there have been periodic extinctions. Some, like the Permian extinction some 225 million years ago which included the end of perhaps 95 percent of all species of marine invertebrates, and the Cretaceous dying which brought the extinction of, among other things, the dinosaurs, have achieved considerable notoriety. But there were many more. Life's history is by no means a smooth progression—it is episodic and capricious.

If inexorable order cannot be abstracted from the fossil record as a whole, what of directional trends within the record? Relative brain size in mammals, for instance, has increased in group after group, in rodents, primates, carnivores, horses, and elephants. This is an evolutionary trend on a large scale and, says Stephen Jay Gould, "we must conclude that more brain is a general advantage for mammals."

Frequently—but wrongly—cited as an example of an evolutionary trend is the origin of the modern horse from its diminutive ancestor of some 50 million years ago. The picture commonly presented, says George Gaylord Simpson, is of "a single line of gradual transformation of *Hyracotherium* into *Equus*." In fact, the history of horse evolution is "more like a bush than a tree," says Simpson, "and even if the tree figure of speech were used, *Equus* would not correctly represent the tip of the trunk but one of the last bundles of twigs on a side branch from a main branch sharply divergent from the trunk."

Like the evolutionary history of many groups, that of the horse records the origin of many different species, some of which were bigger than their ancestors, some smaller; and some of which had more "advanced" features, some less so. The twigs and branches of the bush point in many directions, with differences arising between them in jerky changes rather than smooth transitions. It is true that the earliest horses were small, had multiple toes and relatively small teeth. And it is true that the modern horse is large, has a single "toe," and enlarged molar-like teeth. But there was no steady progression from one to the other. "It is a picture," says Simpson, "of a great group of real animals living their history in nature, not of robots on a one-way road to a predestined end." Trends do occur in evolution, but, says Simpson, "the doctrine of orthogenesis [of continued change in one direction] has grossly exaggerated their frequency, duration, and continuity."

There is a degree of uncertainty in the history of life which we humans find difficult to accept. There is order, there is a certain harmony to be sure—the result of the creative power of natural selection. But reflect on this, as remarked by Gould: "There was just one primate species in the Cretaceous period. If it had become extinct along with all the dinosaurs, there is no reason to expect that primates would ever have evolved again. There would surely have been other complex creatures in their place. But there would be no humans."

Natural selection, limited though it is by certain historical and architectural constraints, is extremely powerful. But its power is directed to the demands of daily life, not to the end point of some grand design.

Colors and texture of the hog sphinx moth blend with tree, an adaptation that improves its chances of avoiding predators.

SHIFTING CONTINENTS

Where mammal-like reptiles once sprawled in the tropical sun amidst abundant plant growth, a leopard seal drifts atop ice chunk on solitary Antarctic journey.

"One day early in 1968, the telephone in my office rang. When I answered it, the voice on the other end informed me that he had just returned from Antarctica and had what he thought was a fossil bone." This, recalls Edwin Colbert, one of North America's most notable paleontologists, was more than just exciting news: "It was sensational," he remembers.

Like many paleontologists, Colbert had for years been hoping that fossil vertebrates would some day be discovered on that vast frozen continent. So when Ralph Baillie, the bearer of this electrifying report, asked Colbert if he would be willing to examine the find, which had been discovered by Baillie's colleague, Peter Barrett, Colbert could hardly contain his intense curiosity. Baillie immediately took the specimen to Colbert's office at the American Museum of Natural History in New York. Colbert unwrapped the three-inch fragment, inspected it carefully, and triumphantly confirmed it to be a vertebrate fossil. Later, Colbert identified the fossil as a fragment of the lower jaw of an amphibian that had lived more than 200 million years ago.

Colbert was himself soon braving the biting Antarctic chill in search of more clues to life forms extinguished long ago on that most hostile of continents. Fossil hunting is frequently carried out under exacting and uncomfortable circumstances; Colbert's prospecting on the frigid exposures of Coalsack Bluff some 375 miles from the South Pole must rate as one of the toughest possible assignments. The paleontology team found plenty of fossils, but for the most part they were too fragmentary to be identified with certainty. Then, on December 4, 1969, came the breakthrough. Paleontologist James Jensen made what would be called "one of the great fossil finds of all time"—part of the upper jaw of a 200-million-year-old reptile named *Lystrosaurus*. At last, here was a fragment whose identity was in no doubt. Colbert was, to say the least, delighted. Two days later the story was

Bundled up against freezing temperatures at Antarctica's Coalsack Bluff, paleontologists David Elliott and Edwin H. Colbert examine a still-embedded bone of Lystrosaurus, left, a mammal-like reptile that thrived in the Triassic period some 200 million years ago. Recent Antarctic discoveries of Lystrosaurus bones—heretofore among the most abundant therapsid fossils in Africa—have provided irrefutable proof that Antarctica and Africa were one continent at the time Lystrosaurus and other animals lived.

announced to the world from the front page of the *New York Times*.

Meanwhile, with frozen fingers, Colbert and his colleagues continued to pry from those ancient rocks a collection of fossils that within a month would fill eight large boxes. In addition to the many *Lystrosaurus* specimens, an assortment of other reptiles and amphibians provided glimpses of life there 200 million and more years ago. The collection, which Colbert described as "looking more and more African in several aspects," added support to the theory of plate tectonics, at the time revolutionizing the geological sciences.

The significance of Jensen's discovery was not just that animals once lived on a continent that is now almost uninhabitable, but that animals very much like those in Antarctica also lived in southern Africa, China, and India. How could this hospitable polar climate—as well as the dispersal of terrestrial creatures across thousands of miles of deep ocean—be accounted for? The answer, according to plate tectonics, is that the animals hadn't moved—the continents had. When *Lystrosaurus* and its fellows were alive, Antarctica, Australia, Africa, China, and India were part of a single giant continent, Pangaea. Pangaea straddled the Equator, and at some point in its history the land that was to become Antarctica experienced a temperate climate. Pangaea later split up and carried the *Lystrosaurus* fossils off to different parts of the world.

Very soon after European map makers began to chart the world's continents with some accuracy, the apparent jigsaw-like fit between the coastlines of South America and Africa was noticed and remarked upon. But no significance was placed on this apparent trick of nature. The world as depicted on maps was viewed as an eternal configuration of stable land masses. Not until the mid-19th century did anyone begin to toy with the possibility of drifting continents. The first serious proponent of the notion was German meteorologist Alfred Wegener, who published his ideas in 1915.

Wegener was impressed by the ease with which South America and Africa could be fitted together along their continental shelves. He could see how virtually all the world's land masses could come together as a single continent, with an almost enclosed Tethys Sea opening to the east and a vast, uninterrupted Panthalassa Ocean covering the rest of the globe. Although Wegener considered the geological evidence to be suggestive of continental drift, he was even more strongly persuaded by the fossil evidence. For instance, how could one account for the occurrence of the small reptile *Mesosaurus* in deposits in South Africa and Brazil and nowhere else? If the two continents were in contact with each other 300 million years ago when *Mesosaurus* was alive, the mystery would vanish. But Wegener was ahead of his time and had, in any case, little hard evidence in support of his theory. Half a century was to pass before most geologists began to be convinced that they inhabited a world of moving continents.

Unwilling to accept the notion of continental drift, paleontologists instead proposed that animals and plants migrated across huge land bridges that had once linked the now separate continents. They suggested that the puzzling distribution of certain dinosaurs in North America and Tanzania, the occurrence of trilobites throughout North America and northern Europe, and the remains of certain seed plants throughout the southern continents could all be explained by the supposed existence of now vanished land bridges.

Geologists, many of whom were not interested in what the fossils implied, told the paleontologists that the proposed land bridges were sheer fantasy—there were simply no signs of vast stretches of continental rock in the oceans. The paleontologists replied that the bridges must have been much narrower than originally supposed. Nevertheless,

First proponent of continental drift, German scientist Alfred Wegener published The Origin of Continents and Oceans *in 1915. Below, Wegener's reconstructions show land masses united in protocontinent Pangaea.*

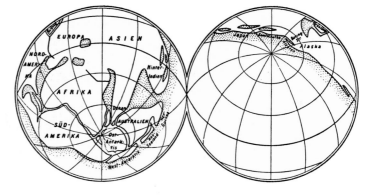

TYPVS ORBIS TERRARVM.

QVID EI POTEST VIDERI MAGNVM IN REBVS HVMANIS, CVI AETER
NITAS OMNIS, TOTIVSQVE MVNDI NOTA SIT MAGNITVDO. CICERO:

while the absence of any direct evidence for ancient land bridges was embarrassing, the traditional view prevailed mainly because no one could think of a good mechanism by which continents could move.

Wegener envisaged the lighter continental masses plowing through the denser rock of the Earth's crust like gigantic granite ships cutting their way across the ocean floor. Could the gravitational attraction of the sun and moon serve to suspend the continents, allowing the Earth to rotate beneath them? No, said the physicists: the force is too weak. The answer came in the 1960s with advances in various scientific disciplines that led to the discovery of the phenomenon known as sea floor spreading.

The Earth's crust, it turns out, is not a continuous skin of rock. Instead, the crust and associated upper mantle, which together are about 60 to 120 miles thick, are broken into sections or plates, half a dozen of which are huge while several others are relatively small. These plates are in constant motion and therefore create a dynamic mosaic: some plates move directly away from each other,

Close fit of South American and African coastlines can be seen in Abraham Ortelius's 1587 map of the world. Three centuries later, scientists aboard pioneer British oceanographic ship H.M.S. Challenger *crisscrossed world's oceans to collect data and specimens from ocean depths and sea bottoms.*

75

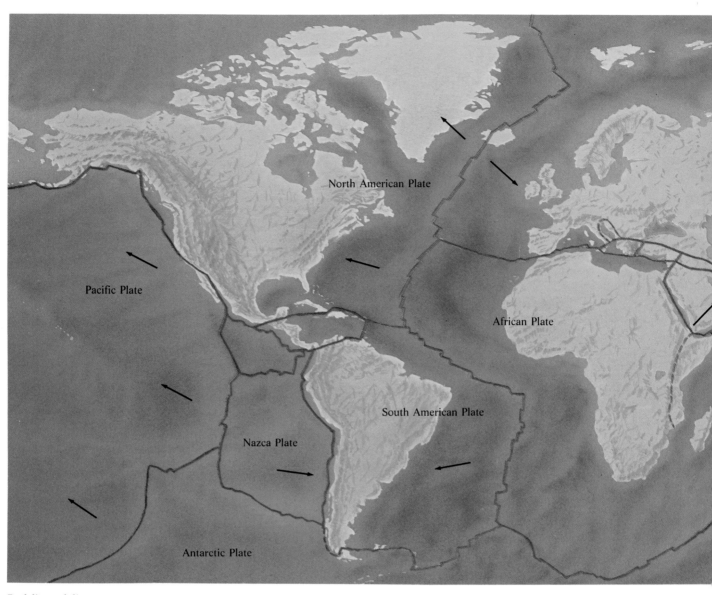

Red lines delineate present-day boundaries of plates, giant sections of Earth's crust. Continents, embedded in some plates, move with them as they spread from midocean ridges. Arrows indicate current direction of movement. Right, volcanic activity along a North Atlantic fracture zone gives birth to an Icelandic island. Far right, stretching like a rough scar across arid land north of Los Angeles, San Andreas Fault marks earthquake-prone juncture of Pacific Plate and North American Plate.

North American Plate

Pacific Plate

African Plate

South American Plate

Nazca Plate

Antarctic Plate

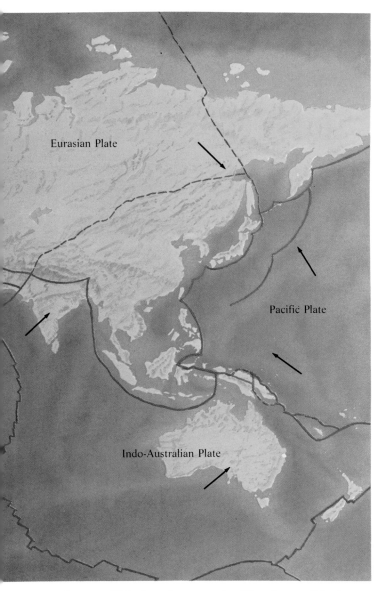

Eurasian Plate

Pacific Plate

Indo-Australian Plate

because the ocean floor is spreading out from a crack (in the case of the Atlantic), the magnetic pattern on one side of the crack directly mirrors that on the other side. The discovery of the magnetically "striped" ocean floor was a key piece of evidence in the discovery of sea-floor spreading.

Plate destruction can take place where two plates collide. If one of them is an oceanic plate and the other a continental plate, the oceanic plate is thrust below the other and dives deeply to its destruction in the molten mantle at what is known as a subduction zone. This is a geologically cataclysmic process, and so it is not surprising that subduction zones are often areas of volcanic activity and earthquakes. Earthquakes are also common where two plates slide against each other, jolting along from time to time as strain builds up at their junctures. California's San Andreas Fault is perhaps the best-known example of this phenomenon.

With the discovery that the sea floor was spreading, the idea of continental drift was quickly accepted as reality. However, Wegener's idea of the continents plowing through the crust like ships through water was clearly wrong. Instead, the continents are embedded in the moving plates and are carried about the globe by the plates as they spread from their zones of origin.

Inevitably, continental masses also sometimes collide. Because the continental rock is less dense than that of the plate in which the continent is embedded, it is not subducted. Instead, the land masses crumple against each other, like a carpet pushed up against a wall. Mountain ranges rise, faulting occurs, and the result can be very rugged topography. The spectacular Himalayan range began to rise when the Indian subcontinent rammed Eurasia about 45 million years ago. When two land masses become sutured in this way, the locked continental masses act as brakes on the carrying plates. Eventually a plate boundary may close and a new one open elsewhere.

The forces involved in the motion of the plates defy imagination. Though the details remain to be established, it seems that heat produced deep in the Earth by radioactive decay powers the slow cycling of molten mantle at many different locations beneath the crust. Each convection current propels the solid plate above it.

The heat engine that through the ages reshaped the physical face of the Earth also drives evolutionary change. The continents' never-ending odyssey across the globe influences evolution in a number of ways. For instance, shifts in climate and

others collide head on, and still others slide laterally against each other.

Where two plates are separating from each other, molten rock rises to the surface between them to add new material to the plates. The most outstanding example of this process is the Mid-Atlantic Ridge, a huge crack with raised edges in the ocean floor that echoes the outline of the continental shelf of the Americas to the west and Africa and Europe to the east. The molten mantle wells up and then cools as it flows both east and west. As it cools, certain minerals, mainly oxides of iron in the crust, become oriented in a north-south direction under the influence of the Earth's magnetic field. Now, it happens that at intervals of about 400,000 years the Earth's magnetic poles reverse. The effect of this is to produce a "zebra stripe" pattern of magnetic orientation on the ocean floor over periods of millions of years. And sea level may be critical to the survival of some organisms. If a large continent is rent asunder to form two smaller land masses, previously unified populations of plants and animals can, through geographical isolation, evolve into different species. And the joining of two lands to form a single continent introduces competition to previously isolated populations. But it is useful to glance back at Earth's history in the light of plate tectonics before looking at some major evolutionary events triggered by continental movement.

Because oceanic crust is constantly running through a process of formation, drift, and ultimate subduction and destruction, it has a relatively limited life-span. Compared with an age of about 3.8 billion years for the most ancient continental rock, the oldest rocks of the sea floor date back "only" 200 million years. Although the pattern of magnetic stripes on the sea floor is an excellent guide to the configuration of continents in the past, the limited life-span of the oceanic crust means that other methods must be used to reconstruct earlier world geographies.

Alfred Ziegler of the University of Chicago is combining clues from a number of sources to do just this. "None of the Paleozoic geographies is similar to that of today's Earth," he says. "In the modern world the continents are grouped into three extensive north-south masses—the Americas, Europe/Africa, and Eastern Asia through Indonesia to Australia. These land masses partly isolate three equatorially centered oceans—the Pacific, Atlantic, and Indian."

"The continents of the Paleozoic were isolated from each other and dispersed around the globe in low tropical latitudes," concludes Ziegler. "The ocean basins were extensively interconnected and the polar regions were occupied by broad, open oceans." The six major continents of the early Paleozoic—Gondwana, Laurentia, Baltica, Siberia, Kazakhstania, and China—presumably experienced equable climates with no extremes due to their distribution at low latitudes and the apparent lack of frigid polar air.

By the end of the Paleozoic, 225 million years ago, the global picture was totally transformed, as was the prevailing climate. All the world's continents were conglomerated into a single supercontinent, Pangaea, which straddled the Equator and linked the two poles.

Pangaea can be divided into two halves: Gondwanaland to the south, which over the past 200 million years has fragmented to form South America, Africa, India, Australia, and Antarctica; and Laurasia to the north, the precursor of North America, Greenland, northern Europe, Russia, Siberia, China, and part of southern Europe.

Because of its vast size, Pangaea would have experienced climatic extremes typical of large land masses—think of today's considerable temperature swings in the North American interior and in Siberia. In addition, easterly winds would have driven the equatorial current into the gaping Tethys Sea, producing an extremely warm and humid climate on its eastern coast. Ziegler and his colleagues, Richard Bambach and Christopher Scotese, theorize that ancient "gulf streams" would have

Research ship Glomar Challenger in Gulf of Mexico, 1968. Vessel's crew drilled deep-sea cores in each of the world's oceans; results confirmed sea-floor spreading.

Sea-floor spreading occurs along seismically active midocean ridges as molten rock rises to surface between two separating plates, then cools and solidifies to form new crust.

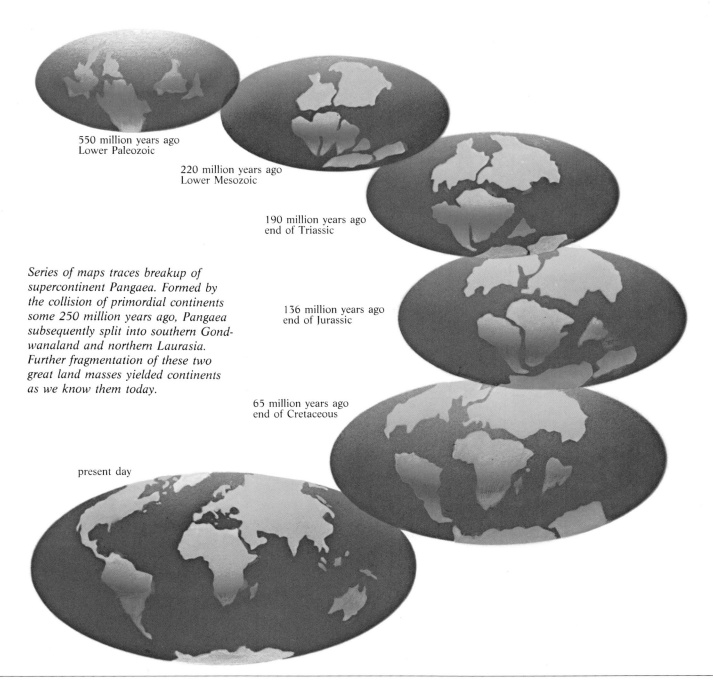

550 million years ago
Lower Paleozoic

220 million years ago
Lower Mesozoic

190 million years ago
end of Triassic

Series of maps traces breakup of supercontinent Pangaea. Formed by the collision of primordial continents some 250 million years ago, Pangaea subsequently split into southern Gondwanaland and northern Laurasia. Further fragmentation of these two great land masses yielded continents as we know them today.

136 million years ago
end of Jurassic

65 million years ago
end of Cretaceous

present day

Collision between oceanic plate and continental plate forces oceanic plate to plunge down under continent into the Earth's molten mantle.

Transform fault marks area where plate edges shear past each other, often creating earthquakes. Example is San Andreas Fault system.

Occasionally continental masses collide. This causes faulting and buckles up mountain ranges such as the Appalachians and Himalayas.

Drift of the continents has reshaped the physical face of the Earth, creating widely varied land forms. Fog rolls through majestic gaps in the Great Smoky Mountains, thrown up by the collision of Africa and North America some 250 million years ago. Right, glacier in Canada's Kluane National Park. Continents' movement may have contributed to the onset of major glacial episodes during the past billion years.

circulated these warm waters into higher latitudes, "causing an especially strong asymmetry between eastern and western Pangaea." As would be anticipated, geochemical evidence shows the interior of Pangaea to have been extremely arid.

The coalescing continents not only dramatically altered the global climate, but they also brought about a substantial fall in ocean levels, a cataclysmic fall as it turned out. As the land masses collided, the continental crust piled up at the point of impact. One consequence was the uplift of huge mountain chains; a second was a drop in sea level, as there was less continental mass available to displace the water.

The effect of the lower sea level was to drain the shallow continental shelves, an event that apparently precipitated the greatest marine extinction of all time: as many as 95 percent of marine invertebrate species vanished at this period. Inevitably, the shape of subsequent evolutionary developments depended greatly on which types of organisms survived this great dying. The drifting together of all the world's continents to form Pangaea was without doubt one of the most catastrophic events in the history of life on Earth.

By 180 million years ago Pangaea had broken into Laurasia and Gondwanaland, which themselves began drifting apart and showing signs of still further fragmentation. North America, though still attached to Eurasia, was starting to edge north and west, with an embryonic Atlantic Ocean beginning to open up. South America, soon to begin its westward journey, was still firmly in contact with Africa although the split was already evident; Africa, in turn, had connections with Antarctica, India, and Australia. Contact between the inexorably disintegrating northern and southern supercontinents was maintained via the North African-Spanish "hinge" point at Gibralter. In spite of the substantial tectonic movement that had occurred by this time, the world was still essentially a system of interconnected lands.

During the next 120 million years or so the outstanding feature of global geography was the emergence of a number of island continents, principally South America, Africa, Australia, and Antarctica. South America and Australia developed highly distinctive animal populations. Except for bats and rodents, placental mammals were unknown in Australia until their introduction by man. Australia had apparently become separated from the other southern continents before modern mammals arrived there, and the marsupial popula-

Hot, dry winds carve ripples and dunes from sands of Southwest Africa's Namib Desert, which stretches 1,200 miles along the continent's Atlantic coast. Its name, derived from the Nama language, implies "an area where there is nothing."

tion evolved in isolation. Australia is the only place on Earth where the most primitive of all mammals, the monotremes (the spiny anteater and the duck-billed platypus), are to be found today. In addition to the herbivorous kangaroo and koala, marsupial carnivores such as the Tasmanian wolf and the tiger cat also evolved in Australia. Interestingly, these creatures bear a striking if superficial resemblance to equivalent placental carnivores that evolved elsewhere in the world.

Marsupials in North America and Eurasia never developed the diversity seen in Australia and South America, presumably because of competition with placental mammals which replaced the marsupials almost completely within the past 10 million years or so. Continental drift, which created the isolated land masses in the first place, contributed substantially to the diversity achieved in mammalian evolution. This diversity was cut

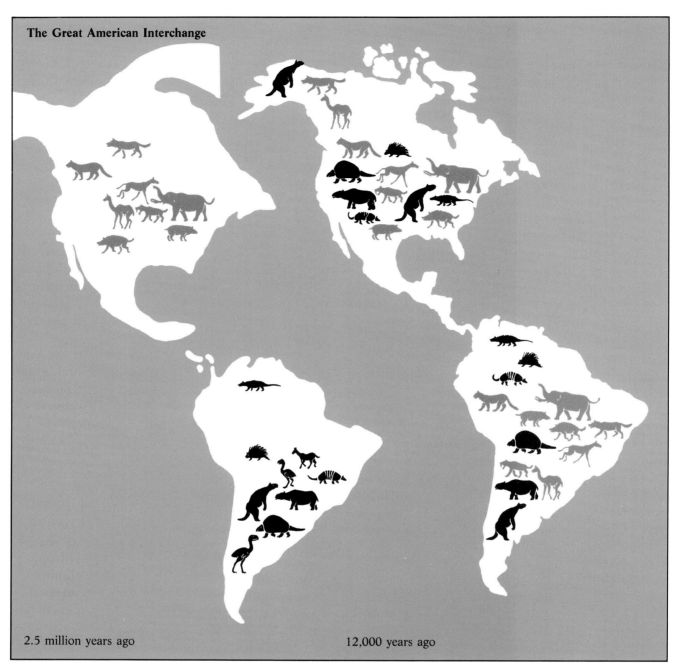

The Great American Interchange

2.5 million years ago

12,000 years ago

Before the Panamanian isthmus arose some two to three million years ago, joining North and South America, the continents' animal forms evolved in isolation. After the land bridge was established, the faunas of the two continents were mixed. The Eurasian-North American forms were more successful in competition with South American types, and the southern fauna declined.

short in South America when North American placental mammals arrived some three million years ago via the Panamanian bridge; recently, in Australia, humans introduced dogs, rabbits, and other domestic animals which displaced some of the native marsupials.

In their journeys northward, both Africa and Australia left behind cool, humid climates and entered warmer, more arid conditions. The dry interiors of both continents are relatively recent developments. When India made its northward trans-equatorial journey it also suffered greater aridity than in its previous history. India apparently had no mammals until about 50 million years ago when it made contact with Eurasia and was immediately invaded by mammals from Mongolia.

The opportunity provided by continents in isolation produces the evolutionary phenomenon known, for obvious reasons, as divergence—the increased diversity of species. The opposite occurs when two previously isolated land masses bearing different animal communities meet and there follows a homogenization of the faunas. The union of North and South America provides a number of good examples of convergence, as this is called. And so was the two-way migration that followed the joining of Africa with Eurasia 20 million years ago. Some native species of each homeland declined or succumbed to extinction as newcomers from the other joined them, and the result was that the African and Eurasian populations ended up looking more alike than they had previously.

This great continental union allowed ancestral elephants to invade Eurasia for the first time. Various species of now extinct elephants also came to North America from Siberia; so successful were they that when the Panamanian bridge was established some two or three million years ago, their descendants were ready and waiting to enter this last major continental region still untrodden by proboscideans. The mastodons became extinct only within the past eight thousand years, at the end of the most recent ice age.

When convergence occurs through the joining of previously separate lands, a seaway is inevitably blocked. So, while convergence may be triggered on land, divergence may simultaneously begin in the ocean: populations of marine invertebrates can become isolated from each other by a widening deep ocean just as much as by a solid land bridge. Certain species of bivalves in the early Cretaceous were common to what eventually were to be the Caribbean and Mediterranean regions. But as the Americas drifted westward, a deep ocean opened up between these shallow basins until the mobile larvae of these tiny shallow-water creatures could no longer drift from one region to the other. The two populations were then free to evolve separately, which they promptly did.

The principal lesson of the influence of drifting continents on the history of life is that diversity is promoted by physical separation. Geologist James Valentine of the University of California at Santa Barbara calculates, for instance, that today's relatively dispersed continents allow for about 10 times as many species of marine invertebrates as could be accommodated by a world with a single supercontinent. And Bjorn Kurtén postulates that the greater diversity achieved by mammals in 65 million years compared with reptiles over a 200-million-year period is largely the result of the breakup of Gondwanaland and Laurasia during the evolution of the mammals.

In recent years biologists have been able to work out the degree of species diversity that land areas of various sizes can support. Over time, new species arise and others fall into extinction. But overall there is an equilibrium which is maintained until something dramatic happens. For the Americas, that "something dramatic" was the establishment of the Panamanian isthmus. Before this strip arose there was a sporadic interchange of generally small animals between the continents—probably unwitting passengers on rafts of vegetation drifting from island to island in the Caribbean. After the strip arose, the way was open for terrestrial travel of species in both directions.

The Great American Interchange, the two-way migration following the union of North and South America three million years ago, provides an excellent example of the overall biological effects of continental drift on evolution. First recognized by Alfred Russel Wallace in 1876, it was termed by George Gaylord Simpson "an experiment without a laboratory, fortuitously provided by nature."

The outcome of the Panamanian bridge interchange in terms of numbers was precisely as might be predicted. The diversity of species on both continents increased for a time as migrants moved from one to another. Later the diversity dropped back to previous levels as competition eliminated many forms. However, the North American species enjoyed a relatively greater degree of success in the competition. Today, for instance, half the mammalian genera in South America have their origins in the north, whereas only 21 percent of North American mammals derive from southern ancestors. The big question about the Great American Interchange is, then, what if anything was special about the northerners?

A unique feature of South America prior to the interchange was its mix of marsupial and placental mammals. For the most part the marsupials were meat-eaters whereas the placentals were herbivores. Carnivores included a marsupial saber-tooth form very much like the placental *Smilodon* in the north, and seven-foot-tall meat-eating birds. Both of these animals became extinct after the interchange, the marsupial succumbing to direct competition from its placental counterpart,

Ring-tailed lemurs, above, are among the 20 or so species of this primitive primate that live without competition of other primates only on the island of Madagascar, wrenched away from the southeast coast of Africa some 55 million years ago. Left, tiny honey possum hails from Australia, whose isolation has nurtured both marsupial and monotreme mammal populations.

and the predaceous bird perhaps to competition with dogs and cats.

Although the popular notion of the outcome of the interchange is that it was a complete rout of the south, this ignores the ever-growing success of the "Virginia" opossum (a marsupial) and the porcupine (a placental). Generally, however, it has to be admitted that the south did fare badly.

In his study of the interchange, Larry Marshall of Chicago's Field Museum of Natural History notes other geological events taking place at this time. The Pacific plate, plunging into oblivion along the South American coast, was simultaneously heaving up that magnificent mountain chain, the Andes. Beginning about 11 million and climaxing between 4.5 and 2.5 million years ago, the elevation of this new towering range threw the country to the east into rain shadow. No longer did the moisture-laden winds from the Pacific irrigate vast tracts of the eastern continent. "The southern South American habitat changed from primarily savanna-woodland to drier forests and pampas," says Marshall. "New opportunities arose for animals able to adapt to these new environments."

As might be expected, one consequence of this increase in environmental diversity was an increase in the diversity of species living in the area. Again, it seems to have been the northern immigrants that grabbed most of this opportunity.

What allowed the northern immigrants to take advantage of new and changing territory? Simpson, who made a long study of the Great American Interchange, had this to say: "North American animals had intermittently, throughout the Age of Mammals and continously in its later part, been involved in the flux and intermigration of the World [Eurasian-African] continent. Those extant in the Plio-Pleistocene [seven million to 10 thousand years ago] were the ones that had been successful in a long series of competitive episodes. They were specialists in invasion and in meeting competitive invaders." By contrast, suggested Simpson, southerners had passed through an unchallenging history. "They had met no impact from outside their own closed economy, and when it came, they had not evolved the required defenses."

Had unremitting challenge sharpened the northerners' competitive edge? It is a well established phenomenon that the constant pressure to survive between predators and prey steadily selects for larger brains. As Harry Jerrison of the University of California at Los Angeles points out, the northern mammals tend to have significantly more brainpower than their southern equivalents.

Meanwhile, plate tectonic forces were causing dramatic changes in East Africa. This time it was the somewhat mysterious uplift that gave rise to Africa's Kenyan and Ethiopian domes, both about one mile high. Believed by some to be the result of upwelling of molten mantle, these domes began to form about 20 million years ago as indications of a probable plate boundary that runs more than 2,500 miles from the Red Sea through Ethiopia, Kenya, and Tanzania and into the Indian Ocean. The forces tearing the Earth's crust apart eventually caused the formation of the Great Rift Valley, a spectacular gash punctuated along its length by closed lakes and active volcanoes.

The rise of the domes and subsequent collapse of the Rift Valley created myriad microenvironments that favored rich diversity of species. But at least as important was the effect of the highlands on the climate. As with the Andes, the East African domes cast a dramatic rain shadow, here stretching to the Indian Ocean. Where lush forests and woodlands had once flourished, there now was open grassland. Efficiently equipped herbivores evolved for the first time, and apes began to take advantage of this more open country. They did leave descendants, however: creatures that were eventually to give rise to *Homo sapiens*, yet another evolutionary product of the engine of plate tectonics.

Once widespread in Northern Hemisphere's temperate regions, ancient giant sequoias today inhabit only western slopes of Sierra Nevada, their territory limited by climatic changes attributable in part to tectonic activity.

BEGINNINGS
IN THE SEA

LIFE EMERGES FROM THE SOUP

Mute testimony to one of the most ancient forms of life, undulating lines of a fossil stromatolite lie embedded in 3.5-billion-year-old rock from Western Australia.

The notice "Laboratory of Chemical Evolution" hangs above the door to the third floor of the University of Maryland's chemistry building. There, biochemist Cyril Ponnamperuma and his many colleagues seek signs of the earliest life on Earth. Analyzing the oldest rocks so far discovered, examining certain types of meteorites that carry faint signatures of potential life-forming processes elsewhere in our galaxy, and simulating the atmosphere of the primitive Earth in laboratory experiments, they are attempting to answer the question, how readily do the building blocks of life arise under purely inorganic, nonliving conditions?

The conclusion from these and similar ventures both in the United States and abroad is striking: life—albeit in primitive guise—arose very soon after the planet condensed from the primordial dust and gas cloud of the solar system some 4.6 billion years ago. "It seems very likely that the first life evolved more or less as soon as the young Earth cooled sufficiently," says Ponnamperuma. "I am very happy with that conclusion because all our experiments show that under the right conditions the inorganic and organic worlds are inseparable. The ease with which the basic chemicals of life are made is incredible."

When Ponnamperuma talks of life emerging on Earth "soon" after the surface has cooled sufficiently, he means after a period of perhaps one or two hundred million years, or around four billion years ago. One or two hundred million years may be a brief instant in relation to the total life of the planet, but in terms of the processes of primordial chemistry and the events that must take place if life is to be formed, it is a very long time indeed.

A volcanic eruption in Guatemala evokes primitive energy sources that may have sparked life-generating chemical reactions on Earth some four billion years ago. Overleaf, long-legged brittle stars crawl over sponge colony off Cayman Islands. Page 87, colorful blenny, Acanthemblemaria castroi, *peers from coral off Galapagos Islands.*

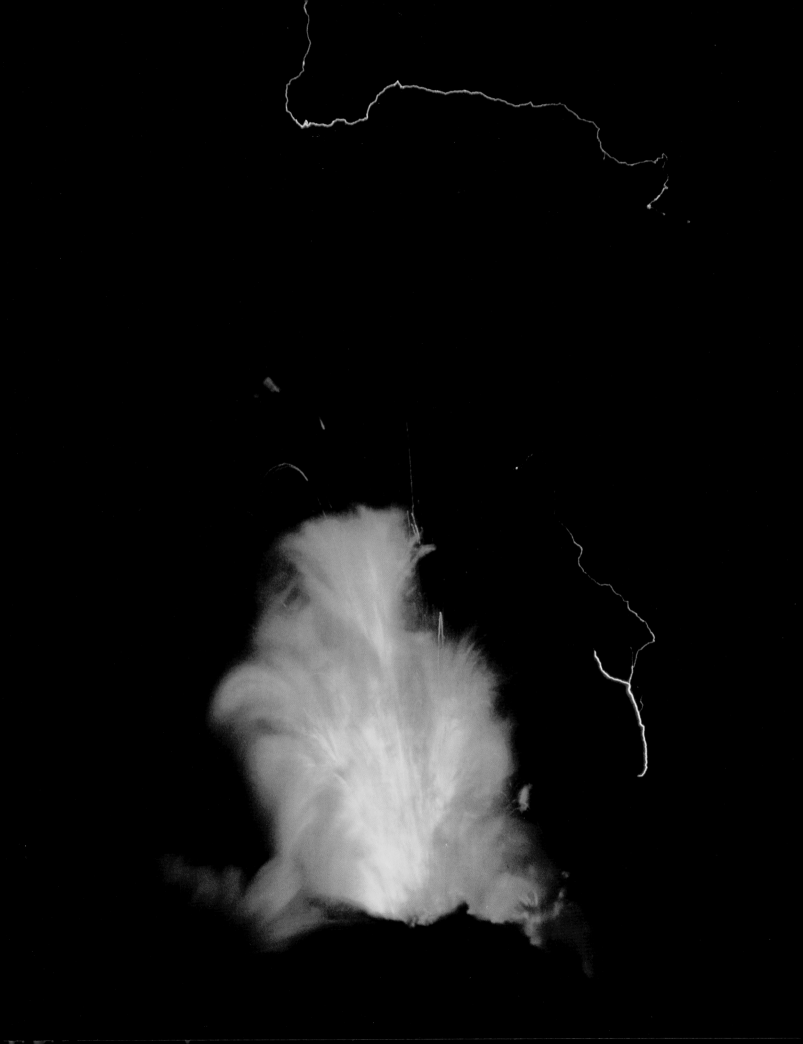

The origin of early life can be broken down into five stages: first, the formation of the Earth from the material spinning in the primordial solar system; second, the synthesis of the most simple chemicals such as amino acids, phosphates, and sugars that are used in living organisms; third, the linking together of these individual building blocks into long molecular chains, or polymers, such as proteins and nucleic acids, carbohydrates, and fats; fourth, the assembly from the primordial soup of minuscule proto-organisms; last, the origin of a mechanism by which these primitive organisms can faithfully replicate themselves.

This is a step-by-step process whose prime component, contrary to popular notion, is not chance. Chemicals react with each other under very simple conditions to form more complex chemicals, as long as some form of energy is added, whether it be heat from volcanic lava, ultraviolet radiation from the sun, or electrical energy from lightning. Chance clearly plays a part in the assembly and breakdown of molecules, depending on local conditions. But if molecules arise that are more stable than others, and if the more stable forms happen to interact with each other in a manner that enhances their own further synthesis, the logic of natural selection dictates that such structures will rapidly come to predominate the local molecular mix.

Although he never examined the question in detail, Darwin expressed his belief that life must have arisen from nonlife "in some warm little pond with all sorts of ammonia and phosphoric salts—light, heat, electricity, etc.—present." Darwin's musings were independently taken up again in the 1920s by Russian biochemist Alexander Ivanovich Oparin and British biologist J.B.S. Haldane. "When ultraviolet light acts on a mixture of water, carbon dioxide, and ammonia," speculated Haldane, "a variety of organic substances are made, including sugars, and apparently some of the materials from which proteins are built up. Before the origin of life they must have accumulated until the primitive oceans reached the consistency of a 'hot dilute soup'."

The Earth's early atmosphere was very different from today's. It was created when the Earth and other planets within what we now call the solar system were formed by the aggregation of cosmic debris. Today, the matter of the universe is 92.8 percent hydrogen and 7.1 percent helium. The heavier elements, the calcium and iron and carbon and gold, and so on, make up just 0.1 per-

The Origin Of Life On Earth

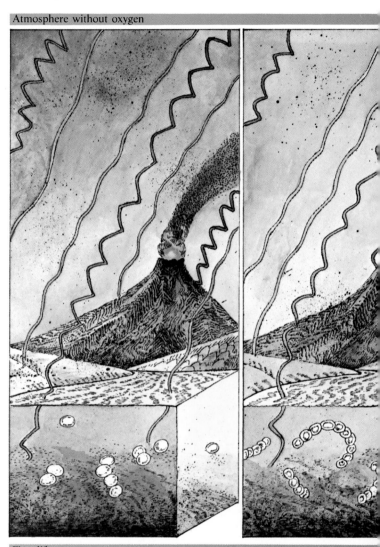

Atmosphere without oxygen

First life processes

cent of the matter. These heavier elements that make up that tiny remainder are what the four inner planets of our solar system, including the Earth, are primarily made of. Under gravitational force, the core of the proto-Earth melted, releasing tremendous energy. Lighter rock rose to the surface and gradually cooled, eventually to become the continents, which "float" on the thin crust. Gases "sweated out" of the molten core, surrounding the new planet with an envelope of water vapor, nitrogen, methane, ammonia, carbon dioxide, hydrogen, and other minor components. Most of the lighter gases, particularly hydrogen, drifted back into space as the Earth's gravity was too weak to hold them. Left behind was an atmosphere—but one that would have been totally alien and toxic to virtually all of life today.

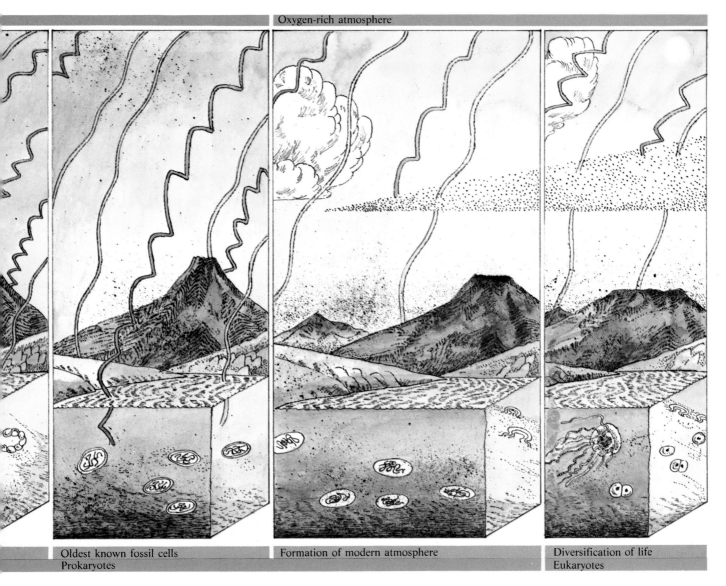

Oldest known fossil cells
Prokaryotes

Formation of modern atmosphere

Diversification of life
Eukaryotes

It was such an atmosphere that Oparin and others, particularly American biochemists Harold Urey and Stanley Miller, attempted to simulate in the laboratory.

The pioneering work of the last decades began a series of discoveries in which many of the important chemicals of life have emerged from a simple mixture of gases bombarded by electric discharge or ultraviolet light. Many important questions remain, of course, such as why a particular set of 20 amino acids, building blocks of proteins, came to be typically used by living organisms. And why only one type of each amino acid—a form called "left-handed" rather than one called "right-handed" —is used. But so far no major chemical barrier has been discovered to stand between non-life and life, given the essential input of energy.

Some four billion years ago the Earth's atmosphere consisted mainly of water vapor, nitrogen, methane, ammonia, carbon dioxide, and hydrogen. Ultraviolet radiation from the sun bombarded the seas, forming complex organic molecules that eventually acquired the ability to reproduce themselves. Free oxygen formed by the dissociation of water vapor gave rise to the "ozone blanket," a layer of oxygen molecules in the upper atmosphere that screened the emerging life forms from lethal ultraviolet. More advanced life forms then evolved, including photosynthesizers that contributed more oxygen to the atmosphere. Between 3 billion and 500 million years ago, bacterial communities and then multicellular organisms arose.

It is intriguing, incidentally, that the cocktail of organic chemicals generated in laboratory experiments matches very closely the chemicals that are found in certain stony meteorites, the carbonaceous chondrites, that occasionally fall to the Earth, and in some lunar samples. Apparently the conditions for the synthesis of these organic molecules exist elsewhere in the solar system, and it may well be that chemicals on these extraterrestrial bodies contributed to Haldane's "hot dilute soup."

During some of Ponnamperuma's experiments he discovered that not only are amino acids readily formed under primitive Earth conditions, but that they readily linked together to form long chains of molecules, or polymers. Polymerization is a crucial step in the formation of life, and clearly it is one that is easily accomplished under the simplest of conditions. If this seems surprising, then a subsequent separate discovery by the University of Miami's Sydney Fox is even more so. Fox has shown that the kinds of proteins called proteinoids or thermal proteins formed in primitive Earth experiments will, when in a watery environment like that of an ancient tidal pool, assemble themselves into tiny spheres that look remarkably like modern microorganisms.

The structure of the curved wall of the experimentally formed sphere and the cell membrane of the microorganisms have important features in common. If these microspheres, as Fox calls them, become too large through accreting more protein molecules, they split to form two "daughter" spheres, just as microorganisms do. The spheres are not microorganisms, but it is apparent that it is the chemical nature of the proteins to behave in this way. "The point is," says Fox, "that the processes are simple enough to have occurred spontaneously on the primitive Earth."

The central property of life is the ability to reproduce: some mechanism is necessary by which an organism can produce progeny that are essentially identical to the "parent." The chemical which in virtually all forms of life encodes information from generation to generation is the nucleic acid DNA. Like protein, DNA is a polymer assembled from single building blocks, all of which are to be found among the products of primitive Earth simulation experiments. The nature of the DNA polymer chain is such that when a new chain is made using the original one as a template, the original structure is precisely duplicated. This precise duplication is the basis for the accurate passing on of genetic information from parent to offspring.

DNA possesses a property of physical chemistry that perhaps provides an important clue to a key feature of the early atmosphere. We have emphasized that the assembly of simple chemicals into more complex associations requires an energy input. Ultraviolet light from the sun is a more or less constant source of energy. The early Earth was bathed in this searing radiation, which would have stirred the chemical soup into many reactions, some of which produced organic polymers essential to the beginning of life. Ultraviolet radiation could have also broken up chains of organic molecules or polymers. However, once created, ancient polymers might then have been protected from ultraviolet in a number of ways—by adsorption onto clay in the bottom of a shallow pool, for instance.

Today's Earth has an umbrella against ultraviolet light in the form of a layer of ozone formed from oxygen high in the stratosphere. Ozone absorbs much of the ultraviolet radiation before it reaches the Earth's surface. In fact, without that umbrella, all of life would perish under the powerful ultraviolet rays. So, the energy that may have been essential to trigger life in the first place is now inimical to it.

The point about DNA is that like all molecules it absorbs radiation of a particular wavelength of energy. And the wavelength which DNA happens to absorb is identical with that which ozone absorbs—ultraviolet radiation. So the chemical—DNA—that was essential to establishing true reproduction in early organisms finds protection from ultraviolet radiation precisely under the ozone umbrella. This is surely more than mere coincidence.

The oxygen in today's atmosphere comes directly from the activity of living organisms: when plants and algae trap the sun's light for their energy, they carry out a process—photosynthesis—which gives off oxygen. So where did the early Earth's oxygen come from, there being no photosynthetic organisms living then? Ken Towe, of the National Museum of Natural History, suggests that there was sufficient water vapor in the primitive atmosphere for a process known as photodissociation to occur. This is simply the breaking down of water into its component parts—oxygen and hydrogen—by ultraviolet light. "The lighter hydrogen would have escaped into space, leaving a small amount of oxygen in the atmosphere," he says.

The suggestion is that this small quantity of oxygen would have been sufficient to establish

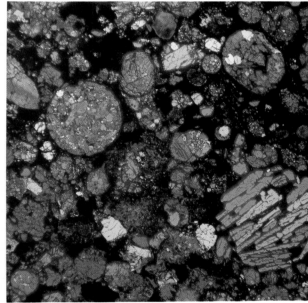

Mitchell Hobish of the University of Maryland's Laboratory of Chemical Evolution watches as electrical discharges bombard a mixture of gases simulating the atmosphere of the primitive Earth. In such experiments most of the amino acids, building blocks of proteins, have been created.

Like stained glass, a photomicrograph of an ultra-thin slice from the Murchison meteorite, above, glows with color. A carbonaceous chondrite, or carbon-rich stony meteorite, the Murchison yielded the first unambiguous evidence of extraterrestrial amino acids, building blocks of proteins in Earthly organisms. Left, rock from Isua, Greenland, dates back about 3.8 billion years.

95

FOSSIL DATING

When a paleontologist unearths a fossil, how does he determine its age? For many years scientists had no direct method for dating their finds. However, by studying the layers of rock in which the fossils were embedded, their sequence from top to bottom could be established. Scientists could then apply the "law of stratigraphy"—in unfolded, untilted beds, the oldest rocks are always on the bottom, the youngest at the top—and tell which fossils were older and which were younger. This method is called relative dating. But no technique existed for determining the absolute age in years of a specimen until the late 1940s, when radiometric dating systems were devised. These all rely on the existence of naturally occurring radioactive forms, or isotopes, of chemical elements. These isotopes are unstable; their atoms decay to form other elements at a rate which can be determined by laboratory analysis. For instance, carbon 14 is an unstable form of the common element carbon, which decays to form another element, nitrogen 14. All living things take in some carbon 14 together with the normal form of carbon and incorporate it in their bodily structures. When an organism dies, it ceases to take in carbon 14. The carbon 14 already in its structure decays at a known rate. When a fossil which still contains organic material is found, its remaining carbon 14 can be measured and converted into the number of years that have passed since the organism died. Carbon 14 dating works well for specimens that still contain organic material and are less than about 50,000 years old. But decay of other radioactive isotopes can be used to date older, completely mineralized fossils and even rocks themselves. Potassium 40, for example, decays into argon 40 and can be used to date very old specimens. Many such isotopes exist and can be used to measure the age of the Earth itself. And other forms of dating, such as protein racemization, can be used. In this method, the rate at which proteins change from one form to another after the death of an organism can be measured to give its approximate date of death.

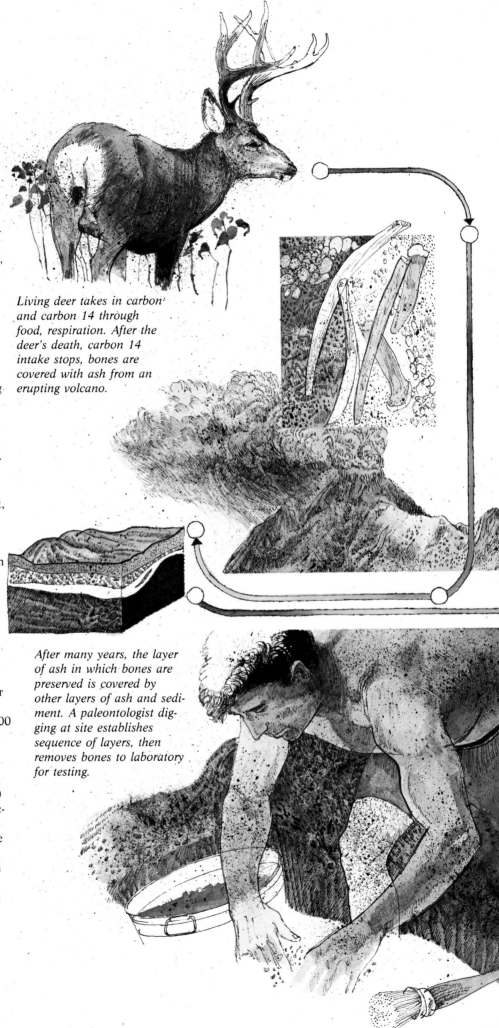

Living deer takes in carbon and carbon 14 through food, respiration. After the deer's death, carbon 14 intake stops, bones are covered with ash from an erupting volcano.

After many years, the layer of ash in which bones are preserved is covered by other layers of ash and sediment. A paleontologist digging at site establishes sequence of layers, then removes bones to laboratory for testing.

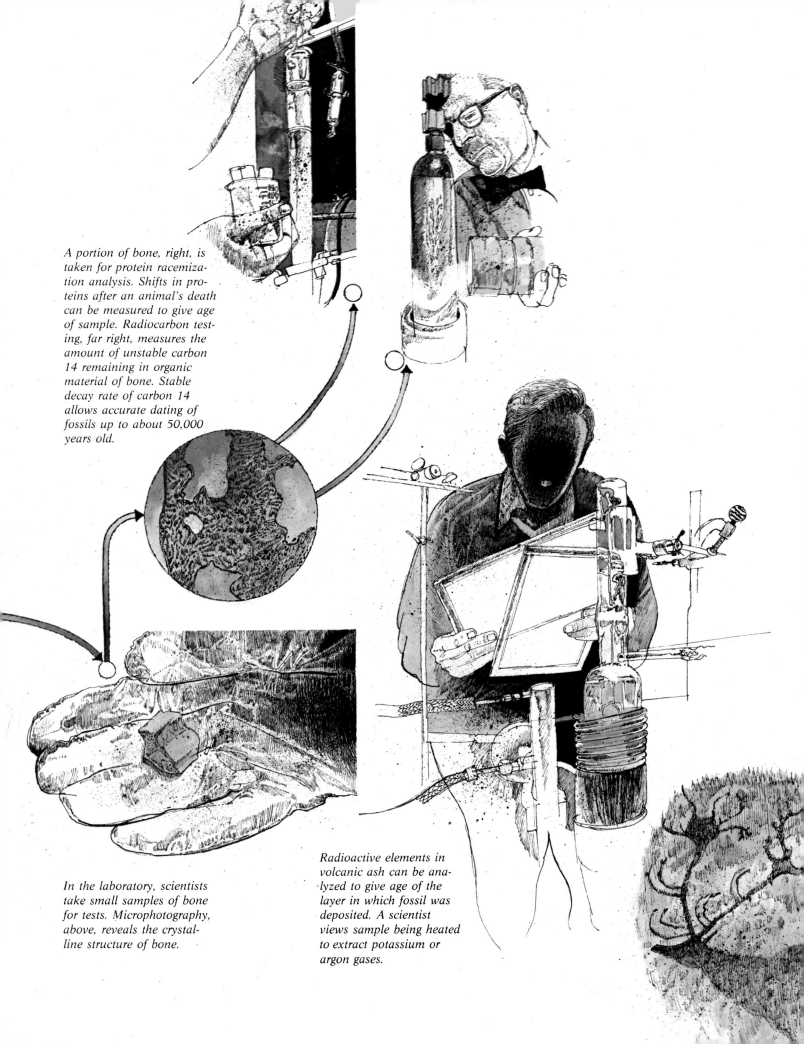

A portion of bone, right, is taken for protein racemization analysis. Shifts in proteins after an animal's death can be measured to give age of sample. Radiocarbon testing, far right, measures the amount of unstable carbon 14 remaining in organic material of bone. Stable decay rate of carbon 14 allows accurate dating of fossils up to about 50,000 years old.

In the laboratory, scientists take small samples of bone for tests. Microphotography, above, reveals the crystalline structure of bone.

Radioactive elements in volcanic ash can be analyzed to give age of the layer in which fossil was deposited. A scientist views sample being heated to extract potassium or argon gases.

some degree of protection from ultraviolet light by providing a minimal ozone layer. "That DNA fits so neatly under the ozone umbrella implies that life must have evolved under that umbrella," says Towe. "Levels of oxygen would have been very small for a very long time, only reaching levels near those to which we are accustomed a billion or so years ago."

To recapitulate the series of events that led to the first organisms on the Earth: ultraviolet light, lightning, heat from volcanoes and other energy sources fire the primitive atmosphere's chemical cauldron, giving rise to organic molecules and some oxygen. The amount of ultraviolet radiation reaching the Earth's surface is gradually reduced as ozone accumulates in the upper atmosphere. Proto-organisms arise, finding shelter under the ozone umbrella. The most primitive organisms are then established and their growth and multiplication are sustained by the "hot dilute soup" that has already accumulated in the oceans.

Such a scenario very quickly runs into a problem. If the energy input from ultraviolet radiation is blocked sufficiently to protect early organisms,

Francis Crick, right, and James Watson pose in 1953 with their original model of the DNA molecule, which established the spiral double-helix structure of this substance, a key to evolution. Right, atoms glitter amidst incredibly complex matrix of chemical bonds in a computer-generated section of a DNA strand.

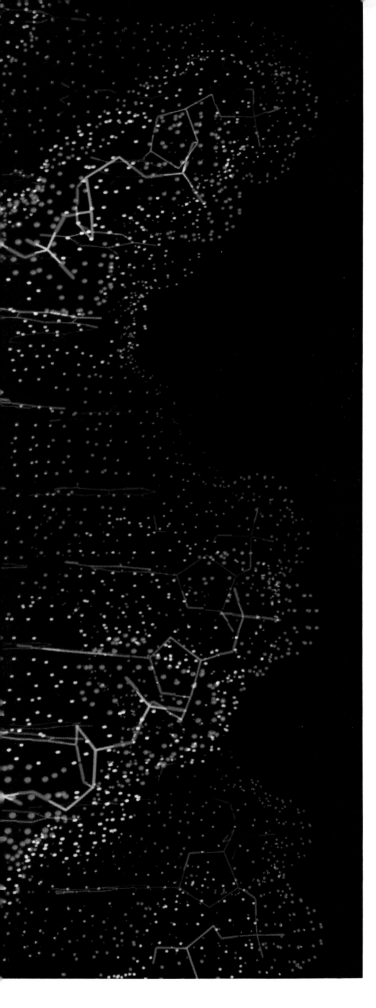

can the production of organic compounds necessary for those organisms' proliferation continue? The answer is, probably not. Other sources of energy already mentioned could help replenish the soup, but very quickly the organisms dependent on this supply of chemicals would face the world's first energy crisis. How would they overcome it? Just as in today's world, the answer is self-sufficiency: in this case it is called photosynthesis.

If an organism acquired a mechanism through chance mutations that could harness the sun's energy and use it to make its own complex compounds from simpler ones, it would have a tremendous advantage over other organisms that depended on a supply of ready-made molecules. On this basis it is a reasonable supposition that photosynthesis was a very early evolutionary innovation. What evidence is there in the fossil record that might illuminate some of this history?

Until the 1950s scientists had found little if any fossil evidence of life prior to about 600 million years ago. It looked as if complex organisms originated from nowhere and proliferated wonderfully. But patient searching through older sediments has now shown that the record of life stretches back almost as far as geological history can go. The oldest sedimentary rocks yet found are from Greenland and India; samples from both sites have been dated at about 3.8 billion years. Although some researchers believe there are chemical indications of life from these ancient layers— "it certainly cannot be excluded," says Cyril Ponnamperuma—there is no direct evidence in the form of microfossils. During their history these rocks have been subjected to high temperatures and pressures, so even if microorganisms had once been fossilized in them, all direct signs would probably have been obliterated.

The oldest unaltered rocks that geologists have access to are around 3.3 to 3.5 billion years old, and in two places in the world they show strong evidence of primitive life. Elso Barghoorn and his colleagues at Harvard have found fossilized forms resembling algae and bacteria in rocks known as the Fig Tree Group in southern Africa. And David Groves and his colleagues in Australia describe convincing evidence of quite complex microbial communities at a place called North Pole in Western Australia. Organisms at both of these sites were apparently photosynthetic.

Through careful geological investigation, the Australian workers have been able to infer that the sediments containing the ancient microorganisms were laid down in calm, shallow tidal pools. Barghoorn says that the Fig Tree microorganisms lived in much the same environment.

In Western Australia's Shark Bay we find something of a glimpse of those ancient times. The water in the bay is unusually salty, and for this reason very few creatures are able to tolerate its environment. Scattered patches of bacteria and blue-green algae, or *cyanobacteria*, which would normally be rapidly grazed by a variety of marine invertebrates therefore manage to thrive. The mats of bacterial organisms appear to rest on small mounds in the shallow water. In fact, the mats have made the mounds themselves. The bacteria and cyanobacteria secrete a viscous substance that traps sediments and sand. Soon the organisms in the mat are covered by the sediments and are therefore forced to migrate up through the barrier, where they then establish a new living layer. As time passes, the piling of sediment layer upon sediment layer forms a mound, a fossil of which is called a *stromatolite*.

Stromatolites are common in the geological record between one and two billion years ago, and sometimes they have complex, undulating formations. There are clear indications of stromatolites in the 3.5-billion-year-old North Pole, Australia, rocks. They are not as complex as the later ones,

Like a lost colony of living fossils, stromatolites—mats of trapped sediment and algae—thrive in the unusually salty and hostile environment of Western Australia's Shark Bay.

but nevertheless they appear to be the product of photosynthetic microbial communities.

In order to harness the sun's rays, photosynthetic organisms must have a pigment with which to trap the light. Unlike most of the green plants and bacteria with which we are familiar, the pigment in the very earliest photosynthetic organisms was probably reddish brown, as in primitive photosynthetic bacteria today. Another difference between today's green photosynthesizers and the ancient forms was their use of hydrogen sulphide rather than water as an essential component of the energy-trapping reaction. Those earliest organisms generated no oxygen in their photosynthesis—their

there are fossil data. However, recent studies of a group of bacteria loosely known as methanogens (because the metabolisms of some of them produce methane, or marsh gas) give an indirect glimpse of an even more ancient past. Carl Woese and his colleague Ralph Wolfe argue that the similarities and differences in certain chemical components of these organisms and the other primitive photosynthesizers indicate that they derive from a common ancestor, a group of organisms that must have existed prior to 3.5 billion years ago. Life does indeed seem to have had an early start on this Earth.

The fact of an early start might lead one to

metabolisms would have been poisoned by it.

As we have seen, the first oxygen producers were the cyanobacteria. They developed the ability to use the abundant supplies of water in their photosynthetic process; as a consequence, they were more flexible in their habits. Under certain conditions they simply switch off their water-using photosynthetic system and revert to the more primitive hydrogen sulphide mechanism. Such a switch may occur when oxygen falls to low levels in the environment. Presumably, cyanobacteria originated at a time when fluctuations in oxygen availability were part of daily experience in the early world. The high level of oxygen in today's atmosphere is the direct result of the metabolism of the cyanobacteria, and the more advanced photosynthesizers that evolved later.

It is clear then that photosynthetic organisms have a very ancient history, going as far back as

Ghostlike behind a branch of dead coral in Palau's Spooky Lake, a diver ascends from a toxic hydrogen-sulfide level of oxygen- and light-free waters in which only bacteria can survive.

expect a continued pattern of rapid change and "advancement." Once the cyanobacteria had arisen, however, life was set more or less in its ways for almost two and a half billion years. Throughout that time cyanobacteria lived in mixed communities with other photosynthetic bacteria, forming mats as the highest manifestation of life.

As the cyanobacteria pumped more and more oxygen into their world, a conflict arose between the old forms of life and the new. As oxygen is toxic to the primitive photosynthetic bacteria, its steady buildup gradually reduced the number of hospitable niches available to those organisms. The old order was inexorably overthrown, and today the diminished ranks of photosynthetic bacteria occupy some of the most extreme and—to us and the rest of the oxygen-dependent organisms—inhospitable environments, such as hot sulphurous pools. This changeover in the established order of life is reflected both in the increasing abundance of stromatolites through the fossil record and in several dramatic signatures in the rocks themselves. The photosynthetically produced oxygen dissolved in the oceans, where it interacted with a soluble form of iron compound (ferrous iron) to form an insoluble form (ferric iron) which then precipitated out of the water, causing the deposition of massive amounts of iron-rich minerals on the ancient sea bottoms. This "rusting" process created the so-called banded iron formations, which were for the most part laid down prior to two billion years ago, and are now the world's principal source of rich iron ore.

Once the ferrous iron had been completely precipitated from the waters of the oceans, oxygen was free to escape into the atmosphere, where it combined with ferrous iron minerals on land. These, too, rusted to give the characteristic reddish brown color of ferric minerals, resulting in extensive deposits which geologists call the red beds. The red beds were formed primarily after two billion years ago. Once these ferrous minerals had fully combined with oxygen, the gas began to build up to substantial levels in the atmosphere.

Although the bacteria and cyanobacteria that were part of the first 2.5-billion-years' domination of the Earth occupied a great variety of habitats, they represented a very simple form of life. They were *prokaryotes*—individual tiny cells without nuclei—which contained a package of metabolic machinery and a set of genetic instructions encoded in a single loop of DNA. Reproduction occurred by simple division of the cell into two "daughter" cells, the DNA having been copied so that each new cell had an identical set of instructions. Apart from some organisms that linked together to form long filaments, all life existed as simple single cells. And sex had not been invented.

At about 1.5 billion years ago a new type of cell begins to appear in the fossil record. It is larger than the organisms of the previous two billion years, and it appears to have a more complex

Bands of algae color the shallow margins of Grand Prismatic Spring, a hot sulphur pool in Yellowstone National Park whose microscopic life may be similar to primitive, hydrogen sulphide-dependent forms.

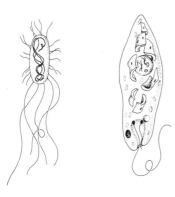

Diagram at left illustrates the structural differences between a prokaryote—a simple, single-celled, unnucleated organism of the kind that dominated Earth for some three billion years, and a eukaryote—a larger, more complex, nucleated cell.

internal structure. This date marks the origin of the *eukaryotic*, or nucleated cell, from which all "higher" forms of life are built.

Eukaryotic cells display several features that separate them from their predecessors, the prokaryotic or unnucleated cells. First, the genetic information (DNA) is in the form of several discrete chromosomes that are collected together inside an envelope termed the nucleus. The enzymes which are responsible for releasing energy from complex molecules are packed inside a sausage-shaped structure or organelle called a *mitochondrion*. And the machinery which carries out photosynthesis is arranged inside other organelles called *chloroplasts*, the photosensitive pigment and associated enzymes of which are stacked in many layers of membrane.

The evolutionary origin of eukaryotic cells is still a matter of some conjecture, but the most attractive speculation is the revival in sophisticated form of a notion that was first contemplated during the last century. Perhaps the new form of cell is the consequence of a once-temporary colonization that eventually became permanent. According to Lynn Margulis of Boston University, mitochondria and chloroplasts may once have been free-living organisms that established a symbiotic relationship with another type of cell: the two smaller cells lived inside the larger host cell. These protomitochondria and protochloroplasts provided their host with a source of useful chemicals and a way of boosting its energy supply. The host offered a stable environment in which the smaller organisms could thrive. Eventually, all parties involved became totally dependent on each other, and a permanent relationship—the eukaryotic cell—emerged.

With few exceptions, eukaryotic organisms require an oxygen-rich environment in which to grow. But the most important feature of this new form of cell is that it offers for the first time the potential for sexual reproduction. The progeny of asexual prokaryotic cells are always identical to the

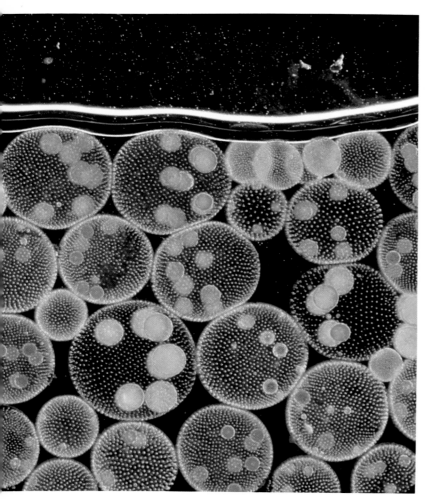

A colony of globular single-celled organisms, volvox, crowds the surface of a pond, above. "Daughter" colonies within will eventually break through parent's wall, right, and swim free.

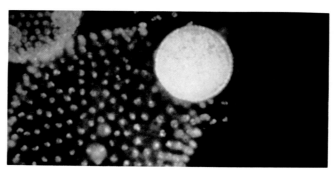

"parental" cell, except where a mutation occurs in the DNA. Variation in prokaryotic organisms was therefore limited primarily to the rare occurrence of mutations. The essence of sexual reproduction is the mixing together of genetic information from *two* parents to form offspring. As a result, although offspring resemble their parents, the mixing and chopping up of DNA that occurs in the formation of sex cells and their fertilization means that there will be differences too. With sexual reproduction, genetic variability—the raw material of natural selection—was possible.

The first eukaryotic cells entered a world in which the most complex form of life was a loose association of organisms in a bacterial mat, and multicellular organisms had not yet arisen. The eukaryotic organisms were also single-celled, of course, although they were rather more complex than their predecessors.

At this stage things remained the same for many hundreds of millions of years. At some point, however, the monotonous pattern of over three billion years was broken: a burst of diversification in the form and habit of organisms swept the primordial Earth.

Where once there had been only single-celled organisms, there were now multicelled creatures. Once again, scientists offer informed speculation, but no firm answers, of what prompted this change. Steven Stanley, a paleontologist at Johns Hopkins University, points to important ecological factors that might have lit the fuse for the diversification explosion that was to come. The organisms of the early phases of life on Earth were all self-sufficient in one way or another. There were no predators—no cell survived by consuming other cells. Stanley points out that in circumstances where there are no predators, the ecological system rapidly reaches a stable state where very little opportunity for diversification exists.

So it was for three billion years on the early Earth: as no organism had developed ways of feeding on other organisms, the environment was dominated by relatively few types. At some point, Stanley suggests, primitive ways of "predation" arose: the first herbivores appeared. As their cropping of shrubs and grasses made its impact, new species would be able to take advantage of new niches, an opportunism probably practiced more by the eukaryotic than the prokaryotic organisms. Once this wedge had been driven into the ecological mix, it would feed back on itself to produce yet more diversification. The world's first carnivores arose to feed on the herbivores.

This, remember, is still at a stage when all of life consisted of single cells, so the terms herbivore and carnivore relate to whether a predator's prey was a photosynthesizer or was perhaps another predator. Nevertheless, according to Stanley, the arrival of organisms that could prey on other organisms caused the massive and explosive diversification that would in the relatively short span of a few hundred million years populate the seas, the land, and the air with complex multicellular creatures.

Other factors must have been at work in this initial efflorescence of multicellular organisms. One suggestion, for instance, has been that until atmospheric oxygen reached relatively high levels, physiological processes basic to building large organisms were simply impossible. One such basic process is the biochemical synthesis of collagen, a fibrous protein that is found in the connective tissue of most multicellular animals.

The new era of multicellular creatures was to witness the emergence of myriad physical forms reflecting the exploitation of different habitats and the pursuit of different life-styles. By contrast, the three billion years preceding this point had been characterized by a series of biochemical innovations encompassed within a relative uniformity of physical form. It had been a time during which life itself had inflicted enormous change on the environment: the atmosphere, the seas, and the rocks were transformed to a staggering degree. Life created a new environment upon which we and all our fellow creatures now utterly depend.

Filamentous blue-green algae, or cyanobacteria, winds through volvox and other freshwater organisms. The first oxygen producers, cyanobacteria modified the Earth in a way that made possible life as we know it.

A SUBMARINE EXPLOSION OF FORMS

Fossil trilobite, Greenops boothi. *A dominant group of early life forms, trilobites were well established by the beginning of the Cambrian period more than 600 million years ago, then died out in the Permian, 225 million years later.*

As was his yearly habit, Charles Doolittle Walcott, Secretary of the Smithsonian Institution and distinguished paleontologist, traveled to the West in the summer of 1909 to search for fossil evidence of life from the ancient era called the Cambrian. Fall was fast approaching in the majestic Rockies of British Columbia when, by great good fortune, Walcott happened upon one of the most remarkable fossil discoveries of all time. He found a window into the past, a glimpse of life in a shallow sea some 530 million years ago.

Walcott made his discovery as he rode on horseback along the trail that runs along the west side of the ridge joining Wapta Mountain and Mount Field. The narrow trail continues through the pass between two mountains, then down into the town of Field. As he rode, Walcott's trained gaze skipped from feature to feature in the landscape. The geology of the region fascinated him. Suddenly, his horse lost its footing and he quickly dismounted. Pausing for a short rest while he and his mount recovered, Walcott picked up a lump of dark shale lying on the track and split it, as geologists are apt to do with any rock that looks even mildly interesting. He was astonished by what he saw, and later wrote in a letter to a colleague that he had spent "a few days collecting . . . in the vicinity of Field and found some very interesting things." He had, in fact, stumbled across the most extraordinarily preserved organisms of an astonishing and distant age ever found.

The following season Walcott returned to the pass with his two sons, and together they eventually located the source of the shale in an outcropping high above the trail. "It is a magnificent spot," says Harry Whittington, professor of geology at the University of Cambridge, England, and noted authority on the fauna of the Burgess Shale,

Charles Doolittle Walcott, paleontologist and Secretary of the Smithsonian, searches for fossils at western Canada's Burgess Shale, a site which he discovered in 1909.

106

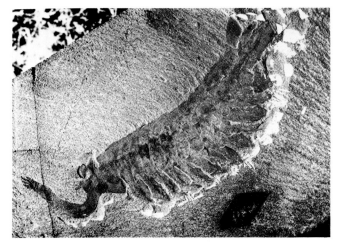

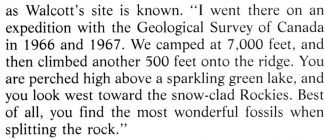

During the Mid-Cambrian, some 530 million years ago, more than 140 species of marine invertebrates inhabited the muddy sediments that are now the Burgess Shale. Stilt-legged Hallucigenia, *above left, and five-eyed* Opabinia, *left, fit no recognizable modern body plan, while ten-limbed* Aysheaia, *above, suggests living land dweller* Peripatus.

as Walcott's site is known. "I went there on an expedition with the Geological Survey of Canada in 1966 and 1967. We camped at 7,000 feet, and then climbed another 500 feet onto the ridge. You are perched high above a sparkling green lake, and you look west toward the snow-clad Rockies. Best of all, you find the most wonderful fossils when splitting the rock."

Continental movement and mountain building have thrust this ancient offshore terrain dramatically skywards, but fortunately the strata have suffered virtually no distortion, unlike most rocks of similar age and history. There is no other known source of such a variety of soft-bodied fossils from this point in the world's past, which is why the Burgess Shale remains so very important.

The Shale reveals more than just a collection of individual species; it represents an echo of an ancient community. "The organisms found here lived on a mud bottom under about 300 feet of water," explains Whittington. "Periodically the mud slipped and the underwater landslide carried the whole community deep into cold, oxygen-free water. Because of the lack of oxygen the animals didn't decay, but instead were slowly compressed in pristine condition as the mud gradually compacted." The result of many such slides is a six-foot-thick layer of shale made up of wafer-thin impressions of life half a billion years ago.

Whittington calculates that an initial one-foot thickness of landslipped mud would eventually be compressed to less than one inch. "You can imagine the problems of trying to determine what an animal looked like if it happened to be compacted at an awkward angle," he says. Not every mud slide carried unwitting passengers to this unusual form of immortality, and so within the shale there are perhaps four or five separate layers, each several inches thick, that abound in fossils. From the ghostly outlines of many hundreds of individuals recovered from these fertile layers, paleontologists have reconstructed a glimpse of life in this ancient community.

Of the 140 species (grouped into 119 genera) identified so far, more than half roamed around on what was then the muddy sea floor or burrowed under it, a third remained fixed on the sea floor, and the rest were free swimmers and floaters. There were sponges, jellyfish, worms, mollusks, and many arthropods (jointed-limbed creatures whose modern marine versions include lobsters, shrimps, crabs, and barnacles). All of these kinds of animals may sound familiar, yet there was nothing with a backbone. No fish existed at this time in life's history. However, one small swimming creature resembling the modern lancelet was entombed in the shale, foreshadowing the phylum Chordata to which the fish would belong.

Once a shallow sea at the edge of the continental shelf, the Burgess Shale terrain now rests 7,000 feet up in the majestic Canadian Rockies, a testament to the great forces of continental movement and mountain building.

Anyone at all familiar with ancient fossils would immediately look for trilobites (a kind of arthropod) in the Burgess Shale. As its name suggests, the trilobite body was divided into three lobes, and in this shallow sea it scurried over the sea floor on jointed limbs. The trilobites were the dominant group of early life, and their rigid and sometimes elaborately "decorated" elongated bodies ranged in size from less than an inch to over two feet long. Many species were totally blind, but some had intricately structured eyes with exquisitely formed lenses made of calcite, a crystalline form of calcium carbonate. So good were these lenses in optical terms and so well have they with-stood the rigors of time that one scientist made photographs through a thin slice of the lens. Trilobites were indeed remarkable organisms, and their evolutionary history stretches over an incredible span of some 350 million years.

The Burgess Shale has its share of trilobites, although compared with other fossil collections of comparable age they represent a relatively small proportion of this assemblage. At this stage in their evolutionary career, most trilobites measured less than three inches long. The trilobites and other arthropods in the shale occupied various niches. Some used brush-like antennae to sweep food particles from the sea floor. Others must have been effective predators and scavengers—the fortuitous preservation of the stomach contents of one specimen revealed the crushed shells of brachiopods.

In addition to the creatures that can be fitted into categories occupied by today's organisms, the Burgess Shale contains some real enigmas—forms that belong to no presently living group. One aptly named specimen, *Hallucigenia*, appears to have moved about on seven pairs of sharply pointed stilt-like spines. A row of seven tentacles, with a pair of strengthened tips at the end of each, waved from its back. Who knows what purpose these appendages might have served? A curious ancient vignette preserved in a sample of the shale stored at Harvard may provide a clue. More than 15 of these strange unclassified creatures lie clustered around a large worm. Were they engaged in a communal scavenge on this juicy meal when a mud slide swept them to their deaths? Whittington and

Mud slumping on the sea floor some half billion years ago trapped and ultimately preserved the ancient community of organisms that is today fossilized in the Burgess Shale.

ANIMALS OF THE BURGESS SHALE

This reconstruction by artist John Gurche depicts a scene set on the floor of a shallow sea during the Cambrian Period about 530 million years ago. Fossils of these and 135-odd other species of animals are found in the Burgess Shale site high in British Columbia's Rockies. Beautifully preserved by burial in underwater mudslides, some of the animals are related to extant forms; others resemble no known living organisms. Five-eyed *Opabinia* (foreground), just three to four inches long including its jointed grasping organ, and stilt-legged *Hallucigenia* are enigmas, belonging to phyla that apparently died out completely. Floating in the background, *Eldonia* are distantly related to today's sea cucumbers. Sponges such as *Vauxia* were common in Cambrian seas. Wispy *Marpolia* is a form of algae. All belonged to a vanished community known today only through their record in the Burgess Shale.

1. *Opabinia*
2. *Hallucigenia*
3. *Eldonia*
4. *Vauxia*
5. *Marpolia*

his colleague Simon Conway Morris have little doubt that they were.

A five-eyed creature called *Opabinia* presents another puzzle. It had no legs, only lateral flaps with which it swam or pushed itself along on the muddy bottom, and a flexible, forward-pointing grasping organ to catch its food. It too fits into no recognized body plan, and so joins the ranks of the eight other enigmatic types in the Shale. "The existence of these unclassifiable creatures suggests to me," says Whittington, "that we are seeing at this stage of evolution a burst of 'experimentation,' the origin of many different forms, some of which later vanished completely."

The unusual thing about the Burgess Shale community is that there are so many organisms that are totally alien to us, yet the majority can be classified with modern living animals according to shared body architecture.

"It seems that the major body plans were established very early in history," comments Whittington, "and that subsequent evolution has brought to dominance those that proved best adapted." The organisms of the Burgess Shale and of rocks of similar age cover the great range of lifestyle and body plan encountered later in history; however, each point in the spectrum is represented by one or a very few species and genera. As time passed, variations upon the themes filled in the "spaces" between them with the origin of new species following the basic designs.

The window of the Burgess Shale undoubtedly reveals a community of complex creatures. Different groups would predominate later, exploiting the sediments more extensively and refining their predatory habits. But life 530 million years ago cannot truly be described as primitive in the sense of being poorly equipped for living in the prevailing environments. The obvious question to ask, therefore, is how long a history does multicellular, complex life have prior to the Burgess Shale? Had there been a slow and steady buildup of more and more complex forms? Or was the life seen in the Shale the result of very rapid diversification following a relatively late origin of multicellular organisms?

One possibility is that multicellular life did indeed arrive with astonishing haste. Another is that the appearance of explosive origin reflects an impoverished fossil record, that the community represented in the Burgess Shale had a long, long history but that the capriciousness of sedimentation failed to preserve it or that paleontologists have yet to find the right sediments.

Sandstone imprint of a jellyfish from the Ediacara Hills in South Australia dates back 650 million years. Site has yielded numerous fossils of soft-bodied Precambrian animals.

Needle-like structures interlock to form the skeleton of a Venus's flower basket sponge, a relic of one of the oldest lines of multicellular evolution.

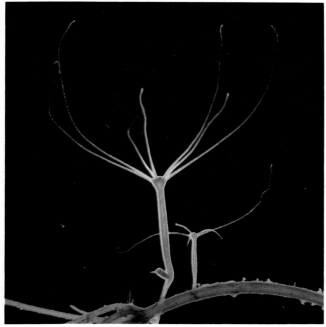

New bud sprouts from the lower body wall of a Hydra vulgaris *attached to a water plant near earlier offspring. Freshwater organisms, hydra reproduce both sexually and asexually.*

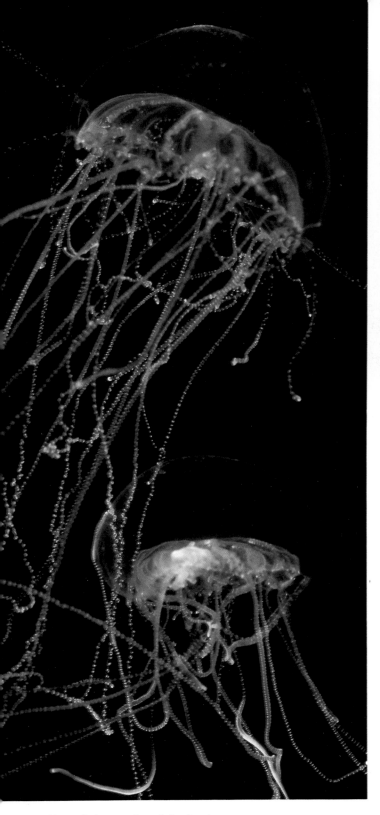

Extended tentacles of the luminescent jellyfish Olindias phosphorica *sweep water for small food organisms. Ancient allies of sponges and corals, jellyfish heralded the arrival of primitive nerves and muscles.*

One inherent difficulty in attempting to trace life's history is that the paleontologist is entirely dependent on the preservation and fossilization of organisms. Even an animal with a bony skeleton has a vanishingly small chance of becoming part of the fossil record, because its most likely fate upon death is disintegration before natural burial occurs. Unless something is buried rapidly after it dies, the process of fossilization cannot even begin. So, if the post-mortem fate of most bony creatures is disintegration rather than preservation, what chance is there for the fossilization of an organism consisting entirely of soft parts? Infinitessimally small, and that is the difficulty in looking for ancestors of the Burgess Shale kinds of organisms.

The animals of the shale left their intricate marks on history because they happened to live on a slope of fine-grained mud which occasionally slid and promptly buried and beautifully preserved its passengers. For this reason, animals with soft parts—jellyfish and sponges, for instance—can be found here in larger numbers than in other deposits of similar age. Only about a quarter to a third of the creatures in the Burgess Shale community had tough body parts, i.e., the leathery outer skeleton of trilobites and the shells of brachiopods. The rest had soft bodies that would have rapidly disintegrated under less propitious circumstances.

113

A pair of shells protects the ciliated food-gathering tentacles of the northern lamp shell, whose ancestors date back more than a half billion years.

Eight overlapping calcareous plates armor the chiton, or coat-of-mail shell, below, one of the most primitive of mollusks. Right, colorful mane of sense organs marks the head end of a spaghetti worm, an ancient form of annelid whose segmented body represents an increased capacity for specialization.

Creatures with hard parts became much more numerous after the Burgess Shale era, and there are good reasons why the evolutionary innovation of such structures would be successful. Hard body parts provide solid support for muscles and might better enable an organism to escape predators. When looking at deposits *older* than the Shale, one expects to find the reverse: fewer and fewer organisms with hard parts. And this is precisely what is found. In the few older deposits that are known to contain fossils, very few fossils of organisms with hard parts are found. But it is also true that signs of *any* complex life fade dramatically as you look back beyond the Burgess Shale.

In Darwin's time there were no fossils known to be older than 500 million years, and the entrance of organisms onto life's stage did indeed appear to naturalists to be instantaneous. But subsequent discoveries have revealed that their entrance was not quite so abrupt. The most important of these earlier fossils first turned up in 1947 when an Australian geologist found impressions of jellyfish, organisms like sea pens, several types of worms, and strange, unidentifiable creatures in sandstone some 650 million years old. The organisms had lived on mud flats in shallow water and had no hard parts other than spicules, little needles of calcium carbonate that provide support.

In the years since its discovery the site, in the Ediacara Hills of South Australia, has yielded several thousand specimens, and so has presented a vivid and comprehensive picture of a community that lived some 100 million years before the animals of the Burgess Shale. These organisms show

no evidence of external skeletons, shells, or other major hard parts, and there are far fewer types of organisms here than are found in the later Burgess Shale community.

At first it seemed that the Ediacaran sandstones' fossil record might be impoverished in some way and therefore unrepresentative of life at the time. But the subsequent discovery of similar groups of fossils in rocks of roughly the same ages in Russia, South Africa, and Newfoundland confirms paleontologists' conclusion that the reduced number and complexity of types 650 million years ago mean that they represent a point on an evolutionary trajectory toward Burgess Shale times, about 530 million years ago.

Further back than the Ediacaran community the paleontological pickings become thin indeed. There are reports of fossil burrows, apparently made by some kind of worm, in the 800-million-

year-old Buckingham Sandstone of northern Australia, for instance. And little else. So where does the story of multicellular life begin? Where are the earliest multicellular antecedents of the creatures of the Burgess Shale?

At some point between 800 million and one billion years ago some single-celled organisms began routinely to aggregate as small coherent communities and thus reap some of the benefits of multicellularity: specialization of cells to do specific jobs, for instance, allows an organism to do certain operations more efficiently than single-celled animals and thereby offers the possibility of adaptation to a wider range of life-styles.

One path of multicellular evolution led to a loose confederation of cells known to us as the sponges. Indeed, so loose is this cooperative alliance of cells that sponges can be disintegrated by passing them through sieves, and the individual

A young boy watches horseshoe crabs gather near the seashore to mate. Not really crustaceans at all but primitive marine arthropods, horseshoe crabs have been present for 200 million years and may be a living link to trilobites.

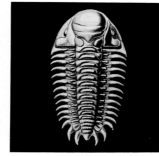

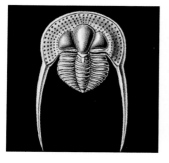

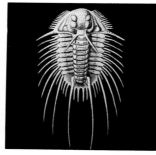

A sampling of trilobites by biologist Ernst Haeckel documents but a few of the highly varied, often elaborate body plans achieved by these now extinct arthropods, whose evolutionary history spanned over 300 million years.

cells will quickly regroup into their old form. Yet the sponges represent something of an evolutionary dead end—they have changed little in all of their long time on Earth.

A second path led to a closer interdependence of cells. This kind of alliance gave rise to the basic designs for the 30 or so complex body plans that the world's living things have used ever since. It is quite possible—even likely—that the different great groups, or phyla, of multicellular organisms arose independently at different times and in different places. Given the vagaries of the fossilization process, our knowledge of those early stages of evolutionary history may always be short on detail. Exactly *when* complex organisms first arose, and, more importantly, *why* they arose from single-celled ancestors with at least two and a half billion years of successful history behind them, remain a puzzle. But these questions do not require firm answers before we can go on to trace the evolutionary history of the rest of life.

The important point here is that the organisms of the Cambrian era do have a long history—they did not arise instantly out of nothing. It is also clear, however, that the origin of virtually all the major body plans we see today was, in geological terms, very rapid. And it is clear that from Burgess Shale times on, the fossil record expands greatly. Is the expansion merely the result of preferential preservation of hard parts that arose substantially then, or was there some real "explosion" of forms?

While the word "explosive" may not be the most appropriate term to use in conjunction with natural processes, history has determined that we are nevertheless stuck with the phrase "Cambrian explosion." In any event, the term aptly describes an event that can now be explained within the framework of evolutionary biology and ecology.

The pearly or chambered nautilus is the sole survivor of a group of cephalopod mollusks that dominated the early Paleozoic era, leaving an abundant fossil record of very diverse shell types.

"The Cambrian explosion," comments Stephen Jay Gould, "represents the first stocking of the world's oceans." The explosive rise in numbers and complexity of types in the corresponding fossil record reveals, he says, "a predictable pattern of evolution in open ecosystems."

And Geerat Vermeij, a paleontologist at the University of Maryland, cautions that this part of life's history looks explosive from a distance and that it is important to gain a true perspective on the time scale. Nevertheless, he does recognize a real expansion of life forms, which he describes as "an unencumbered radiation." In other words, as new types arose they faced relatively little competition in many niches. Evolution would be expected to proceed apace under such circumstances.

Once the oceans were stocked, life might have proceeded in a steady flux of change and variation through time. The reality, however, is quite different. The fossil record of life in the oceans—and on land, for that matter—is punctuated by dramatic periods of mass extinction followed by extensive radiation among the survivors. Geologists divide the Earth's geological successions into periods such as Cambrian, Ordovician, Silurian, and so on. Divisions between periods are not arbitrary, but are marked by the consequences of these periodic disruptions in life's equilibrium. A cataclysmic loss of most of the trilobite families, for instance, signals the end of the Cambrian period, 500 million years ago. The trilobites were hit once again 70 million years later, at the end of the Ordovician; the close of the Devonian, 345 million years ago, reduced them to a mere remnant of their former glory. They vanished in the greatest extinction of them all, the Permian, 225 million years ago.

Coral reefs, those intricate, complex communities of marine life, appear to be particularly sensi-

Extinct relatives of the nautiloids, fossil ammonites and dartlike belemnites encrust a slab of rock from West Germany that dates back 160 million years. Living squids, octopuses, and cuttlefish may have evolved from belemnoid ancestors.

tive indicators of large-scale extinctions. Reef building is the product of interaction between a small number of different organisms, but it is usually only one kind of organism that provides the principal base. With each successive extinction the actors in the drama of the reef frequently change; sometimes entirely new ones enter while others disappear, or perhaps an organism that in one period played a minor part is "promoted" to a leading role in the next. This latter type of accession characterized the career of mollusks known as rudistids, which, until about 120 million years ago, had been obscure members of the reef community for a few tens of millions of years. Over the next 60 million years, they radiated wondrously, supplanting true corals in some areas until the end of the Cretaceous period, 65 million years ago, when they abruptly vanished.

What is it that brings these periodic visitations of mass death? Perhaps each major extinction has its own peculiar cause. Some people theorize, as we shall see in a later chapter, that the extinction responsible for among other things the demise of the dinosaurs resulted from the Earth's impact with a massive asteroid. Whether or not this theory is correct, both geological and fossil records speak of an Earth whose climate has swung through equable and inequable periods, and this pendulum-like change has very probably been important in the periodic extinctions. In addition, as we have seen, continental drift has undoubtedly been a significant cause of extinctions.

Consider the Permian extinction, for instance, the most massive and far-reaching of them all. David Raup, a paleontologist at Chicago's Field Museum of Natural History, has calculated that this great dying spelled the end for up to 95 percent of all marine invertebrate species, a staggering figure that brings home how powerfully such an event could shape the form of subsequent life.

Toward the end of the Permian the continents were achieving an unusual configuration, coming together to form a single supercontinent, Pangaea. A large proportion—almost 90 percent—of marine life existed then as today in the shallow seas covering the narrow continental shelves. When Pangaea coalesced, the area of continental shelf habitat was dramatically reduced, and previously separate populations of organisms were brought into close proximity and into competition. Both factors would work to cause extinctions. In addition, the formation of the continent Pangaea may have caused a drastic lowering of the sea level,

At up to 10 feet long the largest arthropods of all times, now-extinct eurypterids were distant aquatic relatives of scorpions. Eurypterus, shown here, reached only one foot in length.

118

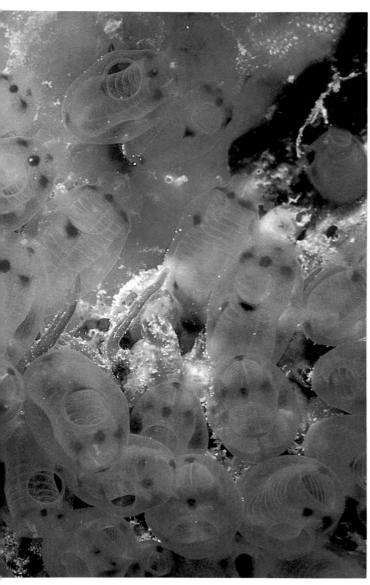

Immobile adult sea squirts, above, develop from free-swimming larvae which may be like earliest chordates, members of the phylum that includes the vertebrates. Above right, sea urchin uses spines as a means of locomotion as well as protection. Earliest stalked types of the Paleozoic lived attached to sea bottom, either directly or by a stem.

draining the shallow seas of the continental shelves and further reducing the available habitat.

This sequence of events provides a highly plausible explanation of the near elimination of marine life at the end of the Permian period. However, the ultimate "success" or "failure" of an organism depends not just on its physical environment, but on its biological environment as well. Competition for essential resources, for instance, such as food and living space, and the burden of predation are key factors in an organism's life.

Life's long history in the sea before it invaded the land presents a dazzling, even bewildering variety of biological environments and responses to them. Indeed, the sheer volume of life there and its apparently endless versatility still far outstrip anything encountered on dry land, a fact that we tend to forget. Beyond the astounding diversity, however, one can discern shifting patterns of biological strategies on a large scale.

In the earliest times of the Cambrian period much of marine life was played out on the sea bed. Trilobites, for instance, fed on food particles on or near the sediment surface. During the Ordovician period, however, a number of other organisms began to flourish. While these organisms displayed a wide variety of physical forms, they all exploited the increasingly rich supply of microscopic plankton, both plant and animal, floating above the bottom. The trilobites continued to flourish, but they were no longer the dominant form of life.

More efficient predators also emerged at this time and, as has happened repeatedly throughout

life's history, the result was a diversification of prey: the predator-prey relationship is like a never-ending arms race. In the Ordovician, the predators triggered in their various prey the adoption of a vast array of protective skeletons, shells, and spines.

The Ordovician also witnessed the origin of the first true corals, already mentioned as sensitive indicators of change. Until this time the few existent reefs were the product of stromatolites, bacterial colonies whose history goes back almost to the very beginning of life itself. Later on, the arrival of grazing animals such as snails and urchins would nearly put an end to stromatolites, which hang on today only in a few marginal habitats. In any case, the newly established relationship between coralline red algae, stony sponges, and the first coral stimulated reef building to a new level of achievement. Reefs are the largest structures made by living organisms, including man. The Great Barrier Reef of Australia stretches some 1,250 miles. Although the fortunes of reefs are subject to drastic fluctuations, they have achieved the richest colonial diversity of any living system.

By the end of the Ordovician, 430 million years ago, forms exhibiting all of the main body plans we see today had evolved, and all of the major marine niches had been occupied.

Then, around 180 million years ago, a dramatic change in the feeding habits of invertebrate life began, involving the invasion of the sea-bottom sediments to a formerly unmatched degree.

Organisms that make their living by extracting nutrients from muddy sediments are sometimes labeled "bulldozers"; in order to obtain sufficient food, such organisms—irregular sea urchins and sea cucumbers, for instance—must be able to burrow into the bottom and plow through large amounts of sediment. These organisms rework bottom sediments much more efficiently than did the burrowers of the Cambrian and Ordovician. When such efficient burrowers are present, the surface of the sediment becomes an extremely

An invertebrate chordate, the Amphioxus, or lancelet, above left, bears the typical musculature of a protofish and can swim as well as burrow. The lamprey, left, a modern jawless fish, may represent a degenerate form of the 500-million-year-old ancestors of the vertebrates.

undesirable place to live, and a rise in the numbers of these efficient burrowers is accompanied by a decline in immobile suspension feeders. Indeed, Charles Thayer, of the University of Pennsylvania, believes that competition between the life-styles might have nudged a number of bottom-dwelling suspension feeders toward extinction.

Why did the "bulldozers" burrow into the sediments at that time? First, they found in the sub-bottom sediments a relatively unexploited resource; second, by burrowing, an individual might escape the attentions of such predators as gastropods or cephalopods that reigned as the invertebrate champions of the seas for hundreds of millions of years. And the starfish, despite their delicate beauty, are highly effective predators that certainly would have encouraged the dive for safety into the depths of the murky sediments.

Inevitably, where the prey went the predators would follow, and a new round in the arms race produced further adaptations to resist attack. Even today the sediments remain a favored place to live, and their continued perturbation by the burrowing bulldozers has prevented the surface-living suspension-feeding communities of earlier times from re-establishing themselves.

The arthropods—the "jointed-limbed"—deserve special mention, not only because of their early successes in the Cambrian, when the trilobites began their 350-million-year history, and their modern manifestation as crustaceans, insects, arachnids, and others, but also because it was members of this phylum that achieved the first successful animal invasion of the land, perhaps as early as 400 million years ago. These terrestrial invaders may have belonged to the subphylum of the arthropods called the Chelicerata, which includes today's scorpions.

Another representative of this group was the so-called sea scorpion, or eurypterid, now extinct. Only remotely related to the air-breathing scorpions, the eurypterids first arose in the Ordovician. Some of their later descendants were the largest arthropods that ever lived. Reaching 10 feet in length, they must have been among the most formidable predators of their seas. However, as we shall see, it is to the smaller members of the arthropod group that we must look to find the first animals that were to make the transition to terrestrial life.

The unquestioned master of the modern seas, the fish, are relative latecomers to the scene. They, of course, have colonized the continents, too, in lakes and rivers. So, from ocean depths of 15,000

The evolution of the jaw began with filter-feeding ancestors of vertebrates. Cilia around mouth drew in water and food, which was strained through basket-like filter bars.

In the next stage, cilia were lost. Filters were modified to pump water and food through strainers, and began to function as gills. Scales migrated to mouth area.

Bones of first gill arch became upper and lower jaws. Scales around mouth were transformed into teeth as animals shifted from filter-feeding to grasping food with jaws.

Finally, second gill arch moved forward to brace jaws at back of skull, and teeth and musculature became fully developed, allowing active feeding on large prey.

Mostly jaw, viperfish has adapted to one of the extreme habitats of fishes, the depths of the oceans.

121

feet and more, to heights of 14,000 feet in Andean lakes, from hot springs to freezing polar waters, fish have flourished on the Earth, counting among their number half the vertebrate classes. Indeed, these ubiquitous swimming creatures outnumber their terrestrial vertebrate cousins both in absolute terms and in number of species.

Before we embark on the history of fishes (and subsequently of land vertebrates), however, it is salutary to pause and reflect that despite the fishes' success, invertebrates outstrip vertebrates in numbers of phyla, classes, genera, species, and individuals—both today and in the past.

Vertebrates have a long history, sketchy fossil indications going back as far as the Burgess Shale. No outstanding fossil candidate exists as an intermediate form between invertebrates and vertebrates, but a look at the larva of a tunicate, or sea squirt, reveals unmistakable signs of material upon which evolutionary processes could have operated in the past. This tiny tadpole-like larva not only has a nerve cord passing down its back, but also a thin, stiff rod running from the tip to the middle of its body, the kind of structure that, with some further development, could serve as a notochord, or primitive backbone. This little rod disappears as the larva matures, and the adult sea squirt emerges without it.

Exhibit specialist Leroy Glenn of the National Museum of Natural History applies the finishing touches to a reconstruction of Dinichthys, a huge, armored, primitive fish that lived some 350 million years ago and attained lengths of up to 30 feet.

Another invertebrate creature that hints at vertebrate origins is the *Amphioxus,* or lancelet. This two-inch-long, slender, translucent creature spends much time with its tail buried in the sand, but it can swim. It is plainly equipped with a thin strengthening rod, the notochord, and has gill slits through which it filters water for "breathing" and feeding. The lancelet surely gives us a glimpse of what the early vertebrates looked like, and indeed, a creature very like it is found in the Burgess Shale.

The first accurate fossil record of true vertebrates, however, is of jawless fish, many of which were bottom dwellers that scooped food-rich sediments into their immobile mouths from the sea floor. Some of these creatures, which first arose around 500 million years ago, had skeletons made of cartilage rather than bone, and in many species their relatively streamlined bodies were covered with bony scales, though the degree of armor differed among species.

These primitive fish flourished during the late Silurian and Devonian periods, 410 to 345 million years ago, but then became extinct, leaving only today's sucker-mouthed, parasitic lamprey and scavenging hagfish as probable descendants.

A new class of fish, the placoderms, probably contributed to the decline of the jawless fish. These fish exhibited two major advances over their predecessors: jaws and paired fins. The placoderms could therefore swim far more efficiently than their predecessors. And they could bite. The combination of the two produced some of the most formidable predators of the Devonian seas.

How, one might ask, could jaws arise from an animal with no jaws? Once again the embryo provides the clue. Embryos of modern fish begin with no jaws; then the first pair of a series of supporting gill arches "migrates" forward and becomes the

From the same family as the larger and heavier great white shark, the mako shark has evolved a beautifully streamlined form that enables it to catch the swiftest prey. An order of cartilaginous fish that first arose about 350 million years ago, sharks are related to skates and rays.

jaws. As the jawless fish obviously did not need jaws to feed, a series of changes that might have led to the formation of a primitive jaw need not have interfered with their lives. It is difficult to see how a half-formed jaw might have been advantageous, so perhaps the origin of jaws should be regarded as a lucky accident. In 50 million years such an eventuality is quite conceivable, and embryology suggests that was how it happened.

The placoderms underwent a tremendous radiation in the Devonian, with some species reaching 30 feet and more. Together with the ceph-

An exquisitely detailed mosaic from a house in Pompeii, Italy, offers a sampling of some of the myriad life forms that have evolved in the seas.

124

alopods, these primitive fish must have applied a keen predatory pressure on both the invertebrate marine community and other fish. But the decline of the placoderms coincided with the origin of two new classes of vertebrates, the cartilaginous, shark-like fish and the bony fish. The placoderms became almost extinct in the Carboniferous, but managed to stagger on in greatly diminished numbers until the Permian, when they were finally completely eclipsed. The placoderms are the only vertebrate class to slip entirely into extinction.

By this time fish had begun to populate fresh water, and much of the Devonian evolution probably occurred in lakes and rivers. The new class of cartilaginous fish, to which modern sharks and rays belong, are, however, marine creatures. Sharks, for instance, are exquisitely streamlined for speed and predation, but they must use their fins for hydrodynamic lift because, unlike bony fish, they have no air bladder. When a shark stops swimming, it sinks.

The bony fish probably arose from freshwater air-gulping ancestors, whose primitive lungs were modified to form the buoyancy-giving air bladder. Freed from the simple but essential function of providing lift, the fins in bony fish have taken on many functions, providing the ability to "hover" and even swim backwards in some cases. Whereas the cartilaginous fish emerged from the ravages of the Cretaceous extinction 65 million years ago with relatively few, though generally successful, forms, their bony cousins proliferated and now pursue every conceivable underwater life-style.

From the outset there appeared two groups of bony fish: the ray-finned fish, whose spectacular success has just been mentioned; and the lungfish and lobe-finned fishes, whose history is unimpressive—as swimming vertebrates, that is. It is, however, to this second group that we look for the ancestors to all terrestrial vertebrates.

Three genera of lungfish survive today, living in freshwater environments on all the southern continents except Antarctica. Some of the more advanced can survive for long periods without water and can use their mobile limbs for crawling in shallows or on mud. While they look like promising candidates for terrestrial vertebrates, in reality they are too specialized. Their skeletons, for instance, lack the sturdiness to carry them effectively on dry land. Although able to inhabit that transitional world between water and dry land, they were unequipped to make the evolutionary transition to terrestrial life completely.

The group of lobe-finned fish that appears to provide a direct link to the first amphibians are the rhipidistians, freshwater predators whose highly mobile fins must have aided in the chase of prey over obstacles in shallow water. Rhipidistians were also characterized by an unusual joint in the top of the skull, which perhaps allowed them to open their mouth independently of the lower jaw. Would such an adaptation have enabled them to snap at prey in shallow water and yet avoid snagging a drooping lower jaw on the bottom? Who knows? It remains something of a puzzle. The coelacanth of the Indian Ocean, an ancient lobe-finned fish once thought to be extinct, displays this same arrangement. Perhaps if one is caught alive and kept long enough for study, this question might be answered.

The rhipidistians breathed by gulping air into the mouth and then pushing it into the primitive lungs, just as modern frogs and salamanders do. While resting in shallow water or on a mud flat, a rhipidistian fish would have found it advantageous to use its front fins to raise its body from the hard surface. Such a strategy would have facilitated this kind of gulp-breathing by preventing the weight of its body from compressing the lungs against the incoming air. This behavior was to leave its mark on all of the terrestrial vertebrate life that followed.

Barnacles ride piggyback on the dome-like shell of a smooth turban, a mollusk in the class Gastropoda which, though most successful in the water, is also represented on land.

UP FROM
THE SEA

Salamander makes its way in same zigzag motion with which its vertebrate ancestors squirmed up on land some 400 million years ago.

Y ou walk down the street and your arms swing left-right-left, in opposition to the swing of your legs. Virtually every four-legged creature does the same in some gait or when changing gait: the right foreleg goes back as the right hind leg moves forward, and the left foreleg goes forward as its hind partners move back.

"It's not a consequence of being four-legged," says Keith Thomson, a paleontologist at Yale University. "It's a consequence of having been a fish." This sounds extraordinary, as none of us looks like a fish. Neither does a horse, a dog, nor even a lizard. Nevertheless, we swing an arm back when the leg on the same side strides forward because, some 400 million years ago, our piscine ancestors moved over muddy terrain by squirming their bodies in reversing S-shapes, using their two pairs of fins. The right front fin goes back as the right rear fin goes forward. "When you start off with a particular architecture," says Thomson, "you are stuck with it."

In spite of this ineradicable vestige of our aquatic heritage, we and other terrestrial vertebrates display many distinctive body shapes that separate us from that distant ancestry. Some of these forms represent adaptations to opportunities offered by life on dry land; some are merely quirks of evolutionary history; but many of these basic changes were forced on us by the severe demands of an alien environment. Organisms of myriad varieties had by turns to face the challenges of a new and hostile world: dry land.

Buffeted though they are by occasional storms, the waters of this Earth are a relatively secure environment. Temperature changes are gradual; constant currents bring a steady flow of food; water supplies metabolic needs without

Bare-hearted frog from Costa Rican cloud forest displays limbs adapted for jumping, features that separate frogs and toads from more primitive amphibians. Terrestrially adapted legs and lungs enabled amphibians to become first vertebrates on land.

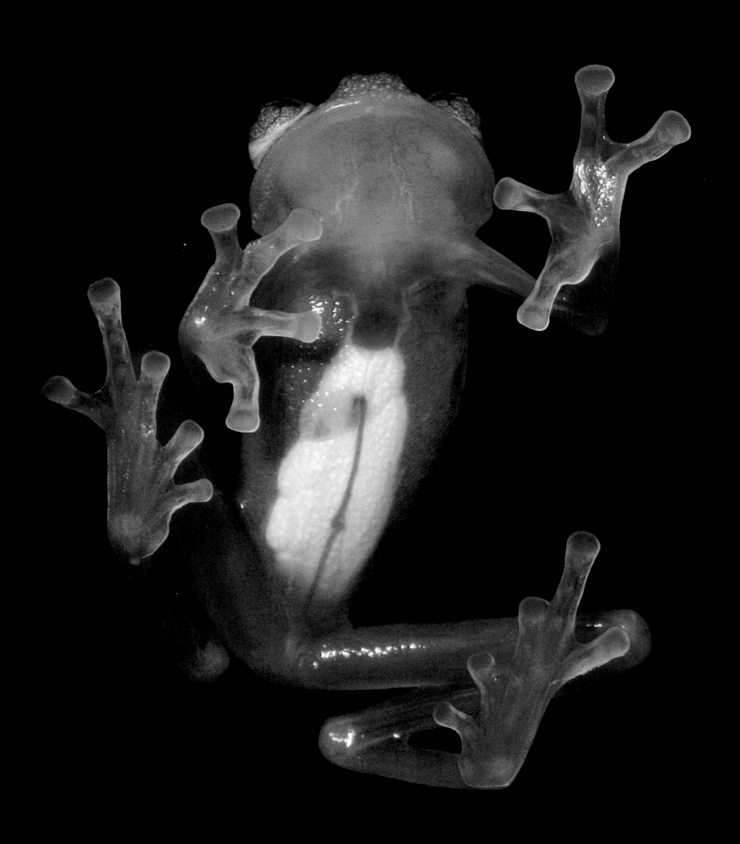

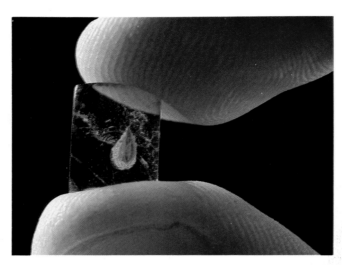

Tiny, transparent tomb of Baltic amber has preserved intact the delicate wing structure of Phatnoma baltica, *the holotype—or only specimen known—of an insect that lived some 50 million years ago. Species similar to this ancient one live today.*

cease and provides a powerful physical prop through its buoyancy. An organism that would survive on dry land must overcome problems not confronted in the water.

First, there is the immediate task of preventing desiccation, or drying up, a crucial day-to-day issue for a mature organism, be it animal, plant, or fungus. Second, the dynamics and mechanics of gas exchange—taking in oxygen and expelling carbon dioxide—are different in air than in water. Third, having lost the buoyancy of water, organisms must cope with the consequences of gravity, whether they are mobile animals or sedentary plants.

In addition to these major areas, certain groups had to face specific problems. Plants, for instance, no longer able to rely on passing currents to waft seeds and pollen to new and fertile nooks, had to find a way of dispersing their potential progeny. Vertebrates had to develop ways of keeping their eyes lubricated, so that vision would not be impaired. They also had to build new ways of sensing sounds—fish had simply exploited the superb sound conduction properties of water.

Numerous benefits counterbalanced problems posed by the new medium. The continents represented a vast unexploited resource, empty territory that offered a haven from predators—temporarily, at least. For plants, life above the waves meant uninterrupted access to their principal resource: sunlight. Uninterrupted, that is, as long as other, taller plants didn't cast them into shade.

One can scarcely imagine the continents as totally unoccupied: not simply *empty* of life, but *untouched* by it. There was nothing to halt scouring erosion; nothing to soften and transform the sands and the clays into organic-rich soils; no sounds beyond those of the physical elements in desolate isolation.

But as small primitive plants established themselves in the transition world between wet and dry, a blush of green spread slowly out from the margins of the seas, rivers, and lakes. Colonization of such an environment occurred gradually, with insects and other invertebrates weaving extra threads into this spreading fabric of life, pushing the hostile frontiers back farther and farther. With a bridgehead of life on land firmly in place, vertebrates began to enrich life's pattern still further.

The conquest of the continents was unquestionably a joint venture, with entangled patterns of dependence arising repeatedly, just as they had among the earlier occupants of the seas. The spread of life on land, then, was the outcome of opportunism expressed through natural selection, and not a deliberate or purposive "improvement" of life's status on Earth.

Although arthropods were not the first to take a foothold on land—as we shall see, that honor inevitably goes to the plants—the arthropods, and particularly the insects, possessed the most suitable characteristics for combating the challenges of a dry environment. They are built with a tough exoskeleton, an external structure that prevents water loss in the dry air and provides support against the pull of gravity.

The arthropods did have to establish a system for the exchange of respiratory gases, oxygen and carbon dioxide. The insects evolved a network of tubes through which air simply diffuses, the oxygen and carbon dioxide exchanged with the tissues through which the tubes run. Such a system is clearly effective—otherwise, insect species would not outnumber all other species three to one. And yet it has imposed a severe constraint on these highly successful animals: the limitation of size.

The system of tubes, or tracheae, works well

over short distances but becomes less and less efficient over larger areas. Some insects have developed various methods for stretching the efficiency of the tracheae to their limits, such as making rhythmic muscular movements that assist in pumping air through the tubes. But such strategies offer only minor improvements, and most insects today and in the past have been small, as compared with animals equipped with lungs. Of course there have been exceptions—the dragonfly-like insects of the past with wingspreads approaching 30 inches, and the Hercules beetle of today which weighs close to 3.5 ounces. But these must still be regarded as small in comparative terms.

The paleontologist interested in the evolution of insects must contend with a fossil record that is patchy at best. Because the insect body has no bones or teeth, its fossilization requires the most propitious circumstances. According to Frank Carpenter, one of the world's great experts on insect fossils, some 40 million years ago there was a lake surrounded by volcanoes in what is now Colorado. "Every now and then great clouds of ash plumed into the air and settled around the lake,

Dragonflies were among earliest flying insects: fossilized dragonfly at top flew Jurassic skies some 170 million years ago. Above, fossil bee from Colorado's Florissant fossil beds lived in Oligocene, about 35 million years ago.

covering the insects instantly. Over 100,000 specimens have been collected there," he says, "some of which are perfectly beautiful, almost as if they have been freshly mounted." But such entomological Pompeiis are rare.

However, one type of exquisite preservation is unique to insects: they occasionally became entrapped in the sticky resin that oozes from certain conifers and other trees, and over time the resin hardened to become a golden yellow semiprecious stone known as amber. An insect so trapped is preserved in every detail of its external anatomy, including mouth parts, sculpturing of body surfaces, and genitalia, making identification of species less difficult.

Handling a hundred-million-year-old ant entombed in an amber bead, then, is comparable to examining a recently dead specimen. But if one attempts to grind away the golden amber, the ancient insect crumbles to dust. What the amber holds is a ghost—a hollow shell complete in every detail but possessing no substance.

The evolutionary career of insects is remarka-

Its wings tucked neatly behind it as it maneuvers through brambles, the lacewing, above, represents the evolutionary burst that followed the emergence of foldable wings. Primitive wings of dragonfly, opposite, remain outstretched at rest as well as in flight.

ble in many ways. It is long, stretching back almost 400 million years, and it is punctuated by four major events: the origin of the first insects, which were wingless; the origin of primitive wings; the origin of foldable wings; and the origin of metamorphosis, in which the young live in physical forms totally different from the adult stage.

The earliest insect in the fossil record discovered so far is a 380-million-year-old wingless creature rather like a modern springtail. The springtail is, however, a rather specialized creature, probably not very representative of the earliest insects. "We have no good record of these earliest insects," says Frank Carpenter of Harvard, "but it is reasonable

Starting sequence of metamorphosis, female periodical cicada slits twigs, lays eggs within. Newly hatched nymphets will fall to ground, burrow, and remain for 17 years. Second stage: just-emerged nymph awaits transformation to winged adult. Third: wings expand as animal struggles to leave exoskeleton, finally shedding it in fourth image. Lastly, discarded nymph exoskeletons hang from leaves.

to suppose that they were similar to silverfish. These are like the primitive winged insects in most respects, except in their lack of wings.'' The silverfish-like insects turn up in the fossil record of 350 million years ago, but their precise origin is yet to be pinpointed. Countless fragments of arthropods at this critical early period in the record give the impression of a great diversity of wingless insects, but no clear image of their identities.

The evolution of wings in insects was a momentous event: the first creatures to take to the air, they would remain lords of the skies for more than 100 million years. In the absence of competition some reached impressive sizes. But it is not so much the size of some that puzzles us, but the fact that wings arose at all. ''Insect wings are the only true wings in the animal world,'' says Carpenter. ''Birds, bats, and the extinct flying reptiles all made their wings by stretching a membrane or putting feathers on an existing limb. The insect wing is not a modified limb structure of this sort.''

The benefits of flight for these early insects must have been pressing enough. ''This was the age of amphibians and small reptiles,'' says Carpenter. ''Scorpions, spiders, and spider-like arachnids, belonging to extinct orders, were abundant. All these predators unquestionably subsisted to some extent, and probably to a great extent, on the

Its wing covers raised above its back, brightly patterned ladybug alights on flower. Modification of the first pair of wings into protective coverings helped ensure success of beetles.

wingless insects, which had no means of escape.'' The question, then, is how did wings arise?

There are several proposals, but no real consensus. As a fraction of a wing would presumably be useless for flight, it is more than likely that wings originated as other structures which then became transformed into wings. Preadaptation once again—not an anticipation of future needs but a fortuitous convergence of different functions on a single structure. One suggestion is that external gills in the young might have provided sufficient lift for an occasional glide to safety after jumping to escape from a predator. Selection for maintaining and enlarging these structures, it is argued, might have eventually given rise to wings.

Is there any evidence for such a proposal? Yes and no. Mayfly nymphs, which live in water, do have external gills of the sort envisioned. What is more, they are equipped with muscles which in some nymphs move the gills at five beats per second, thus increasing the circulation of water around them. In the putative ancestor, these muscles might have evolved into ones that would power flight. But not yet is there good evidence that the young of the early insects had an aquatic stage as in the mayflies.

Fossil evidence indicates that in addition to the two pairs of wings on the second and third thoracic segments, the earliest fliers had a much reduced pair on the first segment. Could it be that the wingless insects originally had three pairs of lobes—function unknown—on the thoracic segments, and that selection of the sort just mentioned favored the evolution of true wings? ''Perhaps these lobes were gills of some sort,'' offers Carpenter, thus combining the two theories.

Although useful, wings in their primitive form were also something of an encumbrance. Like dragonflies and mayflies, the primitive insects were unable to tuck their wings neatly away while at rest. These insects would have been unable to crawl through vegetation, let alone burrow in the ground. Not surprisingly, the next great evolutionary burst followed the origin of foldable wings, an event clearly marked in the fossil record. Modern equivalents of this new stage are the stoneflies and locusts. Just as the primitive winged insects quickly came to dominate their wingless forebears, insects with foldable wings matched and overtook the dragonfly-like forms.

The last major evolutionary advance in insect history—aside, perhaps, from the origin of social insects such as bees—was the development of metamorphosis, which appeared around 270 million years ago. ''It is a tremendous advantage for the young to live and feed in a totally different environment from the adults','' says Carpenter. ''This immediately expands the range of habitats that can be occupied and conditions that can be tolerated.''

At the time when scorpion flies and related forms in the fossil record indicate the arrival of metamorphosis, only about 5 percent of insects followed this life pattern. The figure is now close to 90 percent, dramatically illustrating its great advantages.

Beetles evolved a little after this time, about 230 million years ago. The protective covering for their body formed through the modification of the first pair of wings was ''highly effective,'' says Carpenter, ''making them relatively free from parasites and other pests. This, together with the highly sheltered life their larvae lead, quickly established beetles as the largest family of animals in the world. They represented 40 percent of the insect fauna soon after they arose, and they have maintained that figure ever since.''

Grasshopper falls victim to viselike grip of praying mantis, one of the 1,800 or so species of the family Mantidae. Voracious predators, mantids feed on living insects, small vertebrates, and even other mantids.

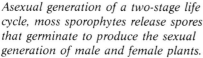
Asexual generation of a two-stage life cycle, moss sporophytes release spores that germinate to produce the sexual generation of male and female plants.

Asked what the products of Creation revealed to him about God, the great British biologist J.B.S. Haldane is said to have quipped, "an inordinate fondness of beetles." Alexander Klots, the eminent entomologist, obviously agreed. He once wrote, "It is difficult to avoid the constant use of superlatives when talking about beetles, for they are unquestionably the outstanding order of insects."

Beetles are almost everywhere, Klots points out: "The beetles have shown a striking ability to penetrate to every part of the land environment where an insect can live, and to adapt to every means of exploiting the food resources available." Not particularly impressive fliers, "they look like airborne trucks in low gear," comments Klots. "Yet they can fly well enough for all practical purposes of mating and distributing eggs." Though most beetles are low in aesthetic appeal, many are decorated with colors and patterns "that vie with those of any other animals, even of the brightest birds and butterflies."

The four major innovations during insect evolution were played out in the million years or so following their origin. "Each period saw an astonishing diversification of the new form," says Carpenter, "and then over time the diversity diminished. For instance, when those huge dragonfly-like insects were flying on wings with a 70-centimeter span, there were others with tiny wingspans of just a few millimeters. We don't see anything like that kind of diversity today." Each innovation was followed by a gradual shift to dominance of the new forms over the original ones, so that, as we have seen, the vast majority of modern species are equipped with foldable wings and undergo metamorphosis.

The evolutionary restlessness of the insect world means that no modern insect species is iden-

Cladonia cristatella, *or red-capped lichen, left, grows on a rotting log. Plant-like organisms that arise from the association of algae and fungi, lichens inhabit some of the harshest environments on Earth. Mosses, lichens, and ferns such as the ostrich fern above are all seedless spore-bearers that represent the Earth's more primitive multicellular plants.*

tical with species living as recently as 10 million years ago. Nevertheless, there is an impressive evolutionary stability about insects, especially when compared with the vertebrates, a point which Carpenter makes: "If you were to be faced with a beetle of, say, 200 million years ago, you'd recognize it as something different from all living beetles, but you would simply describe it as a new species. It wouldn't be considered extraordinary, like coming across a dinosaur or a pterodactyl."

The evolutionary success of the insects is thus outstanding. Despite the very limited raw material available to them, they filled countless highly specialized ecological niches, feeding on animals, plants, and each other. Theirs, for the most part, was a world of teeming individuals, except, as we shall see later, for the social insects, whose evolutionary innovation took them into a new and astonishing biological dimension.

The biological backdrop to insect evolution was, of course, a world of plants, for plants had preceded the arthropods onto the land by at least a few million years. Plants unwittingly provided shelter and sustenance for the emerging insect groups, and at several points in their history complex evolutionary relationships developed between the two.

And a factor almost universally ignored in the origin and continued success of plants is an inconspicuous but vital relationship with fungi, the third of the three kingdoms of multicellular organisms. "The great majority of modern plants have fungi associated with their roots, either externally or within the root, and the same must have been true for the earliest plants," says Peter Raven of the Missouri Botanical Gardens. "It is a symbiotic relationship, with the fungi providing minerals and other important substances to the plant and the plants in return giving a source of food and shelter

A survivor of giant seedless trees that flourished in Carboniferous forests some 300 million years ago, tree ferns spread their great fronds to tropical Malaysian sun, above. Like ferns, horsetails and club mosses were among earliest plants to evolve a vascular system, specialized tissue to conduct nutrients through the plant. Modern horsetails, far right, resemble fossil species, Equisetum winchesteri, right, from Wyoming's Green River Formation.

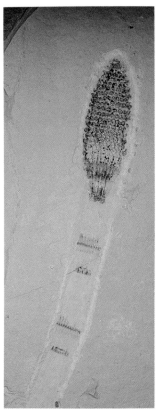

to the fungi." The slow advance of plant life away from the water margins was therefore accompanied by the spread of an increasingly diverse community of fungi.

Plants have passed through three major periods of evolutionary innovation. The first was the origin of the true land plants. These squat, primitive structures that clung to the water's edge arose some 400 million years ago. The second period brought the origin of seed-bearing plants, such as the extinct seed ferns and the extant conifers, which first appeared about 350 million years ago. Once established, they dominated the plant world for 200 million years. Last to evolve were the flowering plants or *angiosperms*, about 130 million years ago. Today, the great majority of plants belong to this group; a smaller proportion are the nonflowering seed plants, or *gymnosperms*.

Unlike the ancestors of the insects, aquatic plants were not preadapted to cope with the demands of dry land. They were both vulnerable to desiccation and devoid of means of standing upright unaided. Plants do, however, have one advantage not shared by other forms of multicellular life: they are capable of both sexual and asexual reproduction. A new plant can arise by the simple extension of an existing one, budding off from an underground stem, for instance. So, in adapting to life on land, plants would have been buffered against periods that were unfavorable to sexual reproduction through simple recourse to asexual reproduction. Animals under equivalent circumstances would perish.

Green algae, from which terrestrial plants evolved, absorb minerals and other nutrients from surrounding water over their entire body surface. The exchange of gases—oxygen and carbon dioxide—follows the same direct route. And sexual reproduction is achieved by the release of free cells that meet and fuse in the passing currents and drift off to become anchored elsewhere as an embryonic plant. The green algae could perform none of these functions in these ways on dry land.

Early stages of terrestrial plant evolution involved natural selection for chemicals that would waterproof the simple green stems and provide strength to support structures a few inches high. But total waterproofing would have prevented the exchange of gases, and so stomata, or pores, arose. Indeed, some of the earliest plant fossils exhibit such pores in microscopic detail.

Another practical consequence of waterproofing was the new need for a vascular system, consisting of specialized structures that could absorb moisture and nutrients and distribute them throughout the rest of the tissues. Only mosses and liverworts among modern plants lack such a system, and therefore are very small.

The seedless plants developed a mechanism of reproduction which, interestingly enough, is in some ways analagous to that of the first land vertebrates, the amphibians. Amphibians live on land, but must return to the water to reproduce. Likewise, these plants have evolved a two-stage life cycle, with one stage absolutely requiring water, or at least ample moisture.

If you turn over the leaves of a fern in late summer you may see dark raised lumps from which tiny black speckles shower. When these spores fall to the ground they eventually give rise to a tiny plant structure called the *gametophyte*, so called because in due time it produces both the male and female *gametes*, or sexual cells. In order for the next stage to be successfully accomplished there must be sufficient moisture on the surface of the gametophyte to enable the sperm to swim to the egg. If fertilization is achieved, a structure begins to grow that eventually forms the familiar fern, the *sporophyte*, which generates spores and completes the cycle.

Many of the key events of plant evolution have to do with modifications of this two-stage cycle, specifically with the protection of the vulnerable stage of sexual reproduction on the gametophyte.

The first simple plants were little more than leafless stems, simply branched, which bore a bag of spores at the tips. This arrangement, fine as a beginning, severely limited the plant's maximum achievable size: when the spore sac developed, further stem growth was halted. "There was strong selection for plants to get taller," explains Bruce Tiffney, a paleobotanist at Yale University. "First, there were advantages in getting the spores up high, as this would aid in dispersal by wind. And second, as light is a principal resource for plants, any increase in height would be beneficial because that individual would no longer be in danger of being in the shadow of its neighbors."

Very quickly new species arose with the spore sac positioned elsewhere. "All possible variations appeared," says Leo Hickey of the National Museum of Natural History. "They were at the tips of side branches, or attached to the side of the main stem—more or less anything you could think of." With the stem's upward spurt unencumbered, plant species steadily got bigger and leafier.

For many millions of years the asexual option of reproduction held sway, the still risky sexual process being subject to frequent failure. "You can see evidence for this in the early Devonian, about 390 million years ago," says Tiffney, "with large areas covered essentially by one plant. As sexual reproduction became more efficient, plant communities became more diverse." As they diversified and moved away from waterside environments toward more terrestrial areas, plants developed more efficient skins for water retention and gas exchange. Improved vascular systems conducted water and nutrients from the roots to the upper parts of the ever-taller plants. Shrubs and then trees appeared, producing vertically layered communities of species.

With the development of more complex biological environments, pressure increased to provide some nurturing of the embryonic plant—one that was provided with even a modest storage of food in the spore would have a better chance of becoming established. Examples of these are the club mosses and the horsetails, both of which included species that were huge trees, some 130 feet in height. These two groups of seedless trees were the most common types in the vast, damp forests that dominated the Carboniferous period 345 to 280 million years ago. We would feel distinctly uneasy in such a forest—not because of the danger from huge prehistoric beasts, of which there were none at the time—but because there would be no flowers or birds, and the air would be ripped by piercing whines and rasps of huge flying insects. Some trees with woody trunks would look relatively familiar, others distinctly alien. Trees of that age adopted many ways of achieving height; some tree ferns, for instance, were supported by a riotous entanglement of aerial roots.

Tree ferns still exist, principally in tropical forests, but they are the only survivors of the giants of those ancient times. The club mosses and horsetails of today are solely herbaceous, their decline having begun at the end of the Carboniferous, when the moist, equable climate gave way to cooler, drier times. We recognize their remains today as the great coal reserves of the world.

The seed-bearing plants had appeared long before the beginning of the decline of the nonseed-bearers. The evolution of the seed, according to Bruce Tiffney, was the single most important evolutionary event in the history of land plants, a crucial aspect of the rise in community diversity during the early Carboniferous.

The key factor in the evolution of seed plants is that no longer is the gametophyte an entity independent from the sporophyte. Instead, the gametophyte is much reduced in size and is retained within the main plant. No longer is the critical event of sexual reproduction—the fusion of gametes—played out in the exposed environment of a tiny, moist gametophyte. The male gamete, produced by a very reduced male gametophyte packaged in a complicated fashion inside a pollen grain, fertilizes the egg. The egg develops into a seed which is richly endowed with stored food. These nonflowering seed plants are known as gymnosperms, which means "naked seed."

This momentous step in plant evolution is equivalent to the vertebrate innovation that gave rise to the hard-shelled egg, and thus to reptiles from amphibians. In both instances, the highly susceptible raw material of sexual reproduction achieved secure protection from desiccation and other hazards.

The evolutionary path that led to the seed plant followed the enlargement of some spores together with the diminution of others. In time these physical differences became linked with differences in function, the large ones being exclusively female and the small ones male—the female sex cell being the one that requires the provision of nutrients for the developing seedling. Because of its tough but light physical structure, the pollen grain is ideal for dispersal by wind, which carries a few grains to a canal at the tip of the *ovule*, or unfertilized cell from which the seed will grow. On the other hand, some pollen was clearly dispersed by insects and animals. With the evolution of seeds and more particularly with the origin of flowers at a later stage of Earth's history the relationship between plants and animals was no longer simply one of adversaries.

The decline of the seedless plants was accompanied by a rise in the gymnosperms, of which there were four major groups: seed ferns, cycads, ginkgoes, and conifers. Except for the seed ferns, all types still exist—indeed, conifers occupy something like 8 percent of the Earth's surface.

By 280 million years ago plant communities had reached a peak of diversity and had begun a slow decline that was accelerated at the end of the Permian, 225 million years ago. This was the time of the great dying in the oceans that is linked with climatic and other changes associated with the conglomeration of all the continents into one supercontinent, Pangaea. Plants were clearly vul-

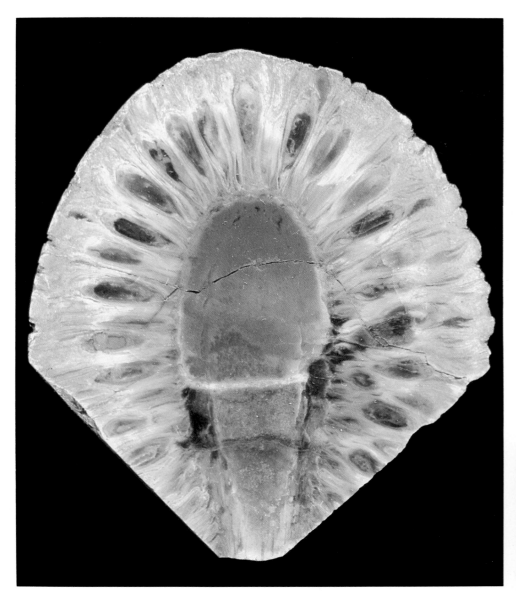

Ancient seeds imprint cross-section of a fossilized cone, above, from an extinct species of Araucarian conifer that lived some 200 million years ago. Among the first seed plants to evolve, conifers today comprise about a third of the world's forests.

Female cycad cone, above, protects egg until fertilization by wind-borne pollen. Left, fan-shaped leaves of Ginkgo biloba, *the only living representative of an order of primitive seed plants that once numbered some 15 genera.*

Crocodile, above, hatches from amniote egg, a reptilian innovation that broke amphibian reproductive bond to water. Spotted salamander, right, still returns to pond environment to lay egg masses.

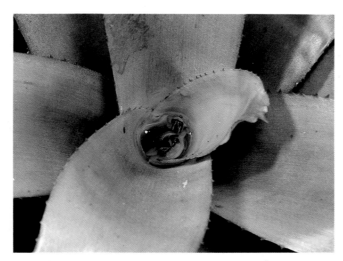

A miniature tree pond, the cup of a bromeliad in Trinidad rain forest provides ample moisture to sustain eggs and tadpoles of bromeliad tree frog.

nerable, but to nowhere near the extent as marine invertebrates. From the evidence available, it appears that the gymnosperms survived the period of extinction rather better than their seedless relatives. The gymnosperms then reigned supreme until the rise and subsequent efflorescence of flowering plants—the angiosperms.

It is worth considering something about the nature of plant evolution as compared with that in animals. Plants, need it be said, are not ambulatory in the sense that animals are. A greater flexibility of response to the environment is advantageous for plants—if they cannot move away from unfavorable conditions, it is better if they can adapt and tolerate them. This kind of flexibility—or developmental plasticity, as botanists call it—is precisely what is found in plants. The variety of leaf shapes found in a typical tree reflects the variety of microenvironments that prevail throughout its canopy.

The evolutionary history of plants on land is inextricably entwined with that of animals both invertebrate and vertebrate. As mentioned earlier, plants preceded animals onto the land, and the evolution of the arthropods and other invertebrate invaders of the land was conditioned by the plant communities in which they lived. Plants, of course, are the primary energy source for all that moves on land, whether eaten directly as food or taken in the form of other animals that do.

Vertebrates, in their transition to terrestrial living, had to overcome the same problems faced by plants—problems associated with desiccation, gas exchange, structural strength, and its associated problem of locomotion. In addition, vertebrates had to modify their mechanism for sensing sound, an alteration that involved a complex integration of many changes that can be traced from fish to humans.

As do insects and plants, vertebrates go through a number of key innovations, the products of which diversify rapidly, assume dominance for a while, and are then overtaken by the next evolutionary wave. There were three major phases in vertebrate evolution, the initial one producing the first true terrestrial vertebrates, the amphibians. Although these creatures had undergone important structural evolution, with the origin of four legs from four fins and the full adaptation to breathing air, they were tied to water for an essential part of their life: reproduction.

The second major innovation was the origin of reptiles, which involved virtually no change in the shape and form of the body but was centered on the production of the amniote egg, which protects the growing embryo. No longer dependent on water for the reproductive stage of their lives, the reptiles radiated remarkably, including in their number the most awesome creatures to have walked this Earth: the dinosaurs.

Eventually, in the third major innovation, the reptilian stock gave rise to mammals on the one hand and birds on the other. The reptilian path to mammals was more extensive than any other evolutionary change in vertebrate history, in that it involved major anatomical and physiological modifications as well as a radical shift in the method of reproduction. Birds and mammals are now the dominant groups of terrestrial vertebrates.

Although many of the key stages have yet to be documented in detail in the fossil record, the consistency of certain themes ties the vertebrate story all together in a convincing way. The fin of a fish and the legs of amphibians, reptiles, birds, and mammals are all constructed on the same pattern, modified in particular ways, of course, but distinctly the same. As Charles Darwin put it, evo-

Skulls and bones of the six-to eight-foot-long late Triassic amphibian Buettneria perfecta *lie jumbled as deposited by a river in what is now New Mexico, about 200 million years ago.*

lution is essentially "descent with modification."

The earliest amphibians, the labyrinthodonts, appear in the fossil record about 350 million years ago, and in many ways resemble the rhipidistian fish, their presumed ancestors. Gills have disappeared, their function replaced by air-breathing lungs, and four terrestrially adapted limbs protrude where the fins would have been. "Protrude" is a carefully chosen word because, instead of supporting the body directly from underneath as would be mechanically most efficient, the upper part of the limbs sticks out horizontally and the lower part then makes contact with the ground. This awkward "half-push up" stance is a direct consequence of the limbs having evolved from sideways-protruding fins.

Why did the amphibians develop limbs folded in the particular patterns that we see in all four-legged animals today, with the elbow facing backwards and the knee forwards? It turns out that the limb is not merely used to lift the body off the ground. The first amphibians could have squirmed along the muddy river banks as some fish do. "It was not as you might have thought, simply to reduce friction between the body and the ground," says Yale paleontologist Keith Thomson, "but because of the way amphibians breathed." Rather than sucking air into their lungs by lowering the diaphragm and expanding the rib cage, amphibians then and now take a gulp of air and force it back into the lungs, more or less by swallowing it. A newly terrestrial animal, unsupported by water for the first time, would be unable to perform this

procedure if it lay flat on the ground. As the weight of the body would make it impossible, "it would have to prop itself up on its forelimbs," says Thomson, "and for mechanical reasons, this means that the 'elbow' would face backwards."

What of the hind limbs? As propulsion and support are their only function, the "knee" joint, also for good reasons, faces forward. "These different functions are the key to the different orientations of the two sets of limbs," says Thomson. "Otherwise they would be very much the same as each other." One therefore must think of the amphibians' posture and locomotion as having been determined as much by a change in the mechanism of breathing as by the need to move around.

The early amphibians had the vertebrate world to themselves for some 75 million years. Their diet was principally insects and other small amphibians; plant eaters had yet to make their mark. Their method of reproduction was hazardous: a mating pair would shed eggs and sperm in shallow water, just as frogs, toads, and most salamanders do today, and after a short time tiny larvae would hatch and begin the frantic bid for growth to adulthood in predator-infested waters. Most young never make it to the adult stage, a fact that points up the selective advantage of a more protected egg and juvenile stage.

Some modern salamanders lay eggs out of water, but they must choose a relatively moist environment. Because the young must be fully able to fend for themselves, this method of reproduction is possible only for species of small salamanders. A

Chart depicts the evolutionary lines and relative abundances of major groups of mammals, reptiles, and birds, all descendants of amphibians. Dotted lines indicate still uncertain relationships.

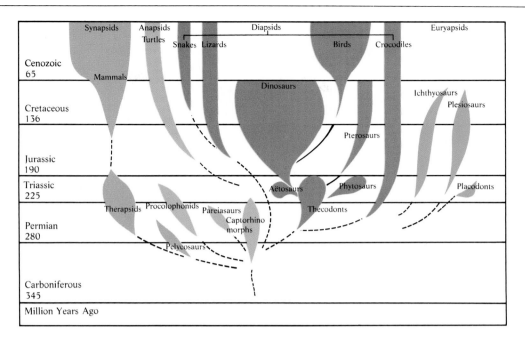

large egg of this simple amphibian sort, in which there is no special mechanism for gas exchange with the outside, would be unable to develop in a terrestrial environment.

The fossil record of the beginning of the reptiles is incomplete, but what evidence exists does indicate that the line began as small animals, as one might expect. And as small animals, they would have depended on insects, that ubiquitous energy-rich source. Although early reptiles may have been small and similar in appearance to amphibians, their mode of reproduction was very different. Robert Carroll of McGill University describes four principal changes that were necessary for this crucial transition which, he says, was "one of the most significant advances in the evolution of vertebrates."

First, there had to be behavioral and anatomical changes to permit internal fertilization. Second, the larval stage so typical of amphibian development had to be eliminated; this was accompanied with an increase in the supply of yolk to the egg so that a complete mini-adult should hatch. Third, the choice of egg-laying sites would shift from shallow water to damp ground and eventually to relatively dry areas. And last, a system of membranes that helped protect and sustain the embryo developed, as did a tough protective shell. Carroll points out that these changes are very much interdependent, and although they would not have occurred simultaneously, all had to be in place before the reptilian condition could finally emerge.

One of the most intriguing evolutionary shifts that begins with the origin of terrestrial vertebrates and goes right on through to mammals concerns the changes in hearing and in jaw structure. Fish detect "sound" in water through a series of sensors along their bodies that respond to pressure changes. The sound waves pass directly into the fish's body, because water and flesh are similar in density. Not so air and flesh. A land animal must have a special structure that transforms pressure changes in the air (sound) into pressure changes in a liquid, so as to be detectable by nerve cells. That structure is a tight membrane exposed to the air and attached to a bone (or bones) that transmits its minute movements to a pressure-sensing device. The structure is called the middle ear.

Amphibians and reptiles have such a structure, located near to the joint of the jaw, and it has a remarkable evolutionary origin. Remembering that embryological development in some cases reflects an animal's evolutionary origin, it has been possible to show that the cavity of the middle ear derives from a gill pocket; that the membrane of the middle ear may have been derived in part from the *operculum*, the gill cover of ancestral fish; and that the small bone or ear ossicle attached to it had been an essential element in the structure of the rhipidistian jaw-gill complex. This evolutionary transition was the outcome of many separate changes reflecting different selection pressures.

The keystone in the structure was the shift from gill breathing to air breathing. Without this change the operculum would not have become available to act as an eardrum. Another restructuring involved the jaw joint which, in ancestral fish,

New Zealand's tuatara is the only living representative of the rhynchocephalians, a group of reptiles that flourished in the Mesozoic era some 200 million years ago.

was unusual because of a curious joint in the brain case. A long bone, the *hyomandibular*, was an important functional part of this joint as well as a connection with the lower jaw, operculum, and gills. The function of this brain case joint is unknown, but in any case, it is no longer present in the amphibians, a change that freed the hyomandibular from one of its responsibilities. The mechanics of the jaw also changed, presumably because of different dietary habits. The gills and operculum were lost with the evolution of air breathing. Thus the release of the hyomandibular was complete. Given the right circumstances, hyomandibular and associated structures were available to reassemble as the middle ear, which they did.

The point of this detailed anatomy is to illustrate the underlying nature of this major evolutionary innovation, which Keith Thomson describes in the following way: "You had a whole series of things coming together. The change in breathing. The change in the structure of the cranium. The change in feeding, which affects the demands placed on the jaw. And there is a need for a different mechanism of hearing. If any one of these had been different, the result could have been totally changed."

With the evolution of the reptiles, the amphibians quickly lost their supremacy on land. In two great radiations the reptiles came to dominate the vertebrate world for 235 million years, a reign that was brought to an abrupt end with the extinction of the dinosaurs at the end of the Cretaceous, 65 million years ago. The first wave of radiation was principally that of the mammal-like reptiles. This diverse, highly successful group has been sadly neglected by the public in favor of the dinosaurs, which constituted the second wave.

The early reptiles, the *cotylosaurs*, were small insect-eating creatures, lizard-like in many ways. They gave rise eventually to a great variety of animals, such as the turtles, those great, armored, tank-like reptiles; and the lizards and snakes we are familiar with today. Some other descendants—the *plesiosaurs* and *ichthyosaurs*—returned to the oceans. And one small descendant group, the *thecodonts*, gave rise to the *archosaurs*, or ruling reptiles, which included crocodiles, the flying reptiles or *pterosaurs*, and dinosaurs in their number. But it was the mammal-like reptiles that were first to become firmly established as the major reptilian group of the Permian and early Triassic periods, from 280 million years ago onwards.

The mammal-like reptiles themselves swept across the evolutionary scene in two great waves, the first group known as *pelycosaurs*, the second the *therapsids*. These groups acquired characteristics that in an ill-defined way were more and more like those of mammals: there are tantalizing hints from the late therapsids, for instance, of the development of infant care, which is what most people associate with being mammal-like. But overall the important changes involved more efficient and faster locomotion, and teeth and jaws that were able to process food more effectively, more thoroughly. It seems that a variety of mechanisms related to controlling body temperature began to appear, so that although they might not have been able to maintain a constant temperature through their own internal metabolic furnace, the later mammal-like reptiles were at least not totally at the mercy of the vagaries of outside temperature. There are indications, too, of an emerging gregariousness that involved true social interaction and was not simply a conglomeration of large numbers of individuals.

The first pelycosaurs were small insect-eating animals, distinguished from other reptiles by a longer jaw, a more developed muscular system for moving it, and a pelvis that probably conferred greater agility. The radiation among this group produced some truly extraordinary creatures such as *Edaphosaurus* and *Dimetrodon*. With great "sails" along their backs, they became the inspiration for the modern-day Disney characterization of the prehistoric. Edaphosaurs had comically small heads, and belonged to a group of plant-eating pelycosaurs, the first animals that had truly exploited this huge food resource. *Dimetrodon*, by contrast, had a huge head with an immense gape. "These animals were effective predators," says Nicholas Hotton of the National Museum of Natural History, "and it looks as if they would have been capable of tackling prey almost as big as themselves."

Though *Edaphosaurus* and *Dimetrodon* pursued very different life-styles, their common possession of "sails" is interesting. Were these structures used for temperature control, being turned full to the morning sun so as to warm up their owners after the chill of night? Possibly. And probably these animals would have been able to control the flow of blood through the membranous sail, and thus radiate heat when they were too hot.

These two creatures represent two of the three main pelycosaur groups or suborders. The third suborder, Ophiacodontia, was also populated by predatory animals. Although the pelycosaurs achieved a tremendous diversity, they did not match the success of their descendants, the mammal-like therapsids.

The group to which *Dimetrodon* belonged were ancestral to the therapsids and, as Hotton points out, they share many features with their descendants. Therapsids arose about 260 million years ago and by the end of the Permian, only 35

million years later, already dominated the vertebrate world. Varying in size between rats and rhinoceroses, the therapsids diversified rapidly. Unlike their predecessors, they began their evolutionary career as well established dog-sized predators. It was only later that some of the smaller forms appeared.

Although therapsid origins were firmly predatory, during their diversification large numbers of rapidly successful herbivores appeared. "The therapsids are virtually unchallenged in their successful diversification," says Hotton. "They filled almost every niche that is now occupied by modern mammals." Paralleling the therapsids' phenomenal radiation was the great ugliness of some of their number. One group earned the name Dinocephalia, or "horrible-headed," in recognition of their grotesque appearance.

The extinction at the end of the Permian period, 225 million years ago, took its toll of the therapsids, but other reptiles and amphibians fared worse. The therapsids marched into the next geological period, the Triassic, bruised but by no means beaten. They began to assume an increasingly mammal-like appearance: their legs were placed more and more directly underneath the body, rather than in the reptilian straddle, and some species may have even sported hair and sensory whiskers. Indeed, the therapsids seemed set for even greater success than before the great Permian extinction. But, within a few million years into the Triassic, their diversity and numbers began to dwindle. Many of the larger groups became extinct. But the smaller, less physically significant ones remained, more mammal-like than ever before and seemingly poised for a highly successful new evolutionary turn.

What happened? The second great wave of reptilian diversification washed over around them. The dinosaurs had appeared on the scene.

Long vertebral spines of the herbivorous mammal-like reptile Edaphosaurus *supported a sail-like membrane that may have served to control body temperature.*

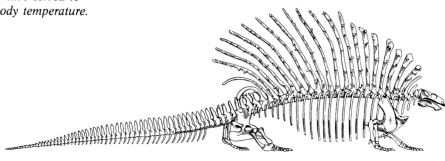

THE LAND
AND THE AIR

THE DAY OF THE DINOSAUR

Petrified eggs of Protoceratops, *a primitive horned dinosaur, were laid during the Cretaceous period some 130 million years ago in what is now Mongolia.*

We live in the third of three great geological eras—the Cenozoic, which started about 65 million years ago. Popularly known as the "age of mammals," these years have seen a tremendous evolutionary diversification of mammals large and small. Were we to be just a little more objective about our labeling, however, we might just as well call our era the "age of birds," or the "age of flowering plants," or even the "age of social insects." Each of these major groups of organisms has blossomed prolifically since the beginning of the Cenozoic and has helped to shape the world that we, as relative newcomers, know.

What would we find if we could go back perhaps 130 million years ago, long before the beginning of our era? The Mesozoic Era—a world with virtually no flowers, no ants, bees, and wasps as we know them, few birds, and no mammals bigger than a house cat. This was the time of the dinosaurs. As Yale paleobiologist John Ostrom has observed, "Dinosaurs are not the most abundant or diverse creatures to have lived. But they are among the most fascinating."

Huge, fierce, grotesque in appearance, and gone forever—dinosaurs fascinate, almost bewitch, the youngest to the oldest museum-goer. While not all dinosaurs fit this stereotype, as a group they would have been extraordinary to behold. But we must not allow their seductive mystery to let us believe that there was something biologically separate about them. A behavioral ecologist would conclude that dinosaurs used resources in much the same way mammals do:

View of the National Museum of Natural History's Dinosaur Hall highlights a few of the many dinosaurs in the Institution's collections. At center, 81-foot Diplodocus *towers above skull of* Triceratops, *foreground; pterosaurs, at rear; right,* Stegosaurus *reconstruction and, above it,* Edmontosaurus, *standing, and the predator* Albertosaurus *in death position. Overleaf, evening sunlight silhouettes lesser flamingos. Page 147,* Chlamydosaurus, *or frilled lizard, adopts defensive posture.*

150

some ate plants, some ate insects, and some devoured each other. The extraordinary size and physical appearance of some were simply manifestations of the anatomical heritage and evolutionary potential of a very long-lived group under particular environmental conditions. As we have seen again and again, variation upon a theme produced change through time, but no inevitable direction. The one inescapable element of all this change is, as usual, the interconnectedness of things.

For example, the long reign of the dinosaurs, from over 200 million to 65 million years ago, had a profound influence on the biological attributes of the stock that eventually gave rise to all of today's

mammals, from the tiny shrew to the gargantuan blue whale. Some people think that the dinosaurs may even have contributed to the origin of flowering plants. Be that as it may, the link between the rise of flowering plants and the spectacular evolution of several insect groups, such as bees and butterflies, is indisputable. So is the close relationship between the appearance of the most successful of all plants—the grasses—and the relatively recent origin of many grazing mammals.

There are around 6,000 species of living reptiles (lizards, snakes, crocodiles, turtles, and the like), about a third more than there are mammal species. In numbers and diversity, however, modern reptiles play a minor role in the animal world. The reptiles have had their fling. At the time when the mammal-like reptiles were the dominant form of terrestrial vertebrates, some 250 million years ago, a small group of reptiles, the thecodonts, evolved from the basic reptilian stock. They in turn gave rise to crocodiles, flying reptiles (pterosaurs), and dinosaurs, all known collectively as the *archosaurs*, or ruling reptiles. "Ruling" because the dinosaurs constituted the second great wave of reptilian evolution. The first wave, the mammal-like reptiles, had been quickly eclipsed.

Thecodonts were generally small animals, but they underwent a wide radiation, both physically and geographically (Antarctica is the only continent where no remains have been found so far). Some became at least semi-aquatic and crocodilian in form, reaching 20 or more feet in length; the main group diversified as relatively small, active, terrestrial carnivores. Some in this group apparently adopted a two-legged stance reflected in part by an increase in the size of the hind limbs and something of a reduction in the forelimbs. It is from this group that dinosaurs are thought to have descended. One reason for this supposition is that, like the dinosaurs, the thecodonts had limbs positioned well under the body and thus were more "advanced" than many of the mammal-like reptiles.

The dinosaurs began their evolutionary his-

tory in the manner common to all major terrestrial groups—as small carnivores which preyed mainly on insects. But within a relatively short period—25 million years—the great dinosaur radiation was well under way, with large herbivores already established, some of which weighed up to five tons.

The term dinosaur, meaning "terrible lizard," was invented by British anatomist Sir Richard Owen in 1842. No longer an official scientific name, its use is still heard informally in academic circles and probably always will be. The terrible lizards are two orders of reptiles named according to the shape of their pelvis: the *saurischians*, or lizard-hipped, and the *ornithischians*, or bird-hipped. The saurischians are distinguished in having in their number the largest-ever terrestrial carnivore, *Tyrannosaurus rex*, and the largest-ever land animal, probably a form of *Brachiosaurus*, as well as the probable ancestors of modern birds. What the ornithischians lacked in physical superlatives they made up for in dramatic form. The multi-plated *Stegosaurus*, the grotesquely featured and three-horned *Triceratops*, and the heavily armored ankylosaurs were all ornithischians.

John Ostrom considers the most interesting of all the dinosaurs to be the theropods, one of the two subgroups that make up the saurischians. *Tyrannosaurus* was a theropod, an 18-foot-high, 49-foot-long monster carnivore which had a huge head and minuscule forelimbs that couldn't even reach its heavily armed jaws. "It seems reasonable to me," says Ostrom, "that *Tyrannosaurus* would have grasped its prey with its hind limbs and torn it apart with its mouth, just as birds of prey do today." All the theropods were two-legged carnivores, though most did not have the diminutive forelimbs seen in *Tyrannosaurus*, that biggest carnivore of all. Other theropods, like chicken-sized *Compsognathus*, were very small, perhaps living on small lizards and insects, mammals, and birds.

The fact that theropods and their immediate ancestors always walked on two legs is intriguing. Apart from hominids and birds, no other animal moves in this way. Bipedalism is actually a difficult way of getting around—greater balancing and coordination skills are required. One of the small theropods is thought to be a possible ancestor of

Though dinosaurs have vanished, plants that flourished during their era continue to thrive today. Alligator, opposite, basks in Okefenokee Swamp, surrounded by bald cypress, ferns, and other vegetation which, like crocodilians, date back to time of dinosaurs. Dawn redwood, left, sheds delicate fronds annually, just as ancient relatives did.

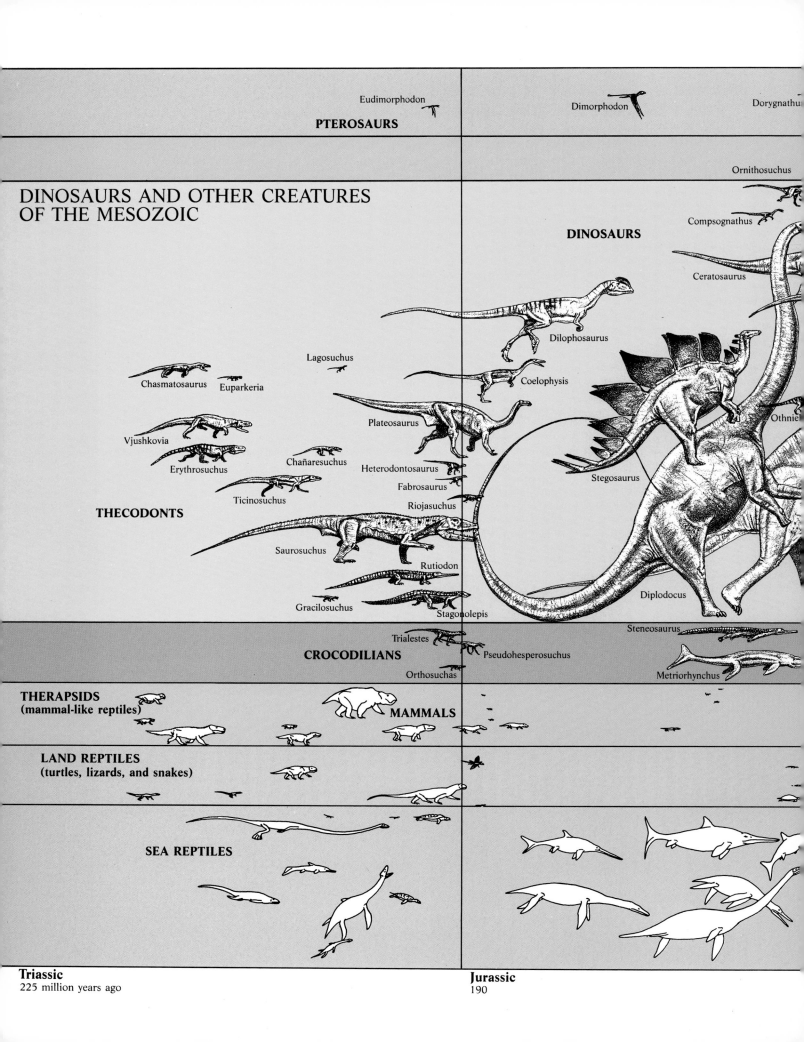

DINOSAURS AND OTHER CREATURES OF THE MESOZOIC

PTEROSAURS

Eudimorphodon

Dimorphodon

Dorygnathus

Ornithosuchus

DINOSAURS

Compsognathus

Ceratosaurus

Dilophosaurus

Lagosuchus

Coelophysis

Chasmatosaurus   Euparkeria

Plateosaurus

Vjushkovia

Othnie

Erythrosuchus

Chañaresuchus

Heterodontosaurus

Stegosaurus

Fabrosaurus

Ticinosuchus

Riojasuchus

THECODONTS

Saurosuchus

Rutiodon

Diplodocus

Gracilosuchus

Stagonolepis

Steneosaurus

Trialestes

CROCODILIANS   Pseudohesperosuchus

Orthosuchas

Metriorhynchus

THERAPSIDS
(mammal-like reptiles)

MAMMALS

LAND REPTILES
(turtles, lizards, and snakes)

SEA REPTILES

Triassic
225 million years ago

Jurassic
190

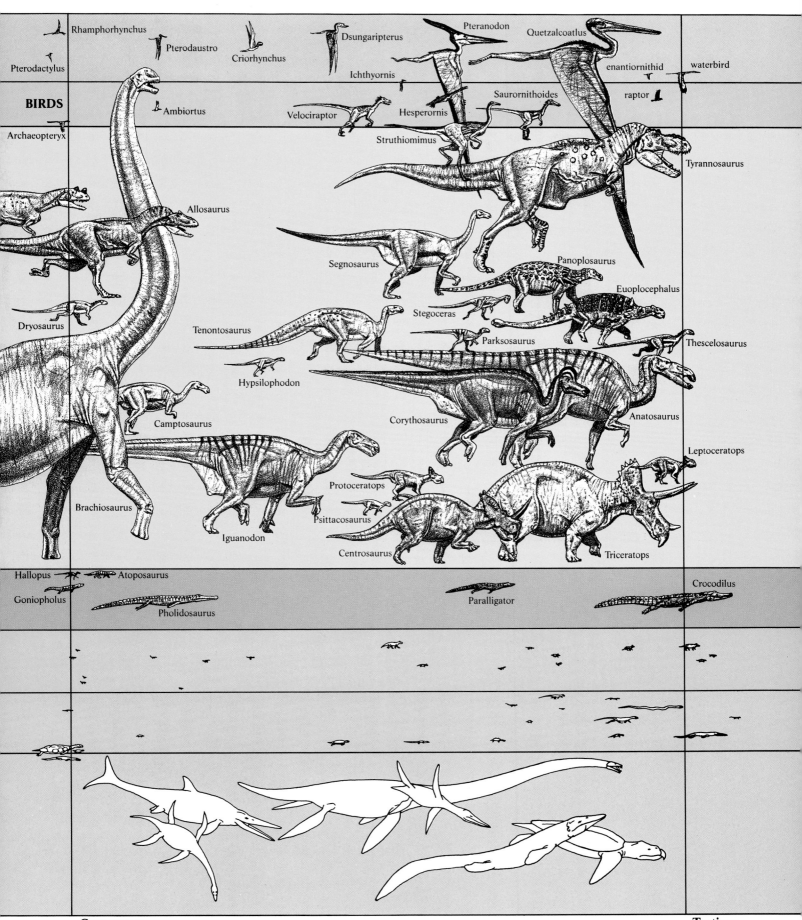

Rhamphorhynchus

Pterodactylus

Pterodaustro

Criorhynchus

Dsungaripterus

Pteranodon

Quetzalcoatlus

enantiornithid

waterbird

Ichthyornis

BIRDS

Ambiortus

Velociraptor

Hesperornis

Saurornithoides

raptor

Archaeopteryx

Struthiomimus

Tyrannosaurus

Allosaurus

Segnosaurus

Panoplosaurus

Euoplocephalus

Dryosaurus

Stegoceras

Thescelosaurus

Tenontosaurus

Parksosaurus

Hypsilophodon

Corythosaurus

Anatosaurus

Camptosaurus

Leptoceratops

Protoceratops

Brachiosaurus

Psittacosaurus

Iguanodon

Centrosaurus

Triceratops

Hallopus

Atoposaurus

Crocodilus

Goniopholus

Paralligator

Pholidosaurus

Cretaceous

136

Tertiary

65

Dinosaurs' legs were positioned directly beneath them, right, rather than protruding from their bodies as do those of modern reptiles. Opposite, tracks of giant sauropod and two-legged carnivore are hauntingly etched in Texas stream bed where hunter may have pursued prey some 120 million years ago. Below, diseased right hip bone of a camptosaur lends poignant reality to distant world of dinosaurs.

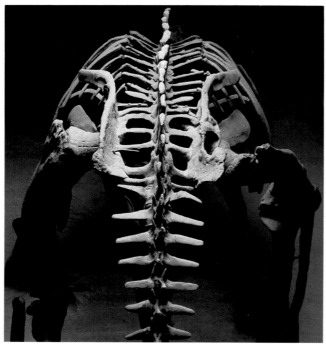

birds, in which case the group's mode of locomotion takes on added significance.

In spite of their unusual stance, the theropods were one of the most successful groups of dinosaurs, being among the earliest to evolve and among the last to become extinct. Of the six types of dinosaurs, theropods were the only carnivores. The rest were browsers, providing ample prey for their carnivorous cousins.

The second subgroup of saurischians were the sauropods, epitomized by the gigantic *Brachiosaurus*, *Diplodocus*, and *Brontosaurus*, properly called *Apatosaurus*. These giant creatures were among the early members of the cast of characters in the dinosaurs' evolutionary career.

One persistent myth about sauropods was that their great bulk doomed them to spend their life partially submerged in water because their legs "surely" could not have taken the strain unaided on dry land. This mistaken view arose before the science of biomechanics had developed sufficiently to determine that a brachiosaur's legs were quite adequate for supporting its massive body on dry land. These creatures had no need to take to the water in order to move; also, the pressure of water on their bodies at any depth would have actually prevented them from drawing air into their lungs.

The evolutionary history of the second major group of dinosaurs, the ornithischians, is much more patchy than that of the saurischians. The plated stegosaurs arose early and quickly became extinct (quickly, that is, in terms of the dinosaurs' overall span). The horned dinosaurs, such as *Triceratops*, arose late and were still a major presence when the dinosaurs as a whole slipped into extinction around 65 million years ago. And the armored ankylosaurs were somewhat intermediate, appearing first about 150 million years ago and then disappearing somewhat before the great extinction ended the entire line.

The fourth subgroup of ornithischians, the ornithopods, had no special protective armor to speak of—they may have relied on their apparently great agility in escaping from the theropod carnivores. Like the theropods, the ornithopods were able to walk on two feet, but probably spent most of their time on all fours. The ornithopods' evolutionary career was longer and less dramatic than their fellow ornithischians. They arose at the beginning and lasted right through to the end of the 150-million-year span.

One of the most tantalizing questions about dinosaurs is why they were so "successful" for so

long. Mammals originated at about the same time, but remained small and insignificant until the giant reptiles became extinct. Why, if mammals are so smart, did they not "assert" themselves sooner?

The mammal-like reptiles suffered many losses in the greatest extinction of all time, the Permian, some 225 million years ago. Although these reptiles, specifically the therapsids, were evolving more and more mammal-like features—canine and molar teeth and ear bones—they still retained much of their primitive equipment. Many of the dinosaurs were almost certainly more agile. They may have been able to process their food more thoroughly, through bacterial colonization of the gut or possibly by using grinding stones in their stomachs or crops, as modern birds do. "You find highly polished stones in some dinosaur deposits," says Harvard's A.W. Crompton. "That's not what you would call firm evidence for cropping, but it has to be a possibility."

Another possibility is that dinosaur social behavior may have been advanced or more advanced than that of the early mammals. Many ornithischian dinosaurs had elaborate, almost frilly armor and other protection, or grotesque excrescences on their heads that appear to have been ornate beyond the need for simple defense. There is the intriguing possibility that they might have been part of an individual's mating display, either in attracting a mate or in contests with rivals. Also relevant is the discovery of multiple tracks of certain sauropod dinosaurs, suggesting that some traveled in herds, with larger animals protecting the more vulnerable mothers and offspring in the center of the pack. Evidence indicates a social life a great deal more intensive and interactive than normally envisaged for reptiles. A recent find revealed fossils of very young duck-billed dinosaurs grouped as if in a nest, with the remains of an

Life-size reconstruction of Dilophosaurus, *an 18-foot-long carnivorous dinosaur that lived 180 million years ago, now inhabits Dinosaur State Park near Hartford, Connecticut.*

Smithsonian paleontologist Nicholas Hotton, above left, holds humerus of Dimetrodon, *one of the mammal-like reptiles that became extinct when dinosaurs arose. Above, paleontologists at Utah's Dinosaur National Monument bring into relief shoulder and leg bones of some large sauropods. Microscopic studies of dinosaur bones, left, have convinced some paleontologists that dinosaurs were warm-blooded.*

adult nearby. Some of today's crocodilians provide parental care of their young, so it is entirely possible that dinosaurs did too.

In any case, the dinosaurs quickly took over the large-animal herbivorous niche and then the carnivorous niche, leaving ecological room only for small insect-eating creatures. This was the slot occupied by the last therapsids and the earliest mammals. Very likely the early mammals, and perhaps some of the therapsids too, had developed metabolic ways of maintaining a steady and relatively high body temperature, though probably not to the degree of refinement we see today. If so, would this not have given them an insuperable advantage over their cold-blooded competitors?

During recent years it has become popular to answer this question by saying, no, because the dinosaurs were warm-blooded, too. By warm-blooded is meant the ability to generate heat internally by burning food to maintain a steady and high body temperature. Dinosaurs were certainly built to be more active than the majority of reptiles, which regulate their body temperature with the warmth of the sun and the cool of the shade. And dinosaurs stood erect in a way that no modern reptile does. A number of scientists, notably Robert Bakker of Johns Hopkins University, have interpreted this information, together with data on the internal structure of the bones and calculations of dinosaurian predator-to-prey ratios, to imply that dinosaurs could indeed control their body temperature by subtle metabolic means.

However, not all scientists agree. "The evidence for hot-blooded dinosaurs simply does not

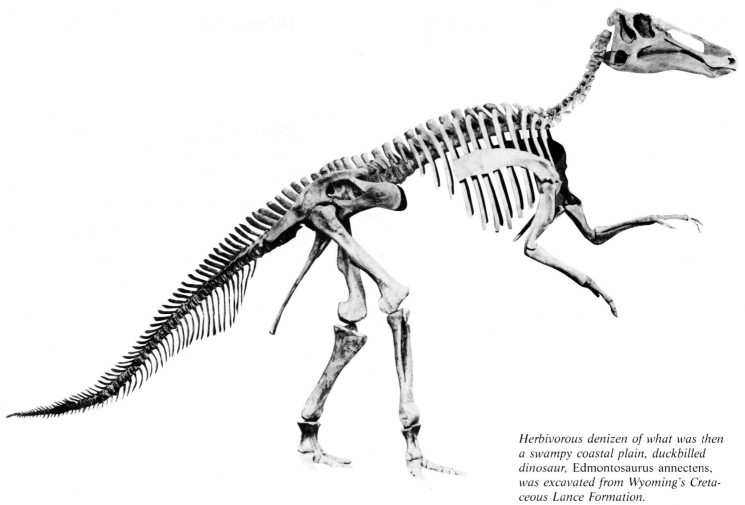

Herbivorous denizen of what was then a swampy coastal plain, duckbilled dinosaur, Edmontosaurus annectens, was excavated from Wyoming's Cretaceous Lance Formation.

Cretaceous boundary lies exposed in this Montana badlands outcrop. Iridium, possibly from a collision of an asteroid with the Earth, has been found in several other similar late Cretaceous exposures.

Evidence mounts of collision between Earth and asteroid, above, some 65 million years ago which may have caused extinction of many species of marine plankton. Declining dinosaurs may have died out before event.

add up,'' says Smithsonian paleontologist Nicholas Hotton, who points to the dinosaurs' generally large size as the important factor in their temperature control, rather than true internal control. And although John Ostrom's name has been associated with those who believe in hot-blooded dinosaurs, he essentially agrees with Hotton. ''A major factor against the idea of hot-bloodedness is the sheer bulk of many of the dinosaurs,'' says Ostrom. ''Just as it costs more to run an engine at high speed, warm-blooded animals need to eat more food than cold-blooded animals.'' The difference in food requirements for these two different metabolic types is between 10 and 30 times, depending on

the size of the animal. Small animals need proportionally more food to keep them going.

''If you consider an elephant,'' says Ostrom, ''it spends about 15 hours a day eating and foraging. Imagine the time needed for 'warm-blooded' animals two and three times its size, not to mention the 70-ton *Brachiosaurus*. There's no evidence that dinosaurs are better equipped to collect food than elephants. In fact, many appear to have been less well equipped.''

The argument, then, is that the simple, practical business of fueling very large ''hot-blooded'' herbivores seems impossible. Ostrom does allow that some of the small carnivores might have generated their own body heat, as mammals do. "The small ones would have been able to gather sufficient food to keep their fast-running metabolism going," he concedes, "and this would fit very nicely with the notion that this group was ancestral to birds, which are endothermic."

Assuming that the advocates of warm-blooded dinosaurs are wrong (and the argument still rages), how could cold-blooded dinosaurs have been so successful? Undoubtedly most of them would have developed behavioral tricks for absorbing heat from the environment or shedding it as conditions demanded, just as modern reptiles do. It appears, for instance, that the staggered array of plates along the back of *Stegosaurus* could have been used as an efficient heat exchanger. The plates were well endowed with blood vessels, and these creatures might therefore have been able to control the flow of blood through them to gain or lose heat. But, surprisingly, the true secret of the dinosaurs' success may lie, as Hotton points out, in the very fact that they were generally so large.

"Large body size could be an adaptation to maintaining an even body temperature," suggests Ostrom. "With their great bulk the big dinosaurs could hold the heat in their bodies much more easily than could small animals." This suggestion seems plausible when one considers the warm, equable climate from near to the beginning of the

dinosaurs' reign until about 75 million years ago. The average temperature was considerably higher than it is now, and most parts of the world experienced no dramatic seasonal change. These are precisely the conditions under which large animals could adequately maintain high, steady body temperatures and thus be as active as hot-blooded creatures, even in the absence of an internal metabolic furnace.

Just as the dinosaurs were dramatic in life—both in physical appearance and longevity—so were they in death. After 150 million years of dominance over the realm of terrestrial vertebrates, the dinosaurs disappeared, signaling the close of the Mesozoic era and the opening of the Cenozoic. Mass extinctions always carry an air of mystery and drama about them, but the one that saw the end of the dinosaurs seems to have been catastrophic rather than gradual, bringing a particularly jolting change to life on Earth.

Paleontologist Edwin Colbert describes the loss of the dinosaurs in the following terms: ". . . the great extinction of the dinosaurs, and the extinction of the large reptilian denizens of the oceans, brought about truly profound changes in the life of the earth. Giant reptiles disappeared from the face of the world. They left empty places on the lands and in the seas, and these places were soon filled by quite different animals, the mam-

Paleontologists encase Triceratops *skull in burlap and plaster to strengthen it for removal from outcrop in North Dakota's Hell Creek Formation.* Triceratops *and relatives were among the last of the dinosaurs before extinction of these reptiles 65 million years ago.*

mals. It is this change in character of dominant life—from reptiles to mammals—that makes the great extinction at the close of Cretaceous times so very important to the student of earth history and to the student of evolution."

Many explanations have been proffered for the dinosaurs' demise, some bordering on the ridiculous. The mammals took a liking to dinosaur eggs, someone once suggested, thus driving the giants to extinction while they were at their most vulnerable. Another idea, that the dinosaurs got so large that the males finally found it impossible to mount their mates, ignored the fact that the small dinosaurs also vanished at the end of the Cretaceous. Inventive though such notions were, they were doomed to failure because they ignored one important fact: it was not just the dinosaurs that met their end 65 million years ago; they were one group in a long list of victims.

One-fourth of the families of shallow-water marine invertebrates vanished in the Cretaceous extinction, as did almost all the marine plankton, all the great marine reptiles (plesiosaurs, ichthyosaurs, and mosasaurs), the flying reptiles (pterosaurs), some land plants, and a selection of primitive mammals. The dinosaurs were part of a curiously patterned mass extinction. Any explanation of the extinction of the dinosaurs must account for the simultaneous loss of many of the other forms of life on Earth.

The idea of an unimaginable catastrophe has long been popular as an explanation of this great global loss—the searing effects of an exploding nearby star, for instance. In 1979, to some scientists' consternation, a team of researchers from the University of California at Berkeley came up with evidence that seemed to indicate an extraterrestrial event of enormous magnitude at the close of the Cretaceous. Led by geologist Walter Alvarez and his father, famed physicist Luis Alvarez, the team claimed that a rich layer of a heavy element, iridium, in worldwide sediments 65 million years old

Smithsonian paleobotanist Leo Hickey takes notes on vegetation and sediment in modern mangrove swamp in Panama for later comparison with features found in sequences of sedimentary rock around the time of the end of the dinosaurs.

The gradual cooling of the climate beginning at the end of the Cretaceous may have brought an end to the dinosaurs' reign. Graph indicates temperatures of middle and higher latitudes of North America.

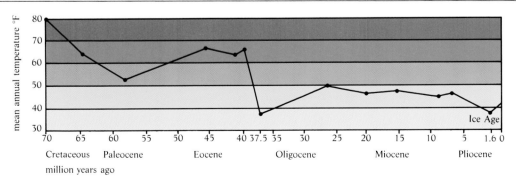

163

was the signature of a collision between the Earth and an asteroid measuring three to six miles in diameter. The impact would have raised a vast dust cloud, blocking out the sun for three years. They proposed that the resultant death of many plants would have been fatal for many animal populations, with only the small species, such as the mammals, being able to pull through by surviving on seeds and other small, long-lasting food items.

Fanciful, perhaps, but by mid-1982 the notion of an asteroidal impact was being taken very seriously by geologists and paleontologists alike. However, the scenario for the associated extinction was refined substantially. "The trouble was," says Smithsonian paleobotanist Leo Hickey, "that if the asteroid had been the sole cause of the Cretaceous extinction you would expect to see all the different animal and plant groups going out of the record at precisely the same time."

In fact, the fossil record shows that as the end of the Cretaceous period neared there was a steady decline in the number and diversity of dinosaurs, accompanied by an equally steady rise in the abundance of mammals. In other words, the switch from a reptilian to a mammalian world was not as

Dromaeosaurus scavenges the carcass *of a* Chasmosaurus *in a dry stream bed in what is now Alberta, Canada. Scene is set in the late Cretaceous, not long before the end of the dinosaurs' 150-million-year reign.*

sudden as has often been imagined. The dinosaurs' decline stretched over a period of more than five million years. Abrupt though this is in geological time scales, it is not the picture one would expect from a single massive global catastrophe.

Hickey also points out that in the western United States, the most pronounced floral change occurred some 20,000 to 90,000 years after the last dinosaurs. "This is not what you would call simultaneous extinction," he comments. The asteroid-as-killer hypothesis is also brought into question by indications that dinosaur and plant extinctions were much less drastic near the tropics than at higher latitudes. And, looking again at the western interior of North America, there is even the suggestion that dinosaurs became extinct well before the asteroid left its signature.

Provided that an asteroid did collide with Earth, it probably did raise a sunlight-blocking dust cloud—but for no more than three months, not three years as earlier suggested. This darkness was probably responsible for a proportion of the marine extinctions, as plankton would have been largely wiped out by even several months of darkness; but it could not account for most of the extinctions on land.

"Data from fossil pollen show that the plants that fared best in the Cretaceous extinction were those in the tropics," says Hickey. "That's not what you'd expect if there had been a long period of darkness. Tropical plants have the least recuperative capacity of all plants." What, then, could explain the terrestrial extinctions? "There is strong evidence of a deterioration of climate toward the end of the Cretaceous," asserts Hickey. "For instance, in Montana the evidence indicates a drop in mean annual temperature from 20–22°C to 10–13°C [68–72°F to 50–55°F], and this would probably mean the occurrence of winter frosts." The cooling of the climate, which continued with periodic fluctuations into the recent ice ages, would have been a serious problem for animals that had become adapted to steady, warm temperatures. Assuming that they were cold-blooded, dinosaurs simply would not have been able to make it through the winter.

The advent of seasonality, with relatively cold winters, caused temperate vegetation to spread where tropical plants had once flourished. Insect populations would have altered, too. Thus, the shifting ecological mix in many parts of the world might account for the extinction of the smaller animals, including some of the mammals.

Exactly what caused the change in climate is something of a mystery. Ocean levels were dropping at the time, draining the sea that had divided North America into Western and Eastern subcontinents. Major changes in ocean levels are often associated with continental drift. The slow and steady shift in the position of continents can alter the pattern of major ocean currents and provoke changes in atmospheric circulation, both of which can influence global climate.

Ostrom believes that climatic deterioration associated with shifting continents is the key to the Cretaceous terrestrial extinctions. Hickey considers the change in climate to have been too great to be accounted for only by the effects of continental movement. Both agree, however, that climate rather than catastrophe was the major instrument in bringing an end to the reign of the dinosaurs. Asteroidal impact might have dealt a coup de grace in some cases, but it was a secondary rather than a primary cause.

Though mystery surrounds the nature of the Cretaceous extinction, the outcome, as Colbert indicates, was strikingly clear. For 150 million years the dinosaurs had successfully occupied the large animal niche, both for herbivores and carnivores, while mammals, principally insectivores, were confined to the small animal niche. Nothing weighing more than 50 pounds survived the Cretaceous extinction on land, and so the beginning of the Cenozoic era offered unlimited ecological opportunities to the surviving mammals. The way in which mammals radiated into this empty ecological space was shaped to a large extent by anatomical and behavioral features they had acquired during their long evolutionary history.

Before examining these features, we must return to some of those other forms that shared the world of the dinosaurs. In particular, the organisms that took to the air to face the greatest challenges and opportunities since their ancestors had invaded the land.

Three-foot-long skull of Edmontosaurus regalis, *a duck-billed dinosaur once abundant in Cretaceous swamps of Alberta.*

LIFE ON THE WING

Wings become blurred as two broad-tailed hummingbirds hover in front of flower cluster and probe for nectar. A family of some 320 species, hummingbirds are the most efficient avian nectar gatherers.

The Galapagos Islands are home to many thousands of frigate birds, aerial pirates that perform unmatched aerobatics. With apparently clumsy seven-foot wingspread, so agile are these huge black aeronauts that they often terrorize other birds in mid-air, forcing the unfortunate victims to relinquish their prey, usually fish. Then, peeling out of attack, the frigate swoops to intercept the free meal before it hits the ground. No other large bird is constructed with an economy and line to compare with the frigate's. This magnificent creature's structure and performance simply invite superlatives.

In fact, superlatives are unquestionably appropriate to the world of birds as a whole. The feats of some of its members are truly astonishing. The wandering albatross, *Diomedea exulans*—the world's largest flying bird with a wingspread of up to 11.5 feet—can soar for hours on motionless wings and cruise the open sea for months on end, coming to land rarely except to breed. The young Arctic tern journeys in August from its hatching place in the Far North via the west coasts of Europe and Africa or through the Pacific to its Antarctic summer grounds, some 10,000 miles away. The following May these diminutive birds turn northward once again as summer returns to the Arctic. Some birds have become so highly adapted to life in the air that they have difficulty on the ground. One Asian species of swift has taken to the air so completely that it boasts not only a level flying speed of 100 miles per hour but it also engages in airborne copulation. The world's smallest warm-blooded creatures, hummingbirds, can hover and fly backward.

If the physical achievements of the avian world are impressive, the variety and elegance of coloring and decoration are certainly no less so. From the restrained but glorious iridescence of sunbirds to the extravagant, blazing plumage of birds of paradise, the class Aves lays exceptional claim to the animal world's peak of sartorial elegance. The secret of birds' vibrant chromatic

Courting male frigate bird inflates bare-skinned throat pouch before female, above. Perhaps the most aerially skilled of all birds except the swift, the frigate bird soars tirelessly on seven-foot wings. Wingspread of wandering albatross, left, reaches 11.5 feet, the widest among living birds.

Halo of feathers encircles head of gray crowned crane, one of the most beautiful members of this ancient family of wading birds.

Bejeweled eastern double-collared sunbird perches on flower from which it takes nectar with its delicately curved beak. Old World counterparts of the hummingbirds, sunbirds number more than 100 species.

expression is the feather, the same structure upon which their superb flying ability depends.

However, birds were neither the first nor the only vertebrate group to take to the wing and thrive there. In fact, a surprisingly wide selection of creatures exploit the air's thin buoyancy to purchase extra distance in their lives. In addition to the bats, which are true flyers, 16 different kinds of other mammals (12 of which are squirrels) are able to fling themselves from branches of trees and glide safely over relatively long distances supported by well developed membranes stretched between their limbs. The most proficient glider is the flying lemur, or colugo, a rabbit-sized inhabitant of the forests of Southeast Asia and the Philippines. Its furry cloak, which is draped between all four limbs and even extends to the neck, can carry these small mammals more than 200 feet in a single leap under favorable conditions. Marsupials, too, have taken

Highly camouflaged Malaysian flying lizard, Draco volans, *planes on flap-like membranes supported by ribs.*

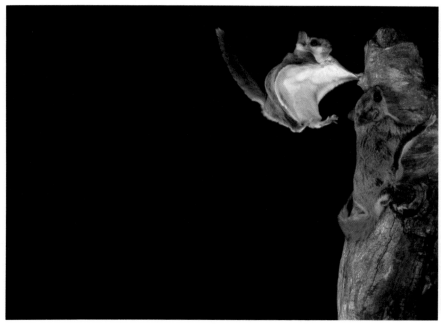

to the air: the several species of the Australasian *Petaurus*, or flying phalanger, have a gliding structure very much like that of the flying squirrels.

Some reptiles can be airborne too. In Southeast Asia abound about two dozen species of the genus *Draco*, a small lizard which planes on two immobile membranes that extend horizontally from its abdomen. Two fossil lizards, *Icarosaurus* and *Kuehneosaurus*, lived some 200 million years ago and apparently possessed flying apparatus similar to the *Dracos'*. A second modern reptile equipped for aerial travel is the gliding gecko, whose airfoils are much more modest in size than the *Dracos'*. Members of the snake genus *Chrysopelea*, again from Southeast Asia, are able to flatten their abdomens and gain aerodynamic support in an astonishing squirming glide.

Sailors and islanders have enjoyed "free lunches"—flying fish—for centuries. These so-

called fliers are actually gliders supported by enlarged pectoral fins but powered by the furious beat of their tails. Some true flying fishes, the tiny freshwater hatchetfishes of South American brooks and lakes, break the surface when alarmed and with a high-speed buzzing of their pectoral fins arch above the water for distances of more than two yards.

There are three known examples of "flying" amphibians, all of which are tree frogs of the genus *Rhacophorus*. These Southeast Asian frogs glide and parachute in a comical fashion supported by exaggeratedly webbed feet.

Intriguing though these airborne variations of normally terrestrial creatures may be, the evolution of true powered and sustained flight is of the most interest. This ability has arisen three times independently in the vertebrates. Both bats, the only really proficient flying mammals, and birds are still

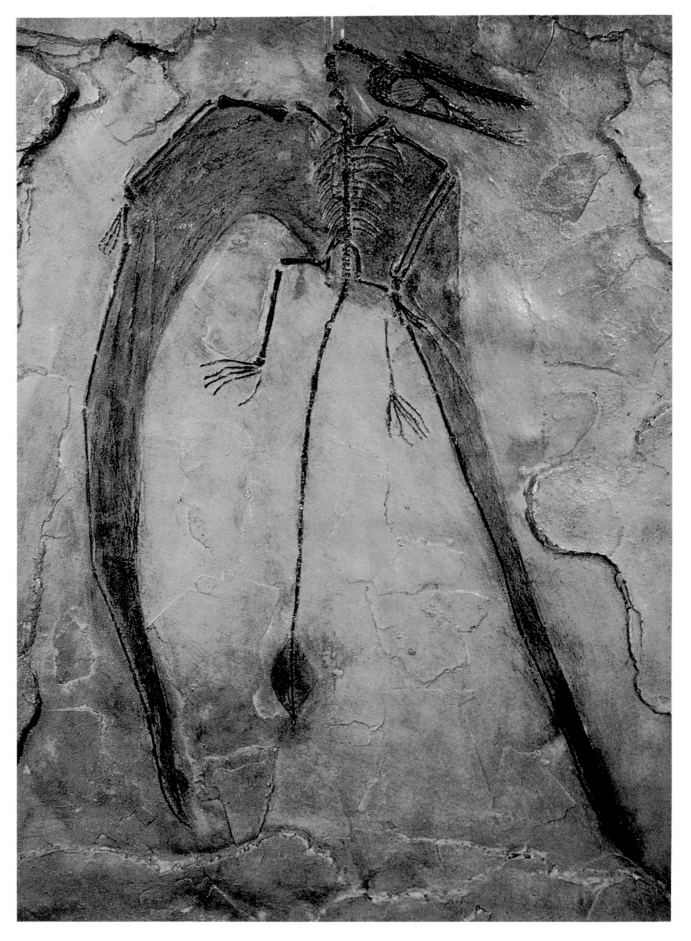

Wing membrane stretches along greatly extended fourth finger of fossil Rhamphorhynchus, *opposite, flying reptile of the order Pterosauria that appeared about 200 million years ago. Below, Smithsonian's reconstruction of pterosaur* Quetzalcoatl northropi, *largest animal ever to have flown, with 35–40 foot wingspread. Compact* Ichthyornis, *far left, and flightless* Hesperornis, *left, hint at many modern forms already in existence in Cretaceous.*

with us. The pterosaurs, a large and highly successful order of flying reptiles, vanished along with the dinosaurs 65 million years ago.

Some 300 million years ago the insects formed the vanguard of the animal world's expansion into the air. The first flying insects seem to have had permanently outstretched wings typical of the modern dragonfly; these eventually gave way to the foldable wings now possessed by most flying insects. Today, the great majority of insects fly, indicating the apparent economic and safety benefits to be had from efficient flight.

For 100 million years the insects had the skies to themselves. Terrestrial and arboreal reptiles and amphibians posed a real threat, but escape from curling tongues and snapping jaws was effected by a few rapid buzzes of the insects' paper-thin wings. No vertebrate predator followed the insects into their aerial refuge until about 200 million years ago, when the first pterosaurs evolved.

The evolution of a flying vertebrate from a previously terrestrial animal demands changes as radical as those involved in the switch from an aquatic to a dry land environment. In addition to the acquisition of wings, the animal's skeleton must be considerably modified. The large muscles that power the flight stroke must be anchored on strong bones. At the same time, the whole skeleton must be made as light as possible. The complex control systems demanded by sustained, powered flight call for greater brainpower and coordination. And, as flying is an intensely energy-consuming business, the body's metabolic rate must be maintained at a high and steady level.

It is clear from the large number of pterosaur fossils now available, which have been discovered in every continent except Antarctica, that these animals did indeed qualify as efficient fliers. They had well developed wings, a very light yet strong skeleton suited for the physical demands of flight, and their brains were enlarged in the areas that would endow enhanced muscular control and vision. Whether or not pterosaurs maintained a

high body temperature—were endothermic—is more difficult to determine. Berkeley paleontologist Kevin Padian points out that two pterosaur specimens have been found in which there is unequivocal evidence of a hairy coat. "This suggests heat insulation in an endothermic animal," he says. In addition to the fossil impressions of fur, certain skeletal characteristics point to a high metabolic rate. "It would be surprising if active fliers, as the pterosaurs undoubtedly were, had not been warm-blooded," surmises Padian.

Pterosaurs have been favorite subjects of animated films for decades. They are usually portrayed as being tentative gliders or, at best, poor fliers while airborne and, when on ground, clumsy beasts stumbling around on nearly useless hind limbs and the "knuckles" of their partly folded wings. "This type of image goes back a long time," explains Padian. "It has its roots in the early misidentification of a pterosaur specimen as a bat."

Attribution of bat-like characteristics—membranous wings linking directly with the hind legs, which were useful only for hanging or awkward walking—has pervaded even the scientific literature on pterosaurs until recently. Padian has made a careful study of pterosaur skeletons. He concludes that the wings would have permitted highly sophisticated flight, and that while on the ground the reptiles would have walked adeptly on their

ARCHAEOPTERYX

Bird-like but not a bird, dinosaur-like but not a dinosaur, *Archaeopteryx* runs, flaps, and glides its way through a Jurassic forest of some 150 million years ago in this reconstruction by artist John Gurche. The oldest bird-like form, known from only six specimens, *Archaeopteryx* had feathers and a wishbone like those of modern birds, but teeth, a tail, and many other skeletal features like those of the small carnivorous dinosaurs called theropods from which the birds seem to have evolved. While the flying skills of *Archaeopteryx* are still the subject of some controversy, the teeth of the pigeon-sized animal would have been suitable for the capture of insects or other small prey. Here, a lacewing insect darts away from *Archaeopteryx* in the gloom of a forest of sequoia-like trees in what will later be southern Germany. A giant sauropod similar to a *Diplodocus* shambles through the forest in the background.

172

1. *Archaeopteryx*
2. Lacewing
   (Mesonymphes hageni)
3. *Diplodocus*
4. Taxodiaceae

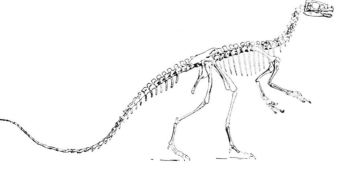

Small carnivorous dinosaurs such as Ornitholestes, *left, may have been similar to ancestors of* Archaeopteryx, *above, possible link between dinosaurs and birds. Fully feathered,* Archaeopteryx *had some skeletal features of modern birds, lacked others.*

hind legs just as modern birds do. "There was nothing clumsy or inferior about pterosaurs," asserts Padian. "They formed an extremely varied and successful group that thrived for more than 140 million years."

The order Pterosauria is made up of two suborders, the rhamphorhynchoids, which first appeared about 200 million years ago and dwindled into extinction around 120 million years ago, and the pterodactyloids, which arose perhaps 150 million years ago and vanished in the great Cretaceous extinction 65 million years ago. Like the dinosaurs whose fate they shared, the pterodactyloids were already beginning to lose ground some few million years before they finally became extinct. Like the dinosaurs, the pterosaurs probably had their ancestral roots in the thecodonts, the small, bipedal carnivorous reptiles of the Triassic. (Together with the dinosaurs, crocodiles, and thecodonts, the pterosaurs make up the archosaurs, or ruling reptiles.)

The rhamphorhynchoids and the pterodactyloids shared the same basic architecture. The forelimbs were enlarged and the wing membrane stretched from a greatly extended fourth finger. Perhaps because the demands of flight pose the same problems for all vertebrates, the pterosaurs resembled birds and bats in their overall structure and proportions. Their shoulder and pectoral girdles were built to support powerful wing strokes. Pterosaurs evolved bones with very thin walls, greatly reducing their skeletal weight. The degree to which these reptiles took this bone-lightening development far exceeded anything to be seen in other flying vertebrates. For instance, the walls of the hollow long bones of *Pteranodon*, one of the larger pterosaurs, were as little as a twentieth of an inch thick. With a wingspread of 23 feet, this displays an astonishing economy of construction.

The differences between the two pterosaur suborders are partly in emphasis and partly in detail. The rhamphorhynchoids, for instance, possessed a long tail which was absent in the pterodactyloids. A membranous flap at the end of the tail may have been used as a kind of rudder. The pterodactyloids had longer necks and a few of them had long crests on the back of the head. The function of these crests has been the subject of lively speculation, with suggestions varying from aerodynamic utility to sexual differentiation. The crest may have been the *Pteranodon*'s version of the peacock's tail.

Although both pterosaur suborders had large and small species, the size range was greatest in the

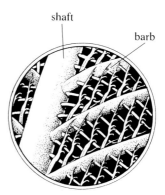

Fossil feather, left, from same Jurassic limestone in which Archaeopteryx *skeletons were preserved. Above, magnified view of flight feather.*

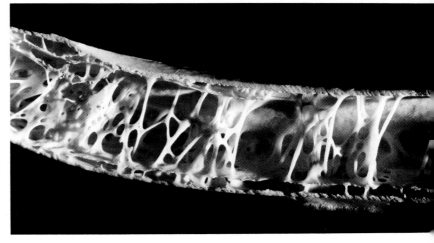

Lightweight, rigid structures such as strut-reinforced eagle wing bone, above, and air sacs in body cavities are among birds' many adaptations to demands of flight.

175

Life in the air is energy-expensive. Like numerous species of birds living for generations in environments free of terrestrial predators, these Galapagos cormorants have lost their ability to fly.

pterodactyloids, stretching from sparrow-sized creatures right up to the largest animal ever to have flown, the gigantic *Quetzalcoatlus northropi*, with a wingspread of 35 to 40 feet. This impressive creature, which takes its name from Quetzalcoatl, a Toltec term for a mythical plumed serpent, and the Northrop Flying Wing, an experimental tailless airplane, has recently been the subject of an adventurous reconstruction. In the Dinosaur Hall of the Smithsonian's National Museum of Natural History it soars over skeletons of creatures with which it shared a vanished age.

The same characteristic that allowed pterosaurs to take to the air so effectively—their extremely light skeleton—conspired with the elements of nature to impoverish their fossil record. Only under the most favorable conditions were the delicate bones of these reptiles turned into fossils. In forests and open country, the chance of fossilization of pterosaurs was practically nonexistent, so the fossil record is biased in favor of those that lived close to, and were therefore trapped in, marine and lake sediments. Nevertheless, it is clear even from this impoverished record that the diversity in size of pterosaurs was matched by a diversity in habit.

One of the small species, *Pterodactylus*, was equipped with tiny peg-like teeth probably suited to a diet of insects. Some larger species had bigger teeth and may have lived on small reptiles and amphibians. Some undoubtedly were seed eaters, while the fossilized stomach contents of the giant *Pteranodon* show that it ate fish. *Pterodaustro*, a relatively large pterodactylid, sported a long beak lined with hundreds of needle-like teeth that formed a sieve similar to that in the baleen whale. The chances are that *Pterodaustro* fed by filtering plankton and other small food items from water.

On what did *Quetzalcoatlus* sustain its large frame? Like *Pteranodon*, *Quetzalcoatlus* had a long toothless beak, so perhaps it too was a fish eater. But it happens that most of its remains found so far have been hundreds of miles from what would have been the ocean at the time. Inland fishing is still a possibility, as is spearing small creatures living along streams and rivers. Some people have suggested that it might even have taken carrion, as the marabou stork of Africa does today. But the extinct pterosaur's long beak might not have been sufficiently robust for that.

The diversity of diet apparent throughout the group is striking and reminiscent of the varied habits of living birds. If the pterosaurs were so widely accomplished, why did they become extinct? "A lot of people assume that they succumbed to competition with birds," says Padian, "but I don't favor that idea. After all, the pterosaurs lived side by side with the birds for more than 70 million years, and it was the pterosaurs that displayed the greater diversity during that period."

The end of the Cretaceous was marked by a significant deterioration in climate. Ocean levels were falling, and environments must have changed dramatically in some cases. Could this have been responsible for the steady disappearance of many of the smaller pterosaurs toward the end of the Cretaceous, eventually leaving only the larger forms, including *Quetzalcoatlus*, to bring down the final curtain on the era of flying reptiles? So far, no one has a good answer; but whatever happened, *Quetzalcoatlus* and its giant cousins failed, like virtually all creatures weighing more than 50 pounds, to make it through the Cretaceous extinction. The skies were then completely open to total domination by the birds, with a secondary role eventually being taken on by the bats.

Flight of small owl demonstrates aerodynamic principles on which all avian wings are constructed. Outer feathers or primaries provide major thrust, flattening for downstroke, twisting to allow air passage in upstroke. Inner feathers on wing's leading edge maintain lift.

Useless appendages on land, flipperlike wings of Adélie penguins propel them gracefully through frigid Antarctic waters. One of six genera of the family Spheniscidae, Adélies have flourished in the absence of land predators.

Birds, which arose some 150 million years ago, share many architectural features with pterosaurs, and their fossil record suffers from the same inherent deficiency as that of pterosaurs. But it is clear from a detailed study of their anatomy that the relationship between these two groups is one of similar function and not of ancestry. Birds are not feathered descendants of pterosaurs. The origin of birds involved a second, independent, evolution of vertebrate flight. Bats, which are mammals, marked the third occasion, arising around 50 million years ago. Their superb echolocation mechanism allows them to fill the hazardous nocturnal flying niche. The origins of powered flight, such a

Gray-headed albatrosses engage in courtship display, one of many such rituals that serve to initiate the demanding mating system of birds.

demanding facility, require careful attention. "It is," says Padian, "one of the greatest challenges to evolutionary biology."

It is perhaps not surprising that to date the fossil record has failed to yield a "proto-pterosaur" that might give some clue as to how flight arose in these reptiles. For birds, however, chance has been kinder to the paleontologists. One of the most celebrated fossils of all time—*Archaeopteryx*—was closely associated with the origin of birds but had not yet attained full status as a bird. It is a perfect example of what paleontologists like to call a transitional fossil.

The first evidence of *Archaeopteryx* came to light in 1861, almost two years after the publication of Darwin's *Origin of Species*, with the discovery of a perfect impression of a single feather in the fine-grained limestone of Solnhofen in Bavaria. The crisp detail preserved in this remarkable ancient lagoon deposit revealed a feather as modern in design as any that helps power the flight of a living bird. And yet the limestone was laid down some 150 million years ago. Soon after the discovery of the feather, several almost complete skeletons were found in between the pristine leaves of closely layered limestone, each about the size of a pigeon and evidently cloaked in feathers. These seemed to be ancient birds (which is what *Archaeopteryx* means). Or were they?

Discussions on the origin of flight in birds have reverberated through the biological world for more than a century, with proposals falling into two camps. The most popular—and intuitively most attractive—notion was that some tree-living reptile developed the habit of leaping from branch to branch and, under the influence of natural selection, evolved wings that allowed it first to glide and eventually to fly. This, roughly speaking, is the *trees-down* or *arboreal* hypothesis.

Its rival is the exact opposite, the *ground-up* or *cursorial* hypothesis. This second, more challenging, proposal envisages a ground-living animal that ran about on its hind legs. Its forelimbs would therefore be free to develop into airfoils which would at first allow assisted leaps but would lead eventually to powered flight. The ground-up idea remained for a long time the less popular of the two, mainly because no one could think of a good reason why the forelimbs might develop wing-like characteristics. In recent years, however, ideas have shifted, and a careful study of *Archaeopteryx* now fits into the ground-up scheme.

Dinosaur expert John Ostrom traveled to England and Germany in the late 1960s to examine the *Archaeopteryx* specimens stored in museums there. He had recently finished an extensive project on theropods, the group of predatory dinosaurs that included the tiny *Compsognathus* and the huge *Tyrannosaurus*. As it transpired, Ostrom's switch of interest from these predators to apparently ancient birds was a great stroke of fortune. "The fact that *Archaeopteryx* was covered with feathers obviously makes you think of it as a bird," says Ostrom, "but I began to realize that if you ignored the feathers and looked at the skeleton, there were many features in common with some of the small theropods. There were too many features

Successful incubation means hungry hatchlings, another time- and energy-consuming responsibility for birds. Above, greater flamingo funnels food to chick through decurved bill.

Nest building remains an integral part of courtship and reproduction, as demonstrated by zealous robin, above, and diligent osprey, top.

for it to be the result of convergent evolution.''

Although the skeleton of *Archaeopteryx* does have a wishbone (two collarbones fused together), which is typical of birds, it lacks the bony breastbone and "keel," structures that are essential for anchoring large muscles required in powered flight. For this reason, and many other details of skeletal construction, Ostrom concludes that "*Archaeopteryx* was a long way from modern birds as far as flight was concerned." (*Archaeopteryx*, incidentally, unlike all modern birds, retained the teeth of its dinosaurian ancestor.)

So, *Archaeopteryx* was bird-like but not a bird, and theropod-like but not a theropod. How-

ever, the probable ancestry of *Archaeopteryx* in the theropods had great significance for those studying the evolutionary route to powered flight. The theropods were habitually bipedal and the ones comparable in size to *Archaeopteryx* were insectivores. Ostrom notes that all the anatomical indications are that *Archaeopteryx* was an agile, bipedal, territorial insect eater. The immediate question to ask is, why did this creature have feathers? More specifically, of what use were the long feathers that made the forelimbs so reminiscent of wings?

A covering of small downy feathers would have afforded excellent heat insulation in an animal that needed to maintain a high and steady body

Fruit bat roosts with its young. The only mammals capable of true flight, bats evolved some 45 million years ago, today number about 900 species.

temperature. As discussed earlier, there are many reasons for thinking that some of the small predatory dinosaurs were endothermic, or warm-blooded. The evolution of a feathery cloak as a means of body temperature control is entirely consistent with this idea. The origin of the "flight" feathers in *Archaeopteryx*, however, demands a secondary explanation.

Perhaps *Archaeopteryx* used its wings to flush out and capture insects as it ran along. Occasional flapping of these proto-wings would have allowed *Archaeopteryx* to leap and capture escaping prey; sustained flapping might eventually have given rise to sustained flight. Ostrom concedes that *Archaeopteryx* was well beyond the simple leaping, insect-catching stage and perhaps was at the threshold of powered flight, but a more rudimentary insect-net stage might have been the evolutionary engine for the innovation.

This was the radical suggestion Ostrom offered in 1974. "It generated quite a bit of interest but apparently very little acceptance," he recalls. One problem with the idea was that it did not really address the all-important flight stroke, the complex maneuver of the wing that gives birds aerodynamic lift. Three researchers at North Arizona University are currently pondering this problem, working toward a simple but elegant solution.

The three are Russell Balda, Gerald Caple, and William Willis—ornithologist, chemist, and physicist respectively. They contend that if a precursor of *Archaeopteryx* used its forelimbs to lunge at insect prey, the effect would be to pitch the animal on its face, unless it engaged in a complex set of counterbalancing movements. As an alternative they suggest that this early pre-bird may have devoted its jaws to catching prey and employed its wings as aerodynamic stabilizers. They note that

with an airfoil capable of lifting just one percent of the animal's weight, a considerable stabilizing effect would be achieved (providing the airfoil was located sufficiently far from the body).

Ostrom is happy to consider this new suggestion as an improvement over the original insect net hypothesis. Kevin Padian is enthusiastic about it too. "It means that the wings should have become enlarged first at the hands—not along the body wall, as in most gliding animals," he says. This is precisely what is seen in *Archaeopteryx*. "An animal that runs along the ground on two legs, leaps into the air to catch prey with its teeth, and uses an aerodynamically advantageous pair of proto-wings to steady its trajectory has all the necessary equipment to evolve active flight," Padian explains. "The first flight stroke may well have been a lunging motion of the forelimbs as the animal leaped from the ground after prey."

A colony of around a quarter million wrinkled-lipped bats emerges at dusk to hunt insects, top. Bats track prey by means of echolocation, a kind of sonar. Above, frog-eating bat in Panama swoops down on toad.

Royal tern opens bill and raises feathers as part of threat display to defend nest against immature reddish egret. Display postures comprise an important part of visual communication in birds.

This ground-up hypothesis of bird evolution clearly does not include a gliding stage. "Indeed, it is difficult to see how it could fit in," comments Padian. Many birds are capable of soaring and gliding, but this should be viewed as a secondary development, not as the primary path of bird evolution. And although most modern birds are arboreal, this is an adaptive zone into which they have moved, not one from which they originated.

As no equivalent to *Archaeopteryx* as a transitional fossil in pterosaur evolution has yet been discovered, there is no direct evidence from which to deduce the route these reptiles took to the air. However, Padian considers that the indirect evidence points to a similar evolutionary story, a ground-up route. He notes that pterosaurs apparently were agile, bipedal animals that walked on their toes, a mode of locomotion seen only in small dinosaurs and birds. In addition, the shape of the pterosaurs' wings is consistent with the demands of the aerodynamic stabilization model. The likelihood is, therefore, that both pterosaurs and birds evolved powered flight in ground-living ancestors.

What of the third group of flying vertebrates, the bats? Like pterosaurs, bats fly with a membranous airfoil, but in these most recently evolved flying vertebrates the airfoil attaches to the hind limbs. Moreover, the anatomy of the hind limbs is such that these small mammals are virtually incapable of walking on the ground. When not flying, bats typically suspend themselves upside down, hanging from branches or from the roof of a cave. For these reasons Padian suspects they acquired their wings by the trees-down route.

"Bats seem always to have been arboreal, nocturnal insectivores," suggests Padian. "In order to evolve flight, it appears that bats must have had to free the hind limbs by developing at an early stage in their history the habit of hanging upside down." This may sound a little odd in isolation, but in fact such a posture in arboreal creatures is an efficient way of escaping detection by predators. In any case, "bats could afford to incorporate the hind limbs in the wing because they employed neither bipedal locomotion nor normal quadrupedal terrestrial locomotion."

Equipped with this unique flying structure, bats extended the nocturnal insectivorous adaptive zone of their ancestors, with new species developing the habit of living variously on nectar, fruit, frogs, and even the blood of large vertebrates. Their flightless arboreal ancestors probably had a primitive echolocation system with which they tracked their tiny prey. This facility became finely tuned through evolution to permit pin-point aerial navigation in the dark.

The long history of the evolution of vertebrate flight is traced only patchily in the fossil record, but in spite of this an extraordinary degree of evolutionary adaptability is immediately evident. Two genera of birds that appeared some 50 million years after *Archaeopteryx* illustrate this very well. One of them, *Ichthyornis*, was a strong flyer, a fish eater, rather like a tern. Another was *Hesperornis*, also a fish eater, but a large creature measuring six or seven feet long. Needless to say, it was flightless. Just as some amphibians, reptiles, and even mammals returned to the seas—at least glancing over their shoulders if not actually retracing their evolutionary path—so have some birds given up the flying habit. The readiness with which flight is abandoned is perhaps a measure of how demanding life on the wing really is.

Birds have typically lost their ability to fly when for whatever reason they have no longer had to face terrestrial predators. Soon after the disappearance of the dinosaurs, large predatory flightless birds such as *Phororhacos* arose in South America, possibly filling some of the niches left open by the dinosaur extinction. The penguins of Antarctica have flourished in enormous numbers in the absence of terrestrial predators. A number of flightless birds living and extinct, such as the kiwi and gigantic moa of New Zealand, the elephant bird of Madagascar, the cassowary of New Guinea,

and the celebrated dodo of Mauritius have arisen on islands free of predators.

Whatever their size, shape or habits, all birds share essentially the same reproductive task, being warm-blooded egg layers. Once laid, the eggs are not normally left to the vicissitudes of the environment, but assiduously incubated to ensure a constant high temperature for the warm-blooded embryo developing inside the shell. Successful incubation calls for patience and devotion, as does nurturing the insatiable hatchlings that result.

The demands of establishing and rearing an avian brood have had a tremendous impact on the social life and appearance of birds. Elaborate and lengthy courtship displays are common before a pair mates. Sometimes a male has to help construct, or even build entirely on his own, a nest acceptable to the female before she will copulate.

The wonderfully extravagant plumage of some male birds—the peacock's tail is a splendid example—appears to be a response through natural selection to birds' unusually demanding mating system. Females, it seems, exercise a considerable degree of choice over their potential mate. The males have therefore been forced to try to outdo each other in ostentatious efforts to attract attention—for instance, elaborate plumage, coloring patterns, or vocalization. Darwin was intrigued by this aspect of competition in nature, and called it sexual selection.

Pterosaurs shared many features with their avian cousins: they laid eggs, flew, and were probably warm-blooded. Did they too build nests in which to incubate a carefully nurtured brood? And did sexual selection produce wild and wonderful physical appearance among the males of some species (such as the large head crest in *Pteranodon*)? These are tantalizing, but perhaps unanswerable, questions.

Crested male common peacock spreads elongated, spectacularly adorned upper tail coverts in courtship ritual, one of the most magnificent sights in nature.

THE MAMMALS'
WORLD

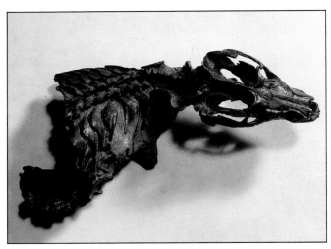

A two-foot-long mammal-like reptile, Thrinaxodon, *lived about 200 million years ago. Finds of* Thrinaxodon *fossils in Africa, India, and Antarctica provide evidence of continental drift.*

It is a sobering thought that had the Cretaceous extinction not occurred, the world might still be dominated by the dinosaurs or their large reptilian descendants. Mammals might still be playing their long-time ecologically restricted role. As it was, the small mammals at the beginning of the Cenozoic era about 65 million years ago began a rapid radiation that involved a great diversification of form in both herbivorous and carnivorous niches. And within a relatively short time, whales, porpoises, and seals had colonized the sea, and bats had taken to the air. Although there was a general increase in size in some lines—in horses and elephants, for example—today about half the 4,000 living species of mammals are diminutive rodents. It is interesting to reflect that when the dinosaurs were alive the vast majority of terrestrial animals were larger than modern cows or horses whereas now the reverse is true, a wonderful example of time and change.

With the passing of the dinosaurs, mammals seem unquestionably to have been the best equipped of the surviving animal forms to replace the ruling reptiles. The small animal niche into which the mammal-like reptiles had accommodated themselves clearly favored active animals that could forage for food at night, provided they were able to maintain a steady and high enough body temperature.

No one knows how well developed the first mammals' endothermic systems were, but they must have had a significant degree of control (as some of the late mammal-like reptiles probably did too). Most modern mammals are equipped with a fur coat that helps retain body heat. The fossil record is mute on the point, but the early mammals were almost certainly similarly equipped.

Worldwide climatic cooling during the Cenozoic, the geological era of the last 65 million years, led to the retreat of lush forests in many areas and the extensive spread of grasslands. Hoofed herbivores such as African wildebeest, right, flourished on newly created open savanna.

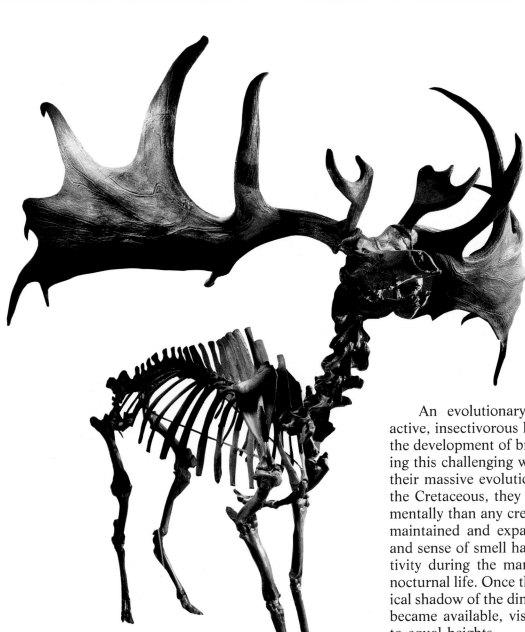

The extinct Irish elk, left, Megaloceros giganteus, *had an antler spread of up to 11 feet, largest of any deer. Irish elk may have survived in isolated areas until 700 B.C. Elephants such as mammoth, right, mastodon, and others roamed Africa, Eurasia, North and South America in huge numbers during the past two million years. To the left of the mammoth, a Pleistocene peccary; to right, a bear.*

An evolutionary consequence of living an active, insectivorous life—probably at night—was the development of brainpower capable of exploiting this challenging world. When mammals began their massive evolutionary radiation at the end of the Cretaceous, they were indeed better endowed mentally than any creatures before them, and they maintained and expanded that position. Hearing and sense of smell had been honed to acute sensitivity during the mammals' 100 million years of nocturnal life. Once they emerged from the ecological shadow of the dinosaurs and the daytime niche became available, visual capacity quickly evolved to equal heights.

A major advantage of mammals over reptiles is the structure of the lower jaw and the associated sling of muscles. As described in Chapter 7, several bones in the reptilian lower jaw became recruited as part of a more sensitive middle ear structure

Evolution of mammalian jaw and ear were linked. Beginning with lobe-finned fish, bottom, and progressing through primitive amphibian to mammal-like reptile and modern mammal, colors in diagram show shifts in size and function of bones.

- Hyomandibular became stapes in ear.
- Quadrate became incus in ear.
- Articular became malleus in ear.
- Angular became middle ear housing, or auditory bulla.

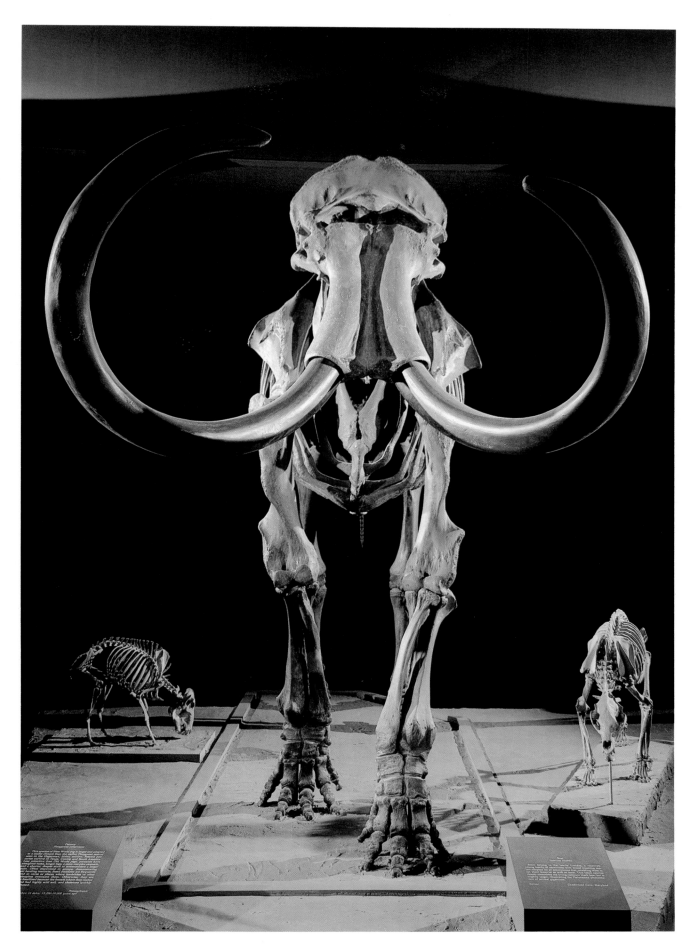

Mammals have evolved into a wondrous variety of sizes, shapes, and life-styles. Primitive tree shrew, right, retains many characteristics of early mammals. Highly specialized whales such as humpback, below, inhabit all of the world's oceans. Many species of jumping rodents like the kangaroo rat, bottom, live in desert environments.

during the evolution of a line of mammal-like reptiles. Eventually, this process gave rise to the mammalian lower jaw comprised of one bone, the dentary. Thus, the change for more sensitive hearing brought with it as an evolutionary bonus a jaw that could be moved from side to side rather than forward and backward only.

"Mammals evolved molar teeth which possessed a complex set of shearing surfaces," says A.W. Crompton. "Upper and lower molars accurately fit one another to produce an effective mechanism for the breakdown of food. Because mammalian molars accurately fit one another, the ancestral type of reptilian tooth replacement which

Adapted for arboreal life, a young orangutan swings through Indonesian forest with abandon. Older individuals weighing 150 pounds or more clamber along branches with care. Orangutans and other great apes—gibbons, chimpanzees, and gorillas—are Mankind's closest relatives.

Another tree dweller, the three-toed sloth, Bradypus, *of Surinam has reversed the usual mammalian evolutionary trend toward speed and agility. A cat-sized herbivore, it relies on sluggishness for concealment. Sloths are related to giant ground sloths, elephant-sized forms that died out within the last 3,000 years.*

continued throughout life was lost because this form of replacement would have disturbed the precise fit between matching upper and lower molars." Reptiles continually replace teeth in an alternate pattern because they need a functional set of teeth when they hatch, and numerous replacements are necessary as the reptile skull grows continuously, he explains. Mammals can get away with a single replacement of the milk teeth by a permanent dentition and a single set of molars which erupt without predecessors. Because young mammals are initially nurtured on milk and because their skulls reach about 60 percent of mature size before the first set of teeth have emerged, a single replacement of the milk teeth and addition of molars can accommodate the limited further growth.

One of the most significant aspects of mammalian life, however, is one that does not become fossilized with the skeleton: the mode of reproduction. "At various localities in western North America," says David Archibald of Yale University, "we have found placental and marsupial mammals from the end of the Cretaceous, together with a third group, the multituberculates." Small and rodent-like in appearance, the multituberculates arose in the Jurassic and for about 100 million years were the most abundant of the mammals. Marsupials were also abundant; when the Cretaceous extinction occurred about 65 million years ago, they were hardest hit. The multituberculates weathered the Cretaceous extinction somewhat better, only to die out completely later in the Eocene about 40 million years ago. The placentals suffered least of all the mammals. The end of the Cretaceous therefore marked a turnaround in the composition of the world's mammals, with the placentals taking over the dominant position they have maintained ever since.

While both placental and marsupial mammals bear live young which are then nourished with mother's milk, the placental mammals retain the growing embryo within the uterus for a longer period of time than the marsupials, and give birth to young that are more mature than newborn marsupials. Marsupials, with their pouches into which the relatively unformed young climb after birth, are common in Australia and include the kangaroos, koala bears, wallabies, and wombats. They were the dominant type of mammal in South America until a few million years ago when the continent became connected to North America. The opossum is one of the relatively few marsupials remaining in South America (where there are upwards of 70 species) and it is a familiar animal in much of North America.

Seemingly the most primitive types of mammal are the egg layers, or monotremes, with the duckbilled platypus and spiny anteater of Australia the only living examples. Although they nurse their young in a fashion analogous to other mammals, their egg-laying habit and apparently primitive skeletal features give the impression that they represent the remnants of early mammalian "experimentation." Whatever the mammalian system of reproduction, it offered the possibility of a degree of parental care hitherto unknown in the animal world, and it also opened up a new potential for long-term bonds and more intense social life.

It is tempting to try to reconstruct the evolutionary history of mammals from monotremes through marsupials to placentals from the fossil record, but unfortunately the traces are few. Virtu-

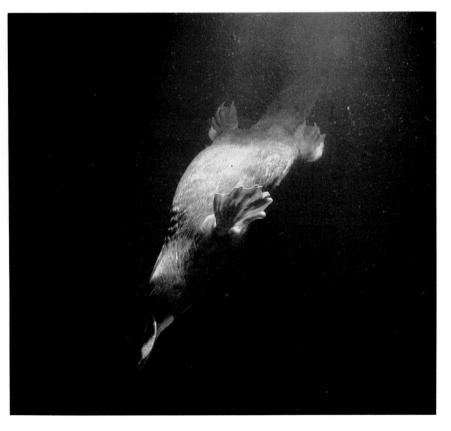

The echidna, or spiny anteater, above, and the platypus, right, are the most primitive mammals. Found in Australia and Tasmania, both lay eggs and feed their young a milk-like fluid exuded from abdominal pores. Echidnas also inhabit New Guinea.

190

ally no fossil ancestors are known for modern monotremes, and the principal clues to early mammalian evolution some 200 million years ago are isolated teeth and jaws. "This is very frustrating," says Farish A. Jenkins, Jr., of Harvard's Museum of Comparative Zoology, "but these tiny creatures are rarely found as fossils."

One of the most intriguing questions about the origin of mammals is whether they arose from a single line of mammal-like reptiles or several. "For quite a while the accepted idea was that different lineages of Mesozoic mammals evolved from different groups of mammal-like reptiles," says Jenkins. "But careful study of the few fossils that have been found in recent years seems to indicate that mammals were derived from a single group of mammal-like reptiles called the cynodonts." If this were the case, one can view mammalian origins as having squeezed through an evolutionary bottleneck, a pattern that is common in much of evolutionary history.

At the beginning of their Cenozoic radiation, the mammals burst out in two main directions: herbivorous ungulates (hoofed animals) and the creodonts, an early group of carnivores. Although animals in both groups filled niches still occupied today by modern equivalents, many early mammals had a far from modern appearance. By 30 million years ago some giant forms had evolved, including

Baluchitherium, a hornless giraffe-like rhinoceros that was at least 18 feet tall at the shoulder and 27 feet long. *Baluchitherium* was the largest land mammal ever to have lived.

During the Oligocene period, about 38–26 million years ago, there was a marked change from the archaic forms to the ancestors of modern mammals, including the true rodents, arguably the most successful of all mammals. The evolutionary explosion that was ignited in the Oligocene continued and culminated in the Miocene period, 27 million years ago. A major factor in this evolutionary phenomenon was the onset of cooler and drier climates causing forests to retreat in many areas. Grasses, members of the group known as angiosperms—flowering plants—previously had been restricted to marshes and swamps; in the Miocene they migrated rapidly to fill the open spaces where lush forests had stood.

The appearance of grassland savanna and prairies had a profound effect on the evolution of grazing animals. Soft and lush though grass may look, it is in fact very abrasive; countless tiny crystals of silica are distributed throughout its blades. Grasses have also developed the ability to grow continuously as a protection against cropping by grazers. The animals that eat grass wear away their tooth enamel very quickly; it is not surprising, then, that grass eaters have evolved countermeasures

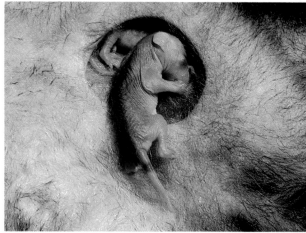

Newborn zebra, left, displays afterbirth that characterizes the reproductive process of most advanced mammals. Baby opossums, above, nurse at teats in mother's pouch. Young marsupials leave the womb at an early stage and crawl to pouch to develop.

191

such as thick enamel or continuously growing teeth.

In addition to changes in tooth and jaw structure, many species became adapted for speed over open ground. The modern horse, which evolved for the most part in North America, is a splendid example of such adaptation.

Between the beginning of the Miocene and the end of the Pliocene periods, 27 million to two million years ago, a greater variety of mammals existed than has before or since. All the modern hoofed animals evolved at this time. Elephants of various types lived in Africa, Europe, Asia, and North America. Apes were as numerous then as monkeys are now, and rodents continued their already tremendous evolutionary momentum.

The climate throughout this time continued its deterioration and culminated in the ice ages of the Pleistocene, beginning two million years ago and lasting until almost the present. Perhaps one of the most intriguing aspects of the ice ages was the evolution of giant forms in several parts of the world. Certain species of elephants, mammoths, horses, bison, wolves, deer, cheetahs, and others grew bigger in the ice ages than at any other time and then became extinct, leaving their smaller relatives to inhabit the modern world.

Until 10,000 years ago, mammoths and mastodons, huge saber-toothed cats, and giant armadillos and ground sloths still roamed North America, then vanished abruptly at the end of the last major glaciation. The sudden change in environmental conditions might well have caused the end of these giants. Some researchers contend, however, that these sweeping extinctions were the work of humans, Stone Age hunters migrating southward and taking everything before them. If this were the case, then it would be the first occasion in which mass extinction was caused by the activity of a single species.

Meanwhile, the main path of mammalian evolution left behind two relics: Australia and South America. A quirk of timing in the breaking apart of the world's supercontinents left Australia populated primarily with marsupial mammals. South America also ended up with many species of marsupials, as well as its share of placentals, although these were mainly herbivores.

Australia has remained separate from all other land masses for the last 64 million years, and its population of monotremes and marsupials provides a glimpse of what life on Earth might have been like if placental mammals had not evolved. The result is exactly what one should expect: a

Bluebells and new green leaves trumpet spring in an English deciduous forest. Dominant flora of the time of the mammals, flowering plants and trees are adapted to seasonal swings of temperate latitudes and flaunt flowers to attract insect and bird pollinators.

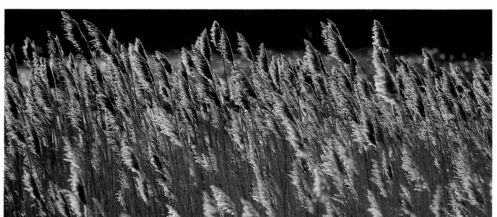

Perhaps the most successful of all flowering plants, grasses have adapted to a wide variety of marginal habitats. Cordgrass, left, thrives in salty sand behind a Long Island beach.

193

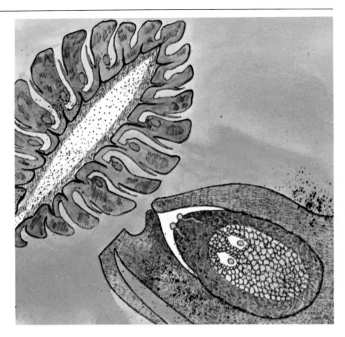

Fertilization of common pine, a gymnosperm, occurs within female or ovulate cone. In close-up, right, pollen grain has germinated, sent tubes toward ovule to fertilize eggs.

Ovulate cones extend from branches of bristlecone pine. In early spring, tiny male staminate cones grow on other branches and eventually produce pollen that drifts to ovulate cones.

range of animals filling the same kinds of ecological niches that are occupied by placental mammals on other continents. Although some Australian mammals such as the kangaroo are novel in form, many display a remarkable parallelism with their placental equivalents. The Tasmanian wolf, for example, shows striking similarities with canine-like carnivores elsewhere in the world, including now-extinct marsupials that once lived in South America. The marsupial mole is strikingly like the insectivore mole (there are only so many ways you can be built and still dig a hole, it seems).

When North and South America drifted into contact around three million years ago, the large cast of marsupial and placental mammals in the south were confronted with many placental species, particularly carnivores, from the north. The upshot was a rout, with many South American marsupials (as well as placentals) declining. Does this imply that the adaptive ability of marsupials is inferior, as is popularly believed? George Gaylord Simpson thinks not. Northern placental populations have been subject to substantial extinctions from which, presumably, more keenly adapted species emerged. It was this honing as occupants of their particular niches that gave northern mammals their competitive edge, suggests Simpson, not their status as placental animals.

While all of these tumultuous changes were

sweeping the animal world, while mammals replaced the reptiles and jostled among themselves for places in a changing environment, a similar revolution had already started among the plants. Where once there had been forests of nonflowering seed plants—gymnosperms such as ginkgoes, cycads, and conifers—a new group, the angiosperms (flowering plants), emerged. The angiosperms appear to have evolved from seed ferns around 130 million years ago. They radiated slowly over the next 65 million years and then spread rapidly, eventually making up 90 percent of all land plants, including grasses, shrubs, and trees.

What was it about angiosperms that led them to displace the gymnosperms so rapidly and so completely? The obvious answer might seem to be the flower itself, a device for substituting the vagaries of wind pollination with the certainty of insect or animal pollination. There is no doubt of the advantages attached to reproduction via flowers, but this is by no means the secret of the angiosperms' success. It turns out that what makes them special is not so much any single characteristic, but rather a package of features which are never found together in the gymnosperms.

What gives the angiosperms their name is the enclosure of the ovule or unfertilized seed within an ovary: "angiosperm" means enclosed seed while "gymnosperm" means naked seed. Once the

*Fragrant magnolia flower attracts
insect pollinators, an adaptation that
along with other reproductive features
has enabled flourishing of angiosperms
over past 125 million years.*

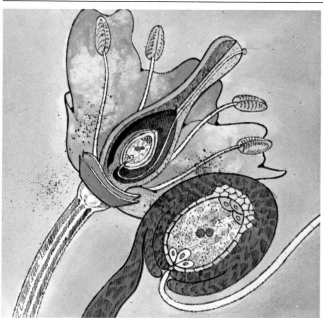

*Deposited on sticky surface of plant's
stigma, pollen grain germinates, forms
tube that grows down style to reach
ovule. Once fertilized, embryo plant
develops in protected environment.*

egg is fertilized by pollen, which has to send its male cells down a long tube to reach the female cell, the embryo plant develops in a highly protected environment. How intriguing that the process is so similar, in a sense, to that of mammals.

One trick of angiosperms that is approached by only a single group of gymnosperms is the process of double fertilization. This simply means that the pollen not only fertilizes the egg cell; it also triggers the development of the food reserve that will serve the resultant seed when it germinates. Gymnosperms almost exclusively build up these food reserves before fertilization takes place, a process that is clearly wasteful of important resources if the ovule fails to be fertilized.

Economy of action is a recurrent theme of angiosperms, whether in the efficiency of insect and animal fertilization, in the process of double fertilization, or in the many economical shortcuts they take in building their various structures. "They've thrown away a lot of the stereotyped development of organ systems that characterize the lower groups of plants," observes paleobotanist Leo Hickey. "They've done this through having tremendous developmental plasticity." In a sense, angiosperms pull up short on the developmental pathway along which gymnosperms pass: they retain the flexibility and simplicity of immaturity, so to speak.

One important consequence of this plasticity or flexibility to adapt is an extraordinary capacity for regeneration after even severe damage, a capacity that gymnosperms lack. And the flexibility is illustrated by the fact that angiosperms have more than 20 ways of making a tree while gymnosperms follow just four patterns. There is an urgency, an opportunism about angiosperms (if such terms can be applied to slowly growing plants) that isn't found in the more stereotyped gymnosperms.

The earliest fossil angiosperm leaves, from around 120 million years ago, come from sediments that were laid down in unstable environments such as floodplains and riverbanks. This gives a clue to the origin of angiosperms' extreme opportunism. Gymnosperms take at least a year and often two to set a seed, thus requiring relatively undisturbed environments in which to survive. A plant that matures and reproduces more rapidly would be able to exploit disturbed environments free from gymnosperm competition. This, apparently, is what happened during the origin of angiosperms.

Hickey points out that if, as seems likely, angiosperms arose through the alteration of developmental processes in an ancestral seed fern, that ancestor would be very hard to find in the fossil record. "You would have to look for stages in the embryological development of the gymnosperms," he says, "and this is next to impossible." Changes in the timing and course of embryonic development are probably important in evolutionary origin of many new groups; this problem of elusive ancestors is a persistent theme of paleontology.

Just as the mammals went through an evolutionary bottleneck at their origin, so too did the angiosperms. "It seems likely," says Hickey, "that the very first angiosperms were small, shrubby plants growing in relatively dry, hostile environments at the periphery of the gymnosperms' growing range. They then gained a foothold in more humid environments as small species arose that could live in unstable riverine environments."

Fertilized by insect-borne pollen, nuts of coconut palms, left, can survive months in ocean currents, then germinate on tropical beaches. In mutually dependent relationship, a flower, right, entices bee with its nectar and scent; bee transmits pollen from flower to flower.

This, it should be remembered, was at a time when the plant world was made up mostly of naked-seed-bearing trees.

Although flowers are inevitably thought of as the major "invention" of angiosperms, the leaves are novel structures too, a fact that is frequently overlooked. Hickey has studied the sequence of change in angiosperm leaves through a series of sediments near Washington, D.C., known as the Potomac series. The leaf begins as a simple blade structure but, within a few million years of its origin, lobed and feather compound varieties have emerged.

Equally striking, however, is the steady consolidation of vein patterns, developing from a fairly disorganized state to greater and greater regularity. "One practical consequence of a regular venation pattern," says Hickey, "is an increased resistance to tearing as a leaf is buffeted by the wind." Such

strength is obviously important in true canopy trees in forests.

As the end of the Cretaceous period neared, the abundance of angiosperms rose in concert with a slow decline in the gymnosperms, a shift that in some ways paralleled the changing relationship between dinosaurs and mammals at the same time. However, there was one important difference. Unlike the dinosaurs, the gymnosperms did not suffer particularly in the great extinction at the end of the Cretaceous; therefore the emergent dominance of the angiosperms was a real expression of their superiority, not just an opportunistic response to a newly vacated niche.

When angiosperms did come to dominate world floras, they did so in a great burst of evolution at the end of the Cretaceous and beginning of the modern period. A second great adaptive radiation, one that marked the appearance of the modern herbaceous flowering plants, occurred during the last 30 million years. Yale University's Bruce Tiffney considers the prime trigger of this radiation to have been the onset of cooler climates with greater seasonal changes, a development that would have put a premium on plants that could mature and reproduce during shortened growing seasons.

With the sharp selection pressure of seasonality in action, and probably as a result of simple evolutionary opportunism, a wide range of woody angiosperms gave rise to small herbs. "It is apparent that the angiosperm trees retained the tremendous degree of plasticity that had initially given rise

Mammalian pollinators, bats, above, plunge into saguaro cactus flowers for nectar, carry pollen to other flowers. Dependent on wind for pollination and dispersal, maple, left, has evolved single-rotor seeds that whirl away on spring breezes.

197

to the group," says Tiffney. "Angiosperm herbs are not a special condition, but rather are an expression of the nature of the group as a whole."

The increase in angiosperm species diversity brought about by the origin of herbaceous forms was closely paralleled by enhanced diversity among many insect populations. In fact, the fortunes of angiosperms in the fossil record are intimately shadowed by changes in the insect world. Insect pollination has become more and more specialized through the ages, with, in some cases, a single plant species and a single insect species becoming totally dependent upon each other for successful reproduction. Orchids, as a group, have developed some truly astonishing structures and relationships with their pollinators. Overall there has been a tremendous diversification in the form of flowers, and an equal efflorescence in the insects that pollinate them. This is a vivid example of the phenomenon known as co-evolution.

The earliest flowers were simple and appear to have been frequented by beetles. Gradually the range of insect pollinators grew and soon included bees, butterflies, wasps, and flies. Birds were also drawn into this fount of evolutionary potential, giving rise to the minuscule and captivating hummingbirds, the honeycreepers of the Americas, sunbirds of Africa and Asia, the brush-tongued parrots of Australia, and many other exquisitely fitted avian partners in pollination.

Mammals, particularly nectar-eating bats, have become involved in this relationship. The targets for these diminutive flying mammals are generally night-blooming flowers such as the calabash tree of America, the saguaro cactus of Arizona, the baobab of Africa, and the cotton trees of Asia. The bats hook their claws into the large flowers and thrust their noses into an often foul-

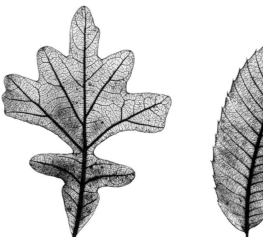

*Spectacular variety of fall leaves,
above, litters floor of temperate zone
forest beneath sprig of evergreen pine
needles. Flowering plants may have
evolved leaf dropping to survive seasonal dry periods. Right, leaves convert
sunlight to sugar through photosynthesis. Leaves are classified in evolutionary sequence by vein patterns.
Complex venation of leaf at far left,
Cinnamodendron brasilense, characterizes most primitive angiosperm leaves.
Austrobaileya scandens, next, and burr
oak are more advanced, while most
advanced is exemplified by parallel
veins of American chestnut.*

199

smelling orifice in search of energy-rich nectar.

The evolution of flowers has been shaped by a fine and ruthless balance between attracting and rewarding an efficient pollinator, and physical security. A flower that is destroyed by its visitors or one in which the highly nutritious and tempting ovule is readily devoured will not last long. Indeed, one of the hallmarks of flowering plants is the battery of toxic chemicals deployed in their tissues as an important line of defense in this essential but uneasy relationship with the insect world. (Incidentally, many of the spices used in cooking are the insect repellents of various flowering plants.)

One great benefit of plant pollination by insects and animals is its efficiency: wind-pollinated plants must produce on the order of 200 times more pollen grains per seed than those pollinated by insects. And because a pollinating insect will generally choose to fly between plants of the same species, those plants are able to thrive scattered over wide areas. But not all angiosperms have retained insect pollination. Some trees, such as oak, beech, hornbeam, and chestnut, and grasses, sedges, and sagebrush among herbs and shrubs, have re-evolved wind pollination. The common factor among the wind-pollinated species is their propensity to live in large stands where wind pollination is at its most efficient.

The bursts of evolutionary change among insects that accompanied (and were to some extent driven by) the origin and diversification of angiosperms produced no new order of insects, simply variations on established themes. Nevertheless, despite its apparent evolutionary stability, the insect world did experience something new and extremely important during the last 100 million years: the rise of the social insects—the ants, bees, wasps, and termites. The social insects display an

The rise of social insects was a significant evolutionary trend in the Cenozoic. African driver ants, above, show physical adaptations to differing roles. Tropical leaf cutter ants, left, use bits of leaves to cultivate underground fungi gardens.

economic and social system quite unknown elsewhere in the animal kingdom, excluding humans. "The result," says Edward Wilson of the Museum of Comparative Zoology, Harvard, "was that the social insects very nearly took over the world."

Wilson has long studied the life-style of the social insects and he is not only impressed with these creatures as insects but also as organisms in comparison with the rest of the animal world. "The social insects challenge the mind by the sheer magnitude of their numbers and variety," he once wrote. "There are more species of ant in a square kilometer of Brazilian forest than all the species of primates in the world, more workers in a single colony of driver ants than all the lions and elephants in Africa. The biomass and energy consumption of social insects exceed those of vertebrates in most terrestrial habitats. The ants in particular surpass birds and spiders as the chief predators of invertebrates. In the temperate zones, ants and termites compete with earthworms as the chief movers of the soil and leaf litter; in the tropics they far surpass them."

It is difficult not to use superlatives when discussing the social insects; their numbers and physical achievements demand it. And yet the remarkable thing is that sociality has arisen only a dozen or so times in the insect domain. The reason is not because the state does not bring advantages (it clearly does), but because it requires a very rare set of complex genetic and behavioral circumstances. In fact, the order Hymenoptera contains all of the social insects save one group, the termites.

Wilson has analyzed the characteristics fundamental to the model of social life upon which each line of social insects has converged. There is always a system of castes and labor roles which change according to age. Elaborate chemical communication coordinates a colony's activity in the most astonishing manner. And nest structures may be extensive, with complicated architectural designs that aid temperature and humidity control.

Why is social life so advantageous? "Among the answers," suggests Wilson, "is the concept of the superorganism. A solitary wasp has to build a nest, hunt and find prey, sting it, and bring it back to the nest. Should any one of these steps go wrong, the wasp has to start again. In a social group there are many backups for each stage, and you simply do not fail. It is a well known engineering principle."

The fossil record of the social insects is, inevitably, rather poor—their tiny, fragile bodies do not readily form fossils. But, because insects occasionally become entombed in resin from certain trees, specimens are sometimes found in pristine condition. One such specimen, which goes by the name *Sphecomyrma freyi*, is surpassingly interesting to anyone interested in evolutionary biology. *Sphecomyrma* relates to the evolution of ants from wasps, but the specimen itself is neither; it is a mixture of both.

"The head is wasp-like," explains Wilson, "and so are the eyes, but the antennae are a perfect mixture of features from ants and wasps. The thorax is generalized ant thorax, and the waist is that of an ant. The rest of the abdomen is typically wasp, and the sting is typically wasp. It is a perfect intermediate between the two forms," he says. "It is a beautiful example of evolution."

Such clear-cut cases of evolution are, as we have seen, rare in the fossil record. Yet the overall trends of the last 65 million years are indisputable. The Cenozoic has been the time of the mammals, the flowering plants, the social insects. Separately and together they have given rise to the biosphere we know, the one into which the first humans were born, such a short time ago.

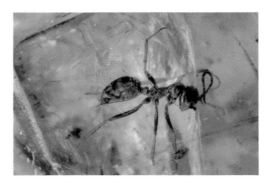

Embedded in amber from New Jersey, Sphecomyrma freyi *is a perfect example of a transitional form in the evolution of wasp from ant. The specimen displays features of both.*

A PORTFOLIO OF THE AGE OF MAMMALS

The scenes depicted on this and succeeding pages are reproductions of sections of murals painted for the Smithsonian's National Museum of Natural History by noted artist and anatomist Jay H. Matternes. The murals present some of the better known animal and plant life from various epochs of the Age of Mammals. In most cases, animal coloring is conjectural. The scene at right, from the Middle Eocene Epoch about 45 million years ago, is set in Wyoming.

Middle Eocene Epoch
Wyoming, about 45 million years ago

1. *Uintatherium* six-horned, saber-toothed plant eater
2. *Trogosus* gnawing-toothed mammal
3. *Ischyrotomus* marmot-like rodent
4. *Mesonyx* hyena-like mammal
5. *Stylinodon* gnawing-toothed mammal
6. *Homacodon* even-toed hoofed mammal
7. *Helohyus* even-toed hoofed mammal
8. *Metacheiromys* armadillo-like edentate
9. *Sinopa* small archaic flesh eater
10. *Saniwa* monitor-like lizard
11. *Machaeroides* saber-toothed mammal
12. *Orohippus* ancestral horse
13. *Helaletes* primitive tapir
14. *Palaeosyops* early titanothere
15. *Sciuravus* squirrel-like rodent
16. *Smilodectes* lemur-like monkey
17. *Patriofelis* large flesh eater
18. *Hyopsodus* clawed, plant-eating mammal
19. *Crocodilus* crocodile
20. *Echmatemys* turtle

Early Oligocene Epoch
South Dakota-Nebraska region, about
35 million years ago

1. *Archaeotherium* giant pig-like mammal
2. *Protoceras* bizarre horned ruminant
3. *Hesperocyon* ancestral dog
4. *Palaeolagus* primitive rabbit
5. *Ischyromys* squirrel-like rodent
6. *Hypisodus* very small chevrotain-like ruminant
7. *Poëbrotherium* ancestral camel
8. *Hyracodon* small flat-footed rhinoceros
9. *Brontotherium* titanothere
10. *Protapirus* ancestral tapir
11. *Hoplophoneus* saber-toothed cat
12. *Hypisodus* chevrotain-like ruminant
13. *Leptomeryx* chevrotain-like ruminant
14. *Glyptosaurus* extinct lizard
15. *Hyaenodon* archaic hyena-like mammal
16. *Hypertragulus* chevrotain-like ruminant
17. *Merycoidodon* sheep-like grazing mammal
18. *Subhyracodon* early rhinoceros

Early Miocene Epoch
Western Nebraska, about 20 million
years ago

1. *Moropus* clawed mammal
   related to horses
2. *Merychyus* small even-toed
   hoofed mammal
3. *Steneofiber* burrowing
   beaver
4. *Daphaenodon* large wolf-
   like dog
5. *Promerycochoerus* pig-like
   oreodont
6. *Parahippus* three-toed horse
7. *Stenomylus* small camel
8. *Diceratherium* pair-horned
   rhinoceros

Early Pliocene Epoch
High plains region from the Texas
panhandle to the Missouri River basin,
about 5 to 6 million years ago

1. *Amebelodon* shovel-tusked
   mastodon
2. *Teleoceras* short-legged
   rhinoceros
3. *Cranioceras* cranial-horned,
   even-toed hoofed mammal
4. *Epigaulus* burrowing horned
   rodent
5. *Hypolagus* extinct rabbit
6. *Merycodus* extinct
   pronghorn antelope
7. *Synthetoceras* snout-horned,
   even-toed hoofed mammal
8. *Aphelops* long-legged
   rhinoceros
9. *Neohippario* extinct three-
   toed horse
10. *Prosthennops* extinct
    peccary
11. *Osteoborus* short-faced dog
12. *Hemicyon* bear-like dog
13. *Pliohippus* ancestral one-
    toed horse
14. *Megatylopus* giant camel

Late Pliocene Epoch
Southwestern Idaho, about 3.4 million years ago

1. *Mammut* mastodon
2. *Olar hibbardi* swan
3. *Pelecanus halieus* pelican
4. *Gallinula chloropus* gallinule
5. *Lutra piscinaria* extinct otter
6. *Chrysemys idahoensis* turtle
7. *Pliopotamys minor* extinct muskrat
8. *Plesippus shoshonensis* zebra-like horse
9. *Ciconia maltha* stork
10. *Tanupolama* extinct llama
11. *Platygonus pearcei* extinct peccary
12. *Castor californicus* extinct beaver
13. *Machairodus hesperus* saber-toothed cat
14. *Rallus lacustris* rail
15. *Mustela gazini* extinct weasel
16. *Cosomys* vole
17. *Cryptotis gidleyi* shrew
18. *Ceratomeryx prenticei* extinct pronghorned antelope
19. *Arctodus* short-faced bear
20. *Phalacrocorax auritus* cormorant
21. *Felis lacustris* extinct mountain lion

Late Pleistocene Epoch
Central Alaska, about 12,000
years ago

1. *Megalonyx* ground sloth
2. *Homo sapiens* man
3. *Bison crassicornus* large-
   horned bison
4. *Equus* horse
5. *Alopex lagopus* arctic fox
6. *Symbos cavifrons* woodland
   musk ox
7. *Alces alces* moose
8. *Canis lupus* wolf
9. *Ovis dalli* dall sheep
10. *Arctodus simus* short-faced
    bear
11. *Gulo gulo* wolverine
12. *Ursus arctos* grizzly bear
13. *Mammuthus primigenius*
    woolly mammoth
14. *Panthera atrox* lion-like cat
15. *Saiga ricei* saiga antelope
16. *Taxidea taxus* badger
17. *Bos bunnelli* yak
18. *Ovibos moschatus* musk ox
19. *Cervus elephas* wapiti or elk
20. *Cervalces alaskensis* stag
    moose

IN OUR TIME

THE BIRTH OF
HUMANKIND

Fragments of the skull and femur of a hominid found in 1981 in Ethiopia's Awash River Valley by paleoanthropologists J. Desmond Clark and Tim D. White may be four million years old.

The many volcanoes scattered along East Africa's Great Rift Valley have witnessed much of human evolution. They have also helped to unravel parts of the tangled story of human origins. Their ash, spewed into the atmosphere through the ages, has settled in layers to form a convenient timetable against which the progression of Mankind's prehistory can be measured. But most remarkable, a series of eruptions some 3.75 million years ago captured a fleeting moment in the lives of three individuals—perhaps a father, a mother, and child—creating a record unique in the annals of paleoanthropology.

The place was Laetoli, some 30 miles south of the famous Olduvai Gorge in what is now Tanzania. The end of the dry season was approaching; storm clouds gathered, and distant thunder rolled across the arid landscape. Rain was near; streams would soon be lacing the slopes of Ngorongoro and Sadiman, two large volcanoes to the east. Subterranean rumblings stirred deep beneath Sadiman, and clouds of ash rose occasionally from its open cone.

As Sadiman's ash settled, it formed a thin gray carpet across which springhares, antelope, elephants, and many other creatures (including a centipede) passed with unhurried steps. A few heavy droplets of rain fell, splashing tiny scattered craters in the fine dust, but the passing clouds yielded no further relief from the drought. Days later Sadiman belched out more ash which settled thickly over the earlier deposit, entombing the footprints in what would become a cement-hard record of that brief moment in history.

Three and three-quarter million years later, the inexorable process of wind and seasonal rain erosion exposed this ancient archive in the shadow

During 1976 dig at Laetoli in Tanzania, Mary Leakey and coworkers found these footprints of three hominids that showed that human ancestors walked erect 3.75 million years ago. Overleaf, dusk descends over skyscrapers of midtown Manhattan, one of the modern world's foremost commercial and financial centers. Page 215, Indonesian farmer transplants rice seedlings near Denpasar, Bali.

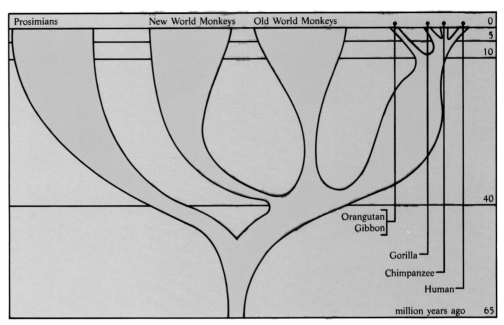

Primates apparently evolved in the late Cretaceous from creatures resembling today's tree shrews. The primate line gave rise to two groups: the prosimians, including tarsiers, lemurs, and lorises; and the anthropoids—the monkeys, apes, and humans.

Prosimians   New World Monkeys   Old World Monkeys

0
5
10
40

Orangutan
Gibbon

Gorilla
Chimpanzee
Human

million years ago   65

of the now quiescent Sadiman. Researchers working with archaeologist Mary Leakey must have passed very close to the area many times after they began work there in 1974. But it wasn't until September 1976 that paleontologist Andrew Hill happened by chance one day to notice that the many small depressions in the solidified ash were fossil footprints. Excavations revealed more than 20,000 footprints of all sorts over a relatively small area, giving the paleontologists a glimpse of an ancient community that could not be matched by the fossil bones common in the era.

As work at Laetoli progressed, Mary Leakey began to hope that among this unique record there might be prints of the *hominids* (members of the human family) already known by fossil evidence to have lived there. That hope was fulfilled, and Mary Leakey describes it as "the most remarkable find I have made in my whole career."

Careful examination revealed the tracks of three hominids who had walked across Sadiman's newly laid carpet of ash. One large individual, possibly a male, walked slowly north, to be followed shortly afterwards by a smaller individual, possibly a female. The second individual walked more or less in the prints already made. "Chimpanzees are known to play 'follow the leader' in terrain where footprints can be made," comments Leakey, "so perhaps this is what the Laetoli hominids were doing." In any case, a third hominid acccompanied the other two, skipping along to one side. At one point this third individual, possibly a youngster, stopped, turned to look west, then went on.

Beyond the emotional effect these prints have on even the least concerned observer, they also convey important scientific information. They demonstrate without doubt that hominids of this long-past age walked with a bipedal stride virtually indistinguishable from that of modern humans. Furthermore, the feet were not those of some supposed simian "missing link"—they were as modern in form as yours and mine.

Although the hominids at Laetoli almost four million years ago clearly walked around in a very human-like way, their brains were still the size of apes'. Not until about two million years ago did the brains of our ancestors enlarge substantially, eventually to lead to modern humans, *Homo sapiens sapiens*. In some ways the Laetoli hominids were at a midpoint in human evolution. In the past their ancestors had evolved a fully bipedal mode of getting around, which no living ape emulates; at some point in their future there was to be a dramatic evolutionary expansion in brainpower, which no living ape matches. These two qualities—upright walking and large brains—are key features in human evolution.

Humans belong to the Primate order, the roots of which go back some 70 million years to just before the beginning of the Age of Mammals. The earliest primates were probably small, nocturnal, insectivorous creatures, not unlike the modern tree shrew. These first members of the Primate order evolved important anatomical features that equipped them well for their demanding, predatory life in the trees: hands capable of grasping, and

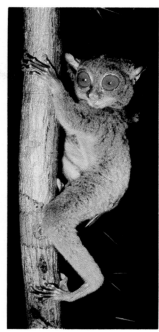

Unlike most other New World monkeys, South American uakari, or red-faced monkey, has a nonprehensile tail, as do all Old World monkeys. Although most monkeys are tree dwellers, some, such as baboons and macaques, forage on ground during the day, retreat to trees at night.

forward-facing eyes capable of stereoscopic vision.

Modern primates are divided into two suborders. One, the prosimians, includes lemurs, sifakas, the slow loris, bush babies, and the diminutive potto. Members of this group are modern representatives of the earliest primates, giving us an idea of what they were like. The other branch, the anthropoids, arose some 40 million years ago. The monkeys evolved first, then the apes, and last the hominids. The members of this suborder had taken to daytime living, were larger than their predecessors, and had acquired color vision.

The close biological relationship between humans and apes has been recognized for a long time. Carolus Linnaeus, the great Swedish biologist, noted this in the 18th century when he classified *Homo sapiens* as relatives of monkeys and apes, although he did not mean to imply that there was any common ancestor between humans and our simian cousins.

In the 19th century, Darwin's friend Thomas Henry Huxley conducted anatomical comparisons between humans and chimpanzees and gorillas. His conclusion that humans are intimately related to these apes has been confirmed in recent years by the demonstration of a close similarity in the genetic material among the three.

Many people take the statement that humans and apes are closely related to imply that we evolved from them, or at least from some extinct ape that looked very much like them. In fact, humans shared a common ancestor with the African apes, and since the evolutionary split occurred

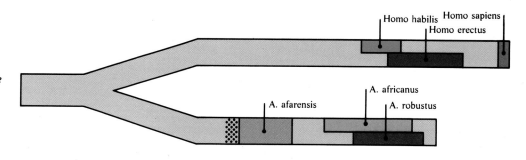

Paleoanthropologists agree on the broad outlines of human evolution, but differ on details of dates and relationships. Two current interpretations of recent finds are shown here.

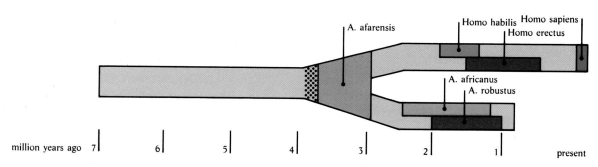

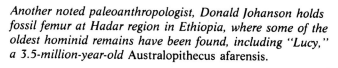

million years ago   7   6   5   4   3   2   1   present

Paleoanthropologist Richard Leakey excavates Homo erectus *skull at Kenya's Koobi Fora, a site that has yielded more than 300 hominid fossils, covering the full range of hominids from between one and two million years ago.*

Another noted paleoanthropologist, Donald Johanson holds fossil femur at Hadar region in Ethiopia, where some of the oldest hominid remains have been found, including "Lucy," a 3.5-million-year-old Australopithecus afarensis.

between apes and hominids a few million years ago, both groups developed their own specialties. Another misunderstanding is that chimps and gorillas are more "primitive" than humans, that they are more like the common ancestor. Actually, some paleoanthropologists speculate that in some respects—in locomotion and tooth structure, for instance—the African apes are more specialized than hominids. In any case, our simian relatives should be extended the courtesy of not being dis-

missed as "primitive." Their specializations are simply different from ours.

As mentioned earlier, certain geological changes that occurred 20 million years ago marked an important milestone along the path of human evolution. Africa collided with Eurasia, the Kenyan and Ethiopian domes began to rise, and an embryonic Great Rift Valley started to form; the local climatic changes induced by uplifting highlands were made more extreme by general global climatic deterioration. These factors caused tremendous reduction in the thick forests that carpeted the African continent at the time. Much of the forest was replaced by open woodland, a change that opened new ecological niches for the primates.

No apes as we know them today lived in Africa 20 million years ago. The ancestors of the *hominoids*—a term encompassing all apes and hominids—were a curious mixture of ape and monkey. One famous example, discovered by Mary Leakey in 1948, is *Proconsul africanus*.

Like modern monkeys, *Proconsul* had a long body and relatively short limbs, an arrangement suited to walking and running on all fours along branches. While *Proconsul* was monkey-like in this respect, its teeth were more like those of an ape: large projecting canines, moderate-sized incisors, and small cheek teeth, or molars. This dentition indicates that *Proconsul* ate mostly ripe fruits, soft shoots, and leaves.

Some time between 20 and 14 million years ago, a new type of hominoid arose, one that was able to survive in open woodland rather than forest. Harvard paleoanthropologist David Pilbeam points out that food in open woodland is generally closer to the ground, often tougher, and less nutritious than that in forests. "The reason for this," he explains, "is that woodland is generally associated with a cooler seasonal climate. Plants have to provide tough protective coatings for their seeds and fruits in dry periods." It is therefore not surprising that the new hominoids that appeared in Africa at this time were equipped for occasional forays on the ground and for processing tough food.

This group of hominoids were, says Pilbeam, much more ape-like than their monkey-like ancestors. "They had shorter bodies, longer limbs, and undoubtedly would have hung vertically from branches rather than walked along them," he says. "Their dentition reflects the tougher nature of the diet. The cheek teeth are larger and now have thick enamel. The canines are still relatively big. And the incisors have become adapted for crushing food

items." The members of this new group, *Ramapithecus* and *Sivapithecus*, were the size of a baboon and orangutan, respectively. A third member, *Gigantopithecus*, was, as its name implies, huge—the largest primate of all time.

The ramapithecids, as the group may be called, apparently were successful; by 14 million years ago they had migrated into many parts of Europe and Asia where woodland habitats were widespread, and it may be that these creatures were much more eclectic in their dietary habits than apes are usually thought to be. In addition to the tough fruits and seeds that Pilbeam mentions, the ramapithecids might well have eaten larvae, birds' eggs, and insects, just as woodland baboons do today.

David Pilbeam hunts fossils in Pakistan where, with Ibrahim Shah of the Geological Survey of Pakistan, he has been working since the early 1970s. The search for fossils goes on among the massive sediments that make up the Siwalik Hills, foothills of the towering Himalayas. The ramapithecids flourished there between 14 and 7 million years ago, when they abruptly vanished as open grasslands replaced their woodland environment. "There was a further climatic deterioration at this time," explains Pilbeam, "a change that affected Africa, too."

As temperate woodland shrank in Eurasia, the hominoids began to be squeezed out of existence there. And in Africa, the climatic change forced a further retreat of forests, expansion of woodland, and the first appearance of open savanna. Grazing plains animals appeared in great numbers and, at some point, the first true hominids evolved from the hominoids. The question is, exactly when?

British paleontologist Peter Andrews and anthropologist Jack Cronin have been looking at this issue. They have come up with a timetable that includes the hominid-African ape split. The evolutionary line that eventually gave rise to the modern gibbon (an Asian ape) seems to have separated from the rest of the hominoids at around 12 mil-

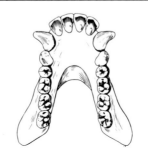
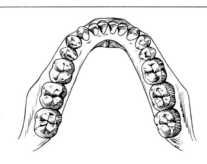

An ape's jaw, right, shows characteristic U-shape, large canine teeth, and backward-sloping chin. Homo sapiens jaw, far right, is arch-shaped, has small canines, forward-thrusting chin.

lion years ago, Andrews says. The orangutan (the second Asian ape) split away around 10 million years ago. And the final division between the African apes and the hominids occurred six million years ago. Such a suggestion, now being seriously considered, would have been summarily rejected by paleontologists just a few years ago. For a long time *Ramapithecus* was thought to be the first hominid, and that would have put the separation between African apes and hominids at least 14 million years ago. But ideas have changed.

"I no longer consider *Ramapithecus* to be the first hominid," says David Pilbeam, "though I suspect that *Ramapithecus* looks very much like

the common ancestor of African apes and hominids." Pilbeam also surmises that the first hominids evolved relatively recently, between six and eight million years ago. One of the great problems in trying to trace the path of human evolution is that, by one of those frustrating twists of fate, few suitable sediments are exposed from the period of four to eight million years ago. Consequently, paleoanthropologists face something of a fossil gap for that slot in the timetable. What then has caused the recent change of mind?

First, as more and more specimens of ramapithecids have been discovered, it has become clear that some of the features that were assumed to be

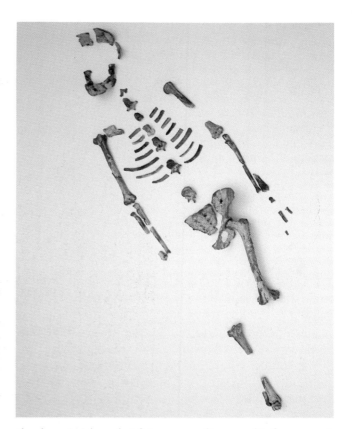

Zinjanthropus, *left, looms before outcrop in Tanzania's Olduvai Gorge where Mary Leakey found 1.8-million-year-old australopithecine skull during 1959 expedition with husband, Louis. Below, Raymond Dart poses with skull, brain cast of first-discovered australopithecine fossil, Taung child, found in South African quarry in 1924. Dart correctly identified it as hominid and published his findings in* Nature, *creating years-long controversy over whether the remains were ape or human. "Lucy," right, extraordinarily well preserved fossil of four-foot-tall hominid found by Donald Johanson and colleagues in Hadar region of Ethiopia in 1974. Dated at 3.5 million years old,* Australopithecus afarensis *walked fully erect.*

advanced and hominid-like—such as thick enamel on cheek teeth—are, in fact, primitive. And one of the prized discoveries from the Siwalik Hills in recent years—a half face and lower jaw of *Sivapithecus*—clearly shows it could well be ancestral to the orangutan, as Andrews believes. Therefore, the sentiment grows that the first hominids must have come later than the ramapithecids, and that the last common ancestor, although different from *Ramapithecus*, might have looked something like it.

University of California biochemists Vincent Sarich and Allan Wilson are watching these developments with wry humor. For more than a decade they have been telling paleoanthropologists that the hominid and African ape lines split from each other just four to six million years ago, not 14 to 30 million as was generally accepted at the time. This early date was based not on old bones but on biochemical analysis. Sarich and Wilson analyzed the structure of certain proteins in humans, chimps, and gorillas; by measuring the differences among them they were able to say how long ago the apes and hominids shared a common ancestor. The measure is based on the fact that through random mutation, protein structure is steadily modified. The more distantly related two species are, the greater will be the differences in their proteins. It is a kind of molecular clock that monitors the passage of evolutionary time.

Recently, Wilson has looked directly at the genetic material rather than at the proteins for which it codes. This approach, he says, allows a greater precision in reading the molecular clock. The answer, once again, is that paleoanthropologists should look around four to six million years ago for the last common ancestor between African apes and hominids. This more precise study has confirmed the conclusion that Wilson and his colleague reached all those years ago.

Although the timing of the first hominid's appearance is undoubtedly important to a reconstruction of the picture of human evolution, it is perhaps more interesting to ask *why* events hap-

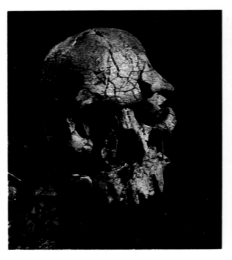
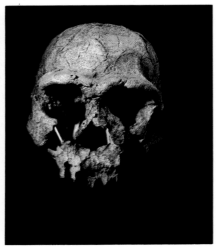

With emergence of the genus Homo *came a steady increase in the size of the brain. Right, skull 1470 belongs to* Homo habilis, *the ancient line that may have eventually gone on to become modern humans. To its right, brow ridges become prominent in skull of* Homo erectus, *first hominid to migrate out of Africa, survive colder climates of Europe and Asia.*

pened the way they did. The first hominids walked erect, had small canine teeth, eventually took to making and using tools, and, in the line that led to modern humans, acquired a large brain. The traditional view is that our ancestors' erect posture and the use of tools were linked in a functional way: the evolutionary pressure for bipedalism was the freeing of the hands for the use of tools.

Furthermore, the ability to make and use objects was thought to be linked with the reduction in the size of the canine teeth. Upright apes that could use tools as weapons would have no need for large dagger-like canines. The last link in the chain—expanded brainpower—was attributed to evolutionary pressure of finer and finer manipulation of tools. You need a big brain to be skillful at making and using artifacts.

The focus of this once popular version of human origins is intelligence—clearly, we are smarter than apes, so this is what must have differentiated us in the first place. "But," says Pilbeam, "we are beginning to look away from the head and toward the stomach for explanations of what went on in our evolution. We are beginning to look for explanations that relate to diet and feeding behavior. Paleoanthropology is therefore getting closer to the studies of other mammals."

With this in mind, how does one contemplate the origin of hominids walking upright? Many primates, particularly the apes, are occasionally bipedal, but it is usually for a brief awkward dash or waddle. Pilbeam points out that if you look at the context in which living primates do stand or walk bipedally, you notice that for the most part it has to do with food and feeding behavior, especially when the animal is on the ground. If the first hominids evolved from a small woodland ape like *Ramapithecus*, Pilbeam reasons, then there would

be a selection pressure for efficient upright walking, especially as open woodland and savanna became more extensive.

Upright walking in the first hominids is therefore seen as a response to diet, not as the result of an inclination to make and use tools. Once hominids had adopted bipedalism the hands were free to develop technology, but this is a secondary event and not the primary cause. The oldest evidence so far of stone tools in the archaeological record dates back to a little more than 2.5 million years ago, whereas the footprints at Laetoli, and a magnificent collection of fossils from the Hadar region of Ethiopia, demonstrate without doubt that bipedalism had fully evolved at least a million years earlier.

Hominid teeth are different from those of *Ramapithecus* too, but some would argue that the differences are of degree rather than kind. The greatly reduced size of the hominid canines might have been a consequence of chewing tough or fibrous food that needed more grinding than that eaten by hominoid ancestors.

The shift in style of locomotion for an occasionally upright *Ramapithecus*-like ape to an habitually upright hominid was clearly a vital step in human evolution, but the change itself was not revolutionary. Compare this with the mode of locomotion of today's chimps and gorillas. They move about by means of "knuckle walking," supporting themselves on the knuckles of their front limbs in a unique quadrupedal gait. "It is only just beginning to sink into people's perceptions that these features are specialization in the African apes," comments Pilbeam. "They are in some respects more specialized than hominids."

Human evolution was once viewed as a simple ladder, with ancestors acquiring more and more advanced characteristics until the fully modern

226

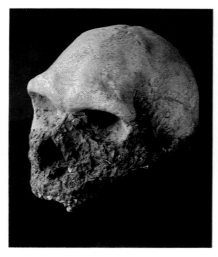

form finally emerged. It was a straight path from the primitive to the sophisticated, a path that was strongly redolent of inevitable progression. More probably, human prehistory followed the sort of evolutionary sequences experienced by other groups of animals: that is, complex and multi-branched. Fossil evidence of those branches—both the one that survived and those that didn't—has been unearthed over the past six decades in Africa.

Raymond Dart, later aided by Robert Broom, discovered the first early hominid remains in cave deposits in South Africa during the 1920s, '30s, and '40s. Named *Australopithecus africanus* and *Australopithecus robustus*, these two different types of australopithecine hominids unquestionably walked upright but had brains the size of today's apes'. The average male *africanus* probably measured on average a little over four feet and *robustus* about a foot taller. Both had large, thick-enameled molar teeth and were apparently principally vegetarian.

In the 1950s and '60s the major focus of paleoanthropology shifted to East Africa with the discoveries at Olduvai Gorge by Louis and Mary Leakey. And in 1968 their son Richard began working at the remarkable fossil-rich deposits east of Lake Turkana in northern Kenya. A large team of researchers has been working there ever since. From the early 1970s attention turned to the Hadar region of Ethiopia, where a joint American/French team hit upon ancient sediments even more fossiliferous than those east of Lake Turkana. The result has been a flood of new fossil evidence confirming just how complex the picture of human evolution really is, but at the same time allowing at least some of the details to be sketched in.

In addition to the two australopithecines living in Africa about two million years ago, another hominid, more delicate but bigger-brained, appears to have existed then too. Discovered first at Olduvai Gorge in 1961, and then again in 1972 at Lake Turkana (the famous specimen number 1470 skull), this new hominid was named *Homo habilis,* or able man. Some theorized that this creature represents the line that eventually went on to modern humans, while *Australopithecus africanus* and *robustus* became extinct, probably about a million years ago.

The probable descendant of *Homo habilis* is *Homo erectus,* which first appears in the fossil record about one-and-a-half million years ago. Good examples have been found at Olduvai and particularly at Lake Turkana. It was this member of the hominid line that moved out of tropical Africa and into the temperate regions of Europe and Asia. *Homo erectus* was a taller animal than *Homo habilis* and was brainier. *Erectus* had a brain capacity of 775 to 1,300 cubic centimeters compared with *habilis'* of around 800; the australopithecine brain size was in the region of 450-550 cubic centimeters. (The brain size of modern humans ranges from 1,000 to 2,000 ccs.)

Although it is clear from the abundant fossils recovered from the deposits along the shore of Lake Turkana that several different types of hominids coexisted there two million years ago, what is not so clear is where these branches of the family lead back to. It seems likely that *Australopithecus robustus* arose as a side branch of *A. africanus* and then became extinct. But did *Homo habilis* also derive from *A. africanus,* or has it always been separate? And if so, what came before?

Some remarkable discoveries made at the end of 1975 by Don Johanson, Maurice Taieb, and their colleagues in Ethiopia surely have a bearing on this question. In what turned out to be a paleontologi-

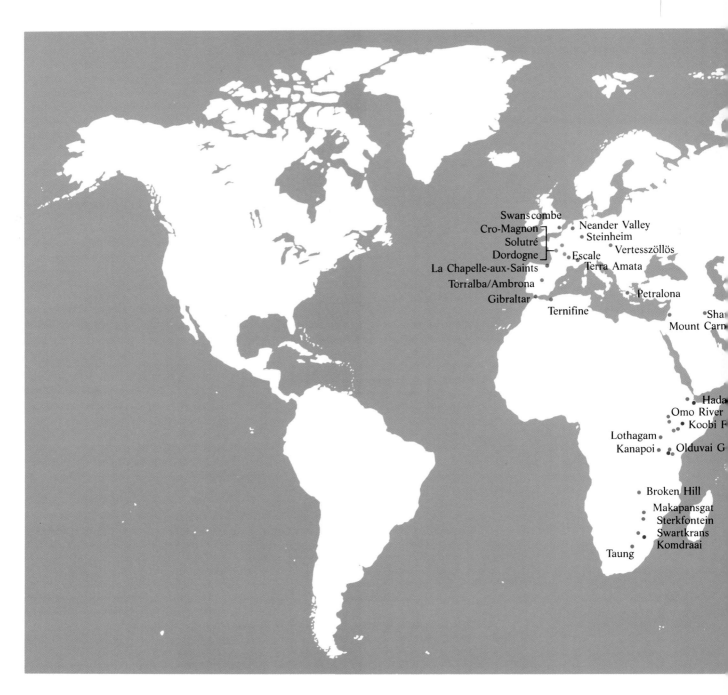

Swanscombe
Cro-Magnon
Solutré
Dordogne
La Chapelle-aux-Saints
Torralba/Ambrona
Gibraltar
Ternifine

Neander Valley
Steinheim
Vertesszöllös
Escale
Terra Amata
Petralona
Sha
Mount Carn

Hada
Omo River
Koobi F
Lothagam
Kanapoi
Olduvai G

Broken Hill
Makapansgat
Sterkfontein
Swartkrans
Komdraai
Taung

Taung child, Australopithecus africanus, *estimated at around two million years ago, South Africa.*

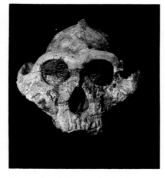

Australopithecus boisei, *an australopithecine, about two million years ago, Koobi Fora, Kenya.*

Skull 1470, Homo habilis, *about two million years ago, Koobi Fora, Kenya.*

Homo erectus, *approximately half a million years ago, Lantian, China.*

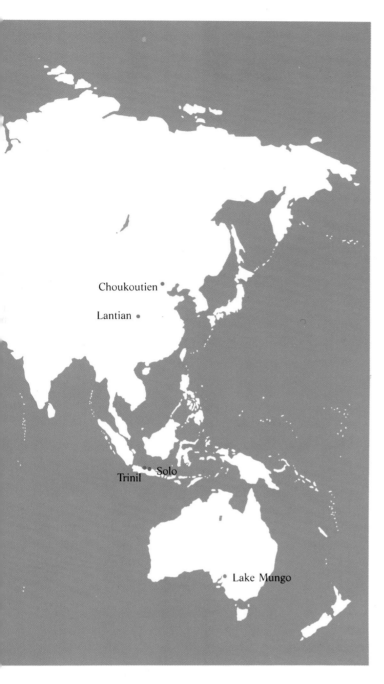

Choukoutien •

Lantian •

Trinil • • Solo

• Lake Mungo

cal bonanza, Johanson and his coworkers came across more than 200 hominid bones representing at least 13 individuals (immediately dubbed "the family group"). Nothing like it had ever been found before, and it was an especially important discovery because the deposits from which the fossils came are thought to be at least 3.5 million years old. A year earlier Johanson and his colleague Tom Gray had found the now-famous "Lucy" skeleton, a diminutive hominid dating back to this crucial early period.

Johanson initially considered some of the "family group" to be a primitive form of *Homo* and some to be early *Australopithecus*. This would put the origins of the *Homo* line back to a relatively ancient date, in agreement with Richard Leakey's ideas. Later, however, Johanson changed his mind and at the end of 1978 published a paper with colleagues Tim White and Yves Coppens stating that all the fossils belonged to one species, *Australopithecus afarensis*. The idea was that this species was ancestral to all subsequent hominids, thus pushing the origins of *Homo* to a late date once more, to about two million years ago. The proposal created an uproar in the world of paleoanthropology: *A. afarensis* was the first new hominid species to be designated in 15 years, and it was supposed to give rise to all later hominids.

Although some researchers quickly came round to support Johanson's and White's proposal, others, including Richard Leakey, said that the fossils were clearly of two species, not one as claimed. There is definitely a wide range in the size of the individuals represented in the Ethiopian fossil collection. Johanson and White say the group is made up of large males and small females, showing size differences similar to those in modern gorillas. Leakey and others suggest that the spread

Groupings of major hominid fossil sites show early Man's beginnings in Africa. Gradually spreading to Asia and then to Europe around a million years ago, Man finally journeyed across exposed Bering land bridge into North America some 40,000 years ago.

- Australopithecines
- *Homo habilis*
- *Homo erectus*
- Early types of *Homo sapiens*
- Cro-Magnon Man

Homo sapiens neander-thalensis, *c. 35-45,000 years old, La Chapelle-aux-Saints, France.*

Cro-Magnon Man, Homo sapiens sapiens, *40,000 years ago, France.*

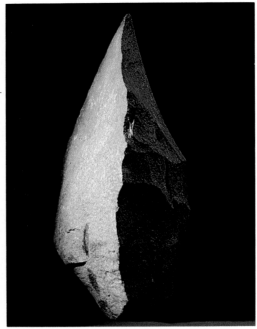

Stone tools of primitive Man: top left, earliest chipped-pebble choppers from Oldowan culture; above, Acheulean hand ax; left, flint core and flakes from neandertal Mousterian tool kit.

is too large to be encompassed by one species. Furthermore, there are other anatomical details indicative of two species, they claim. Meanwhile, Coppens has reconsidered and now believes there to be two species, or perhaps even more, represented in the collection.

The extent of the disagreements over the Ethiopian fossils indicates one thing: that a clear judgment cannot be made with the available evidence. If Sarich and Wilson are right about the date of the split between African apes and hominids, then the Ethiopian fossils would be very close to that branching point. In that case the fossils might well represent one single ancestral hominid species. On the other hand, if more than one hominid species lived at this time, and it had only recently arisen from an ancestor, it might well look very similar to that ancestor. In *that* case it would be very difficult to distinguish one species from another. As Leakey says, "We really won't be able to answer this one properly until we find more fossils of a similar age from other parts of Africa."

Once again, questions about the timing of events are somewhat secondary to questions about the cause of those events. If the first hominids arose as an adaptation to food available in the woodland environment, what was responsible for the emergence of a large-brained species? Some cite the intellectual demands of making and using stone tools as the driving force of brain expansion. But, if this were the case, it would not occur in isolation—there has to be some kind of social or economic context in which tool use was important. One popular notion—known as the "hunting hypothesis"—declares that hunting was the behavior that drove an evolutionary wedge between the australopithecines and *Homo*. Proponents of the hunting hypothesis see the technological and social demands of a hunting way of life propelling primitive *Homo* down a new evolutionary path. While there is no doubt that later hominids such as *Homo erectus* were proficient hunters, evidence for a well developed hunting pattern as early as two million years ago is pretty slim. Our ancestors at this point in their history apparently did eat meat, but probably as opportunistic scavengers rather than as systematic hunters.

As a direct reaction against the aggressive image inherent in the hunting hypothesis, a number of anthropologists, notably Adrienne Zihlman and Nancy Tanner, have suggested that the focus of evolutionary change was on the females. The female-offspring bond, strong in all primates, provided the binding force in early hominids' social life, they say, and the females developed the very simple but effective technology required for gath-

Photomicrographic studies of stone tool cut marks on a modern bone, top, and a fossil bone, above, show that marks match, proving that our ancestors used such tools to butcher meat.

Paleoanthropologist Henry Bunn examines cut marks on a fossil bone from Kenya's 1.5-million-year-old Koobi Fora exposures. Discovery of tool marks on bone indicates the probable presence of a camp at that site even in the absence of stone tools. Tools of similar age have been found nearby.

ering nutritious roots and other plant foods. The males are seen as tagging along in this arrangement, steadily becoming more and more involved in taking care of the offspring. This, roughly speaking, can be termed the "gathering hypothesis."

An alternative to these two combines elements of both: it is the "food-sharing hypothesis" developed principally by Glynn Isaac of the University of California, Berkeley. Although most modern primates are intensely social creatures, they don't actually share food with one another. Each adult individual collects and eats its own food, usually on the spot. There is now good archaeological evidence that hominids as long ago as one and one-half million years, and perhaps longer, regularly established a kind of home base to which food was taken to be consumed. "It seems very likely to me," says Isaac, "that such a focus of social activity would serve very well the purpose of sharing food among members of an established troop."

The business of survival has to do principally with gaining ready access to important resources, especially food. "If hominids started to include meat in their diet, even on an opportunistic and occasional basis, they would immediately widen their economic base," says Isaac. "This would be a tremendous advantage." Isaac suggests that the new way of life may have begun with the exploita-

tion of accidentally discovered carrion. The next step required manufacture of a simple, sharp stone flake to cut up the meat. The conception and execution of this effective cutting edge must be regarded as one of the major technological breakthroughs in the history of human evolution.

Casual collecting of carrion could be extended to active scavenging. Circling vultures could lead to carcasses that might still have some pickings after the more established carnivores had eaten. Direct competition with carnivores would be difficult for creatures not equipped with sharp teeth and claws, but a sharp wit may have helped make up for this. And as most carnivores operate at dawn or dusk, leaving open a niche for a daytime predator, the early hominids might have eventually filled this niche. Nevertheless, the relatively secure availability of nutritious plant foods must have formed the stable economic base on which these early hunter-gatherers depended, just as it does among today's hunting and gathering peoples.

The wider resource base provided by the food-sharing economy was probably important in allowing *Homo erectus* to spread beyond the tropical habitats of most primates. When bands of *Homo erectus* drifted north into Europe and Asia about a million years ago, they took with them a simple but effective stone tool technology and a

San peoples of Botswana, above, and BaMbuti in the Congo region, opposite, are among few living representatives of the hunting-and-gathering way of life that evolved between a million and half a million years ago.

Most hunter-gatherers live in groups of about 30 people, their mainly vegetarian diet supplemented by meat and fish. Although they must move often when local resources are depleted, way of life affords much time for socializing.

highly developed social and economic system. The mixed economy of hunting and gathering placed demands of social skills on individuals that are matched nowhere else in the animal world.

The question of why large-brained hominids arose when they did, two or more million years ago, may have no single answer. There may, in fact, have been no specific causative event, and the rise of the large-brained types may have been just an evolutionary quirk that worked. But C. K. Brain, director of the Transvaal Museum in South Africa, thinks he sees a clue in the geological record. "There was a significant climatic deterioration at this time," he says, "and it triggered evolutionary change in many different groups of animals. The origin of *Homo* among the hominids might well have been a response to this change." Brain concludes that "had it not been for temperature-based environmental changes in the habitats of early hominids, we would still be secure in some warm and hospitable forest, as in the Miocene of old, and we would still be in the trees."

Homo erectus fossils have been discovered over a wide area of Eurasia. Although they show some distinct geographical variations, *Homo erectus* remained a stable species until something less than half a million years ago. After that, indications of modern features begin to appear. A skull about 300,000 years old from Petralona, Greece, for

instance, is considered to be something of a mosaic of ancient and modern features. The same applies to the front part of a skull from 400,000-year-old deposits in a cave in the foothills of the French Pyrenees. Certain specimens from England, Germany, and North, South, and East Africa seem to indicate that something was happening to the long-established *Homo erectus*.

This issue of possible evolutionary change focuses on the origin of modern Man. The famous fossils from the Cro-Magnon caves in France show that the fully modern human form had arisen by 40,000 years ago. But earlier there had been the dramatic rise and fall of European, Asian, and African neandertal people, a history that started about 130,000 years ago and ended some 100,000 years later. Caricatured as brutish and dim-witted, the neandertalers were in fact quite modern in form, a fact that is recognized in their designation as *Homo sapiens neanderthalensis*.

Named for the German valley in which their remains were first found, many of the neandertalers thrived for much of their existence in the harshest of conditions in Ice Age northern Europe. Because of the lack of trees in those frigid lands, the neandertalers used mammoth and other bones to build shelters, presumably covered by animal skins, and even burned bones for fuel. Tool technology developed to a high degree in neandertal

Magnificent legacy of pre-historic art in Europe, vivid images of bulls stampede across vaulted entrance to Hall of Bulls in Lascaux cave in southwest France.

times. Poignant evidence of their spiritual concern is to be seen in careful burials in which flowers were arranged around the body. Although they were stockily built, they were less so than some of their *Homo erectus* forebears. Surprisingly, their brain size was slightly larger than that of today's humans. The fate of the neandertalers is therefore a matter of some interest to paleoanthropologists. Did modern humans evolve from *Homo sapiens neaderthalensis*? Or were neandertals replaced by *Homo sapiens sapiens*, today's humans, that had evolved elsewhere?

Unhappily, there is no consensus on this question. Some argue that there was indeed a "neandertal phase" through which our ancestors passed. Others see too many important anatomical differences between the neandertalers and later *Homo* for one to be ancestral to the other. There is some

fossil evidence that modern humans may have arisen in southern Africa some 90,000 years ago, and then spread out over the globe. But this evidence has to be regarded as equivocal at best, and the problem remains to be resolved.

Whatever was the fate of the neandertals, it is clear that fully modern humans were established by 40,000 years ago. And it was at about this time that populations from northern Asia were able to cross the Bering land bridge into North America. Ocean levels had fallen because of extensive glaciation, providing a migratory route across the temporarily dry Bering Strait.

Human history over the past three million years has been marked by an extraordinary increase in brain capacity and a rising sophistication in tool technology.

The pattern of stone tool development

Carved of reindeer antler some 12,000 years ago, bison figurine celebrates exquisite craftsmanship of ice-age artists. Bull appears to be craning its neck to lick an insect bite.

through the ages has an interesting aspect. The earliest stone tools were simple flakes and pebbles, dating from around 2.5 million years ago. This simple "Oldowan" tradition of tool-making persisted for about a million years, to be joined by a slightly more sophisticated technology, the Acheulean, which is characterized by teardrop-shaped handaxes. Acheulean tools gradually replaced the more primitive tool kit, but then remained more or less unchanged until some 100,000 years ago. And although style varied somewhat from area to area, the products were remarkably uniform regardless of where they were made.

With the emergence of the neandertalers, the pace of technological and stylistic change began to increase. Compared with the dozen or so implements included in the Acheulean tool kit, the Mousterian technology—as one of the neandertalers' most common tool-making traditions is known—had upwards of 60. Many of the Mousterian tools were fine implements crafted from bone, a new development at that time. From 40,000 years on there were greater stylistic differences in tool technology between neighboring valleys than there had been between different continents in earlier times. Changes in prevailing style now took place over periods of 5,000 years rather than 500,000, as had previously been the case. Clearly, utilitarian demands were not the only forces to guide the hands of the new tool makers. Artistic whim and aesthetics now played their part.

Humans had become supremely cultural animals, fashioning their physical and social worlds in inventive and arbitrary ways. The core of this must have been the evolution of language, a capacity that sets us apart from all our fellow creatures, notwithstanding the sign language accomplishments of some apes.

Language, the key to many aspects of human history, is of course virtually invisible in the fossil record. Neither an idle conversation nor an elaborately sung ritual leaves a tangible impression that can later be read by archaeologists. One has to turn to more indirect evidence. The breathtaking cave paintings of France, Spain, and parts of Africa surely are silent testimony to an elaborate language ability. As these paintings were crafted between 30,000 and 10,000 years ago, it is perhaps not surprising that our ancestors then possessed sophisticated language. But what about the neandertals? What about *Homo erectus*?

An individual's brain etches a crude signature on the inner surface of his skull, and it is therefore possible to reconstruct the rough outline of a brain in a fossil skull. Ralph Holloway of Columbia University has perfected this skill to a high degree. He finds that as far as one can tell, there is nothing in the general shape of the brain of neandertals that would preclude language ability; for that matter, neither is there in *Homo erectus* and *Homo habilis*. It is certainly easy to imagine that the large-brained hominids of two million years ago were capable of more extensive spoken communication than non-human primates, but it is doubtful that this matched the ability we have today.

Glynn Isaac suggests that the gradual imposition of order on the range of stone tools from two million to perhaps 100,000 years ago might be echoing a more and more ordered mind, one capable of controlled speech increasingly rich in information. The nuances of the neandertalers' physical and spiritual worlds clearly betray a highly developed language. But was it as developed as ours?

Possibly the key event in the evolution of *Homo sapiens sapiens* was the improvement of language to the level we enjoy today.

An endocast of the skull of a robust australopithecine from the Swartkrans cave in South Africa reveals basic shape of human brain, poses tantalizing questions concerning origins of language.

BEYOND BIOLOGY

Student employs high technology in the education process, long a central function of culture. Computers have created a world-embracing fascination with electronics.

ise man, *Homo sapiens*. Indeed, there is no doubt that human intelligence, in all its keenly analytical, creative, and compassionate forms, is the hallmark of our species. In art, in science, and in systems of ethics and justice, we express the uniqueness of humanity among the rich pattern of life that constitutes our world.

Alone among our fellow creatures we ask the big "Why" questions. Why are we here? What is the purpose of it all? As Dostoyevsky put it: "Man needs the unfathomable and the infinite just as much as he needs the small planet which he inhabits." This is a hunger we experience; it is manifested repeatedly in various forms in cultures throughout the world. If humanity is truly the product of evolution, it is surely legitimate to ask why we have this hunger.

Charles Darwin and Alfred Russel Wallace discussed this issue in correspondence over many years. At the end of the exchanges Darwin was left saddened: although his friend accepted the power of natural selection in fashioning life's rich diversity, Wallace could not see how the human mind, with its virtually infinite powers of reasoning and morality, could also be counted as the product of a strictly utilitarian force. Darwin wrote to Wallace in 1869 saying, "I hope you have not murdered too completely your own and my child."

In spite of repeated appeals from Darwin, Wallace continued to believe that the otherwise ubiquitous and inescapable laws of natural selection did not act on that most human essence of *Homo sapiens*, the mind. Wallace hoped that one day all would be explained "by the discovery of new facts or new laws, of a nature very different from any yet known to us."

Wallace failed to be fully consistent in attributing all of life, including the human mind, to the

Traditional ornament bolsters cultural identity for a young Masai woman of Kenya. Artistry in its manufacture allows for an individuality not found in assembly-line products.

Lapp life revolves around traditional rights and obligations imposed by the rigors of reindeer herding in northern Scandinavia. Caravaneers pass by famed Buddhist sculpture at Bamian in Moslem Afghanistan, a land which has felt the sway of successive Asian cultures.

creative powers of natural selection. It was not that he was fearful of the probable social response to such a suggestion, or because he considered natural selection to be limited in its effects. Rather, he thought our more remote ancestors would have had no need for such a wondrous capacity as the human intellect. How, Wallace argued, could natural selection favor the evolution of something for which there was no evident use?

Unlike most scholars of his time, Wallace judged technologically primitive people to be as intelligent as members of Victorian society; Victorians differed in that they benefited from instruction and the "refinements" of civilization. If primitive peoples' lives were as undemanding as they seemed to be, why, Wallace questioned, should they be so generously endowed mentally?

"A brain one-half larger than that of the gorilla would . . . fully have sufficed for the limited mental development of the savage," reasoned Wallace, "and we must therefore admit that the large brain he actually possesses could never have been solely developed by any of those laws of evolution, whose essence is, that they lead to a degree of organization exactly proportionate to the wants of each species, never beyond those wants." Wallace guessed that natural selection could have given rise to a brain slightly superior to that of an ape, but surely not to one that is "very little inferior to that of a philosopher."

For Wallace, the human brain was simply too exquisite an organ of sensibility to have been the product of selection in the humdrum business of day-to-day survival. He was also skeptical that certain other human attributes were solely the outcome of natural selection. "The structure of the human foot and hand seem unnecessarily perfect for the needs of savage man," he wrote, "in whom they are as humanly developed as in the highest races." Wallace also suggested that the larynx gave powers of speech and song "beyond the needs of savages." These refined qualities, he argued, could not have been acquired by "survival of the fittest."

Wallace noted that natural selection could not have given rise to the human brain so that Beethoven could soar to musical genius, or Newton perceive the elegance of universal physical laws. But this is an extremely narrow interpretation of function. "Objects designed for definite purposes can, as a result of their structural complexity, perform many other tasks as well," comments Stephen Jay Gould. "Our large brains may have originated 'for' some set of necessary skills in gathering food, socializing, or whatever; but these skills do not exhaust the limits of what such a complex machine can do." A computer built to issue paychecks and manage a factory's accounts can also solve differential equations and play a passable game of chess.

The question that must be addressed, therefore, is, what endowed us with our extreme mental capacity? What made us human? Philosophers and paleontologists alike have wrestled with this prob-

Farm people meet to mix business and pleasure, above, with a barn raising in Pennsylvania Dutch country, and in Louisiana for a quilting bee. Filling the homesteader's kit through community action became one of pioneer America's major cultural features—one honored today.

lem, and here we are concerned primarily with the thoughts of the latter group.

Paleoanthropologist David Pilbeam points out that prevailing social attitudes have had a great influence in shaping scientists' responses to the question of what separated humans from apes. "When Darwin was talking about human origins more than 100 years ago," says Pilbeam, "many people believed that the most important development in hominids was their use of tools as weapons. By the turn of the century, in the heyday of Edwardian optimism, the original prime mover of human evolution was seen as having been the brain. In the 1950s, an era of tremendous techno-

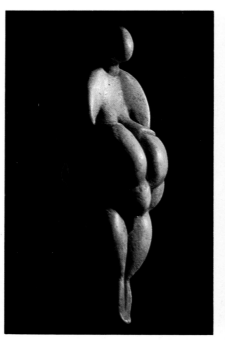

Across the ages, artists have increased people's awareness of their coming of age, as suggested here. Carved from ivory, prehistoric fertility cult figurine was found in Lespugue, France. Self-portrait of Rembrandt, age 53 (detail), is considered a classic study of a man entering full maturity.

logical expansion, man the tool maker came into vogue. Later, with the ever-growing impact of the media, language capacity became popular." The fear of global destruction through nuclear war saw the rise of man as hunter, the product of an unswervingly aggressive predatory ancestor. Pilbeam adds, "And I don't think it coincidental that at the time of the women's movement we find man the hunter becoming man—human, that is—the gatherer-hunter in a cooperative society."

Skills of tool-making, demands of language, hunting skills, and the complexity of a cooperating society all have been cited as important forces in human evolution. No doubt each has to some degree been influential, but can any single factor be identified as having played the predominant role? Nicholas Humphrey, a psychologist at Cambridge University, believes it can.

Some years ago Humphrey contemplated the "problem" of why humans were apparently so excessively intelligent. He soon found he had to ask the same about chimps and gorillas. After all, the great apes can do the most complex tests of cognitive skill in the laboratory, some of which challenge normal adult human accomplishments. Why would apes in the wild need brains capable of performing impressively difficult intelligence tests?

"Many people have considered the main role of creative intellect to lie in practical invention," says Humphrey. "But I would suggest that subsistence technology, rather than requiring intelligence, may actually become a substitute for it." Humphrey spent some time observing gorillas in the Vir-

unga Mountains of Rwanda, and has this to say about what he saw: "I could not help being struck by the fact that of all the animals in the forest the gorillas seemed to lead much the simplest existence—food abundant and easy to harvest (provided they *knew* where to find it), few if any predators (provided they *knew* how to avoid them) . . . little to do in fact (and little done) but eat, sleep and play." Our ancestors might have experienced similarly undemanding conditions, says Humphrey. "Studies of contemporary Bushmen suggest that the life of hunting and gathering typical of early man was a remarkably easy one."

Where, then, is the source of intellectual demands in the lives of early humans and apes? "I have suggested that the life of great apes and man may not require much in the way of practical invention," Humphrey says, "but it does depend critically on the possession of a wide factual knowledge of practical technique and the nature of the habitat. Such knowledge can only be acquired in the context of a *social* community—a community which provides both a medium for the cultural transmission of information and a protective environment in which individual learning can occur." Humphrey proposes that "the chief function of creative intellect is to hold society together."

Social life is more demanding, more unpredictable and more difficult to control than any aspect of subsistence technology, suggests Humphrey. "It asks for a level of intelligence which is, I submit, unparalleled in any other sphere of living. The more complex society is, the more skillful you have to be in order to be successful." Hence, humans are more intelligent than the great apes which, in turn, are smarter than monkeys.

Life in a complex society demands a great deal of time. Commitments such as maintaining alliances, placating potential threats, and being solicitous of relatives build extra demands. "If an animal spends all morning in nonproductive socializing, he must be at least twice as efficient a producer in the afternoon."

Thinking of the consequence of all this for our ancestors, one can conceive of a sharp evolutionary pressure along the following lines. Hunting and gathering is a highly complex economic system that requires close social cooperation. Close cooperation requires highly developed social skills not matched elsewhere in the animal world. And this degree of socialization requires that hunting and gathering be especially productive. The two aspects of life—social life and economic activity—feed back on one another.

Many animals, especially primates, live in societies. Individuals interact extensively, perhaps even learning some rudimentary traditions, cooperating, competing, and participating in common activities. "If we ask how human societies differ from these other animal societies," says Kenneth Bock, a sociologist at the University of California, Berkeley, "we can answer that in all . . . respects . . . human societies manifest such traits in far greater degree of intensity, scope, and effect, and that this is a consequence of qualities in human beings—most notably, symbol-making and symbol-using power—that other animals do not possess in anything like the same degree."

But such an answer only goes part of the way, says Bock. Referring to culture, that richly woven fabric of human existence, Bock notes that all species are products of the evolutionary time process. "But, for given periods of historical time, *Homo sapiens* differs radically from other species in the degree to which his social life changes with no apparent reference to evolutionary changes. . . ."

Countless threads intermingle in human culture, from utilitarian artifacts of subsistence through styles of dress, housing, and self-decoration, to high art, community beliefs, values, and religion. Culture, elaborated by the society in which those individuals live, touches every action, thought, or interaction with another individual. Humans make culture, but they are also products of their culture.

A perceptive study carried out by British anthropologist Ian Hodder illustrates the essential element in culture. Two tribes, the Tugen and the Njemps, live among the rolling hills of the Lake Baringo region in northern Kenya. Both subsist in semi-pastoral, semi-agricultural economies; yet in styles of dress, decoration, village architecture, language—in fact, in anything that is important in their daily lives—the Tugen and Njemps are distinctly different. While understandable if the two groups had no contact with each other, this is far from the case. Their villages are located in close proximity. There are frequent meetings between the two peoples, trade is common, and even intermarriage, but the cultural distinctions remain intact. Tugen women who marry Njemps men quickly adopt the customs of their new tribe.

Hodder interprets what he sees as an important need to express and maintain group identity. Confrontation with the unfathomable and the infi-

Music and solemn finery mark funerals in many lands. The Eureka Brass Band marches in a cemetery at New Orleans, also home of jazz music.

Provisioning for the afterlife, a concern since neandertal times, found its fullest expression in Egyptian tomb furnishings. This wooden model of a plowman and team was entombed with a nobleman to work for him in the hereafter.

nite is translated at the tribal scale into a deep commitment to group identity, stated emphatically through the products of culture. It is interesting to reflect that all humans share a common genetic endowment that permits the expression of culture, and the result worldwide is variation on the cultural theme limited only by the number of peoples existing. Ironically, the common genetic capacity for culture, expressed according to different social ideologies, serves to divide community from community, nation from nation.

It might be tempting to think of ourselves, friends, and strangers as humans clothed in a cultural cloak, naked beings given security and identity by layer upon layer of cultural protection. But the image would be inaccurate. Culture is not layered *upon* us, it permeates *through* us, through our every thought and action. It has been said that one of the remarkable features of humans is the ability to learn. In fact, more remarkable is the tremendous amount that *must* be learned in order that we might function at all. And all that we learn is flavored by the culture in which we live.

The evolutionary process that endowed our ancestors with an ever more profound cultural capacity not only led the way to manifold expressions of identity, but, at least as important, it gave us a degree of freedom not enjoyed by any other species. The gibbon is superbly adapted to acrobatics in the trees, the frigate bird to split-second timing on the wing, and the anemone to unhurried but effective predation in tidal waters. All species are suited to a particular type of environment, and as a corollary are constrained by it. Only *Homo sapiens* has broken loose of these constraints to such an astonishing degree, a liberation facilitated by an extraordinary adaptability and the capacity to elaborate a material culture.

Homo erectus was first to break the shackles that bound primates to tropical climes. Even with a relatively simple technology, these ancestors of ours ventured deep into Europe and Asia, taking their hunting and gathering economy with them. Early *Homo sapiens* pushed geographical frontiers even farther, often surviving under the most demanding climatic conditions with a culture that was discernably expanding. Culture displayed a trajectory that was to curve ever upward, a path

The leap from the plow to the planets took more than 5,000 years. But the great technological push—witness the auto engine and the rocket voyage that landed Edwin E. Aldrin, Jr., on the moon—occurred in one century. It happened roughly between the date of Darwin's theory, 1859, and Detroit's heyday of the 1960s. Artwork, left, is a detail from Diego Rivera's mural "Detroit Industry."

along which our ancestors increasingly created their own environment.

Biological evolution has not fitted *Homo sapiens* to a particular environment. In an important sense, we are the least specialized of all creatures. "Among the multitude of animals which scamper, fly, burrow, and swim around us," wrote that great polymath Jacob Bronowski, "man is the only one who is not locked into his environment. His imagination, his reason, his emotional subtlety and toughness, make it possible for him not to accept the environment but to change it. And that series of inventions, by which man from age to age has remade his environment, is a different kind of

evolution—not biological, but cultural evolution."

In the long run, and through the uncertain processes of evolution, animals might adapt to new environments through a change in their genes—give rise to a new species. Birds evolved from reptiles that did not fly. Whales and porpoises evolved from mammals that in a sense retraced their evolutionary path and returned to the sea, not as reborn fish but as swimming mammals. Humans have conquered the air and the deep by building airplanes and diving bells. We create specialized equipment to take our unspecialized bodies to all parts of the Earth, and even into space. We buffer our interaction with the environment using creations of the mind. ". . . cultural evolution," said Bronowski, "is essentially a constant growing and widening of human imagination."

Cultural evolution has two main features, style and pace. Unlike the randomness of genetic varia-

tions, change in cultural habits is directed by individuals; if approved, the new forms are often passed between individuals of one generation and often to those of the next generation. While selection operates among cultural inventions according to their success in the prevailing environment just as it does among genetic variations in biological evolution through natural selection, the origination of new cultural traits is a conscious, directed process. In this sense the style of cultural evolution is Lamarckian, not Darwinian.

The pace of cultural evolution is, without question, its most dramatic feature. "Cultural evolution has progressed at rates Darwinian processes cannot begin to approach," says Stephen Jay Gould. "From perhaps one hundred thousand people with axes (50,000 years ago) to more than four billion with bombs, rocket ships, cities, televisions, and computers—and all without substantial

Conflict has long marred benefits of culture. Bayeux tapestry, left, chronicles William the Conqueror's invasion across the English Channel in 1066. His Normans fight from horseback, with several of the defending Britons shown as casualties.

Need for order has concerned cultures through the ages. Above, the Security Council of the United Nations works to avert warfare. Top, Egyptians conceived Maat, goddess of Truth and Social Order.

genetic change." And all on a timescale that is too short to be measured in the lifetime of a typical species in the fossil record.

In a world where change previously was measured in units of millions of years, the pace of human cultural invention is truly staggering. The pace accelerates through the Agricultural Revolution around 10,000 years ago, through the rise of cities, states, and nations just a few thousand years later, through the Industrial Revolution two centuries ago, to the ages of technology, space, genetic engineering, and home computers. "Biological evolution is neither cancelled nor outmaneuvered," says Gould. "It continues as before and it constrains patterns of culture; but it is too slow to have much impact on the frenetic pace of our changing civilizations." The future of *Homo sapiens*, in other words, is now firmly in its own hands, its own responsibility.

The quintessence of the culture-laden human mind is a quality that is at once so profound and yet so evanescent that it evades easy definition. It is the quality of consciousness, of a far-reaching awareness of self, of others, and of death. With its origin in the expanded human brain of our immediate ancestors, the nature of intelligence in the animal world changed not just in degree but also in kind. When it arose, consciousness was something new, something truly novel in the history of life. It didn't simply allow those who possessed it to move, eat, or interact with others in a more effective fashion. It opened up a new window on the world through which no creature had previously gazed.

The German psychologist Eric Fromm describes the view from this new window in these terms: "Man has intelligence, like other animals, which permits him to use thought processes for the attainment of immediate practical aims; but Man has another mental quality which the animal lacks. He is aware of himself, of his past and of his future, which is death; of his smallness and powerlessness; he is aware of others as others—as friends, enemies, or as strangers. Man transcends all other life because he is, for the first time, life aware of itself." Yes of course an animal knows things, but in the terms of deep consciousness which humans experience, the animal does not know that it knows.

Self-awareness is clearly a finely honed tool with which to understand the actions and feelings of others. You can put yourself in another's place and imagine what he might be feeling or what he might do in certain circumstances. In this sense, self-awareness is precisely what might be expected

245

to arise in highly social animals such as humans.

When this transcendental awareness began to flicker in the mind of our ancestors, concern about death must have arisen for the first time, concern about what happens beyond this newly sharpened experience called life. When, 60,000 years ago, a group of neandertal people in the Zagros Mountains of northern Iraq buried one of their number curled in quiet repose and surrounded by flowers, they surely were expressing awareness of life and death in poignant terms. Many burials of that era involved a carefully positioned body and the inclusion of objects that might have been important to the individual or perhaps to the group as a whole. Without doubt, this was a nod in the direction of the unfathomable and the infinite.

As one peers further back in human history, the signs of transcendental awareness fade rapidly. But one finding in a 300,000-year-old springtime camp of *Homo erectus* in southern France is tantalizing. Among signs of a carefully constructed shelter, scattered with stone tools and bones, there is a single piece of sharpened ochre. Was this simply an inconsequential artifact? Or was it perhaps used to color the individuals' bodies or to draw symbolic designs on nearby rocks? No one will ever know. But it is conceivable that the quality of consciousness that burns brightly in the modern human mind was already beginning to smolder at that great distance in our past.

Religion was undoubtedly seeded in the human mind with the origin of true awareness, and it has flourished to become a major thread in virtually all cultures. "Among the two million or more species now living on earth, man is the only one who experiences the ultimate concern," wrote geneticist Theodosius Dobzhansky. "Man needs a faith, a hope to live by. . . . " Intimately bound up with religion in most cultures are the concepts of morality and justice. "Justice is a universal of all cultures," wrote Jacob Bronowski. ". . . It is a tightrope that man walks, between his desire to fulfill his wishes, and his acknowledgment of social responsibility." Animal societies are guided by rules of biology that are ultimately selfish: the individual that commands the most resources, including mates, is in evolutionary terms the most successful. In human societies, an individual's behavior is constrained by rules that are imposed by the group, rules that are guided by a sense of what is right and what is wrong.

In most cases the "oughts" and "ought nots" do not equate with what might be predicted from a

simple interpretation of "survival of the fittest": they are instead the artificial product of that unique being, the "ethicizing animal," to use British embryologist Conrad Waddington's term. The ability to make ethical decisions is surely the cornerstone of human society, and we ignore at our peril the security it gives us.

There has been a propensity in recent decades to tie human behavior to an animal nature lurking within us all, from which there is no escape. Initiated by the theories of South African paleontologist Raymond Dart, and propelled by the popular books of playwright Robert Ardrey and English academic Desmond Morris, there has grown the notion that humans are nothing but animals wrapped in a desperately thin cloak of culture and civilization. Humans make war because, at heart, we are aggressive animals; we arose from blood-lusting predators, so the argument goes. In recent years, scholarly, and some less scholarly, texts have added to the discussion with the suggestion that virtually every human behavior, including the less savory side of life, is somehow dictated by our genes. Rape, adultery, urban violence and poverty—many blots on the face of human society are said to be rooted in our animal nature. This is an "attractive" notion, not because such behaviors are laudatory, but because if they are indeed an immutable part of our nature, then there is nothing that can be done about them, and we therefore need no longer disturb ourselves by feeling guilty. "How satisfying it is to fob off the responsibility for war and violence upon our presumably carnivo-

Western civilization seeks to surmount uncertainties of biological life. Mechanized agriculture creates a new landscape and nurtures a heavy flow of food, above. Students at the National Zoological Park, left, harvest a crop of knowledge—product of a complex scientific and educational establishment. At right, a mother-to-be undergoes a sonogram to determine the size, shape, and placement of her unborn child. Other advanced techniques permit diagnosis of certain illnesses before birth, allowing surgical and chemical treatment within the womb.

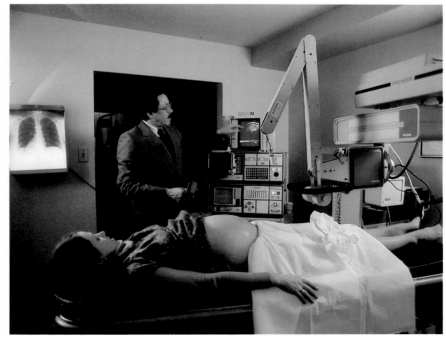

rous ancestors,'' jibes Gould. "How convenient to blame the poor and hungry for their own condition—lest we be forced to blame our economic system or our government for an abject failure to secure a decent life for all people.'' And how convenient to forget that, as the only ethicizing animal in this world, such decisions are ours to make; they are *not* written indelibly in our genes.

Unforgettable suffering through war, oppression, and neglect litter the pages of human history. But progress and improvement also inspire the reading. It was not long ago that the Earth was thought to be flat, that diseases were thought to be visitations by evil spirits or retribution for wrongdoing. Now, with the aid of spacecraft and television, we can see the Earth as an orb in space, blue and lovely, almost fragile. And many diseases are no more bothersome than remembering to take antibiotics three times a day. At a time of an apparent groundswell in anti-intellectualism, it is worth remembering what our collective intellect continues to achieve.

For some time now many have viewed science with increasing suspicion, as responsible for potentially dangerous food additives, chemicals that despoil the environment, and weapons that may destroy us. Uncontrolled or used unwisely, science can, of course, be a threat. But, like art, science is one of the greatest of human endeavors. It is continued ignorance that will destroy us, not new knowledge carefully applied. "Knowledge," said Bronowski, "is our destiny."

Knowledge gives us an understanding of our physical and living environment. But contrary to what is sometimes suggested, the removal of mystery through understanding does not diminish that which we gaze upon. An understanding of life and physical laws brings an awe of the beauty of it all, a deep wonder at the rich and never-ending variations in nature. Some people see the influence of a higher being in the physical laws that shape the patterns we see. Others have no such need. In either case, the patterns before us are enhanced, not diminished, by pursuing knowledge.

The new knowledge that Darwin brought to the world of the mid-19th century was seen by some as a dismal message. After Copernicus and Galileo had dislodged the planet Earth from the center of the universe, along came Darwin, apparently downgrading the human being to the status of a "mere animal." "I can scarcely imagine a judgment more mistaken," wrote geneticist Dobzhansky. "Evolution is a source of hope. . . . Man, this mysterious product of the world's evolution, may also be its protagonist, and eventually its pilot."

Humans are not just a part of the rich pattern of evolving life; through possession of our sense of awareness, we know we have evolved and are evolving still. "The fact that man knows that he evolves entails the possibility that he can do something to influence his own biological destiny," observed George Gaylord Simpson. He also recognized that this represents not only a unique opportunity but also a heavy responsibility. With our expanded brain has come, perhaps inevitably, an expanded view of our own importance. But we are not, and never can be, separate from the natural world. Through a deadly mixture of commercial greed and ignorance, countless numbers of animal and plant species are plunged into extinction each year in the name of progress. Of course we could live without the snail darter, the orangutan, the humpback whale and most of the other endangered species. But our world is diminished by the loss of each and every one.

Extinction is the ultimate fate of every species,

to be sure. But before the rise of *Homo sapiens*, the mass extinction of species at the hands of another species was unknown. Our expanded brain is blessed with conscious awareness, and this brings with it a responsibility with which no other species is burdened. We must exercise that responsibility assiduously, allowing for the needs of expanding human populations while at the same time recognizing that *Homo sapiens* is just one species among all of the others. As Gould notes, "We live in an essential and unresolvable tension between our unity with nature and our dangerous uniqueness."

Darwin's friend Thomas Henry Huxley in his book *Man's Place in Nature* wrote, "The question of questions for mankind—the problem which underlies all others, and is more deeply interesting than any other—is the ascertainment of the place which Man occupies in nature and of his relations to the universe of things."

"The universe of things" is that from which we arose and that upon which we will always depend. This is what humans have sought, and must continue to seek, to understand. Simpson, in his unmatched eloquence, crystallized Man's place in nature when he wrote the following: "In degree, man's social and intellectual complexity is something new under the sun, but man remains a part of nature and is still subject to all of nature's laws. Man is only one of earth's manifold living creatures, and he cannot understand his own nature or seek wisely to guide his destiny without taking account of the whole pattern of life."

Evoking a medieval woodcut, Flammarion's 19th-century artwork suggests Man's ageless curiosity about the universe, a characteristic of scientific culture. Earth—arena of biological and cultural evolution—faces grave threats to its very survival because of human cultural activity.

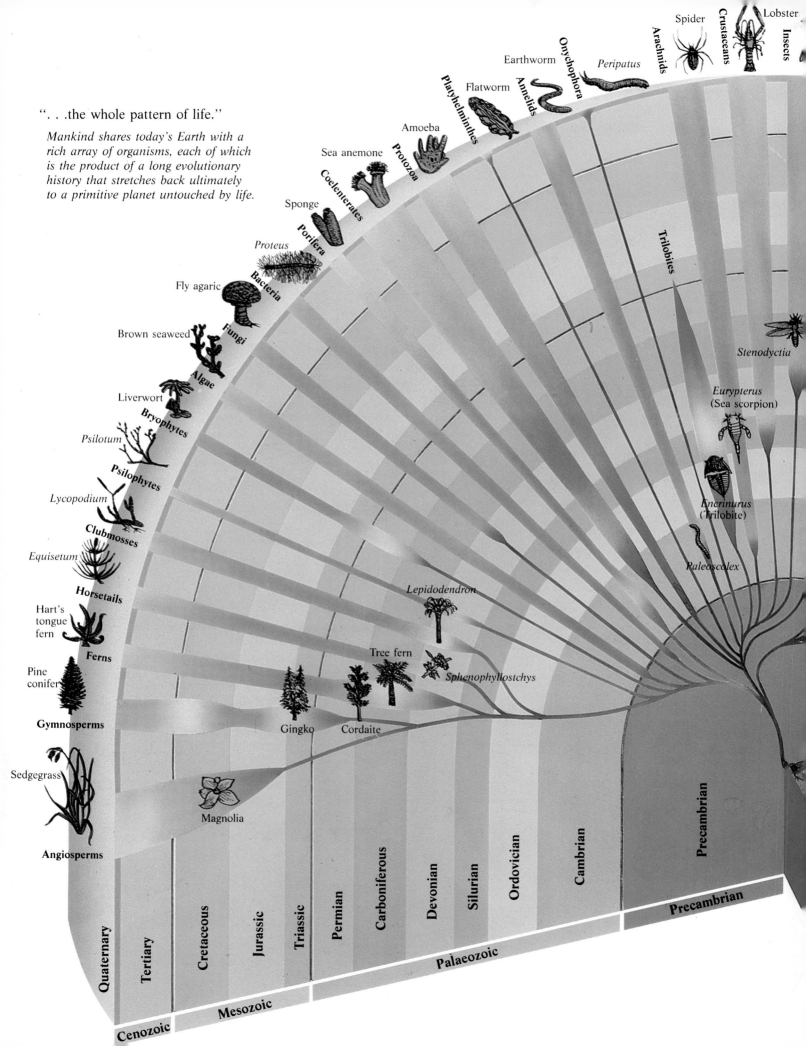

"...the whole pattern of life."

Mankind shares today's Earth with a rich array of organisms, each of which is the product of a long evolutionary history that stretches back ultimately to a primitive planet untouched by life.

Spider
Arachnids
Crustaceans
Lobster
Insects

Earthworm
Onychophora
Peripatus

Flatworm
Annelids
Platyhelminthes

Amoeba
Protozoa

Sea anemone
Coelenterates

Sponge
Porifera

Proteus
Bacteria

Fly agaric
Fungi

Brown seaweed
Algae

Liverwort
Bryophytes

Psilotum
Psilophytes

Lycopodium
Clubmosses

Equisetum
Horsetails

Hart's tongue fern
Ferns

Pine conifer
Gymnosperms

Sedgegrass
Angiosperms

Magnolia

Gingko
Cordaite
Tree fern
Sphenophyllostchys
Lepidodendron

Trilobites

Stenodyctia

Eurypterus
(Sea scorpion)

Encrinurus
(Trilobite)

Paleoscolex

Quaternary
Tertiary
Cretaceous
Jurassic
Triassic
Permian
Carboniferous
Devonian
Silurian
Ordovician
Cambrian
Precambrian

Precambrian

Palaeozoic

Mesozoic

Cenozoic

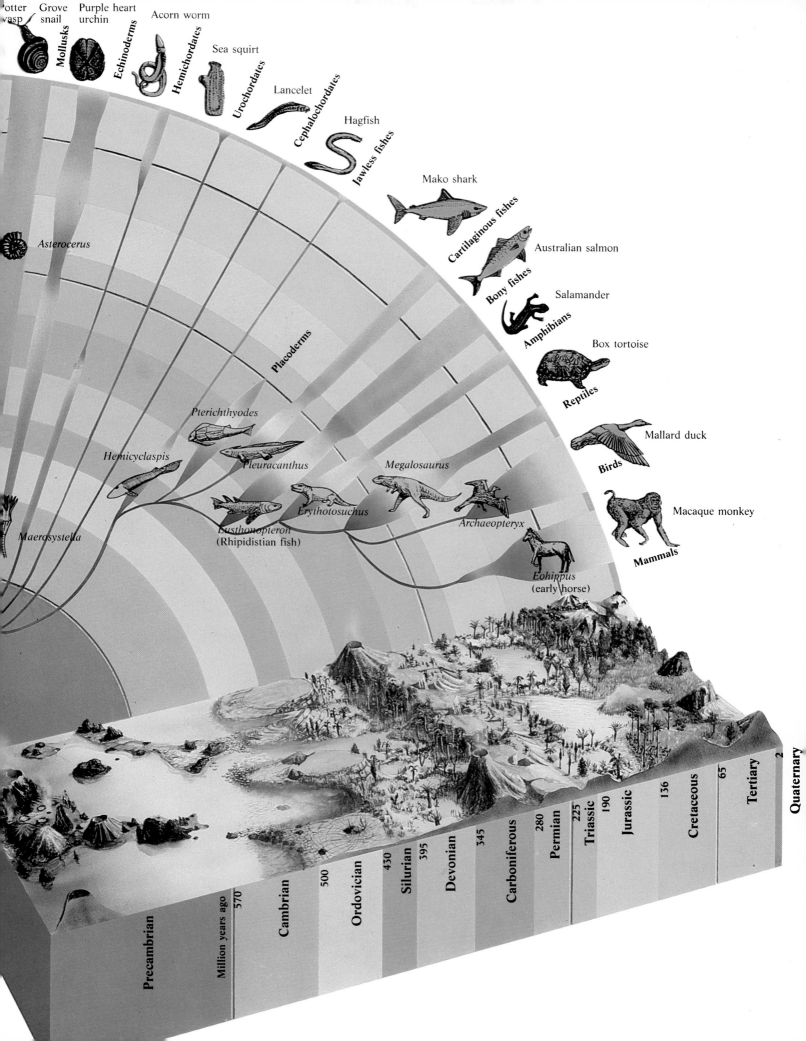

Otter wasp

Grove snail

Purple heart urchin

Mollusks

Echinoderms

Acorn worm

Hemichordates

Sea squirt

Urochordates

Lancelet

Cephalochordates

Hagfish

Jawless fishes

Mako shark

Cartilaginous fishes

Australian salmon

Bony fishes

Salamander

Amphibians

Box tortoise

Reptiles

Mallard duck

Birds

Macaque monkey

Mammals

Asterocerus

Placoderms

Pterichthyodes

Hemicyclaspis

Pleuracanthus

Megalosaurus

Erythotosuchus

Archaeopteryx

Maerosystella

Eusthonopteron
(Rhipidistian fish)

Eohippus
(early horse)

Precambrian

Million years ago 570

Cambrian

500

Ordovician

430

Silurian

395

Devonian

345

Carboniferous

280

Permian

225

Triassic

190

Jurassic

136

Cretaceous

65

Tertiary

2

Quaternary

INDEX

Illustration and caption references appear in *italics*.

PICTURE CREDITS

Jacket: Tom & Pat Leeson.

Back Flap: Chris Jones.

Front Matter: p. 1 Francisco Erize/Bruce Coleman Inc.; 2–3 Charles H. Phillips; 4–5 E.R. Degginger/Bruce Coleman Inc.; 8 (left) Zig Leszczynski/Animals Animals; (center) Tom McHugh/Photo Researchers, Inc.; (right) Jane Burton/Bruce Coleman Ltd.; 9 (left & center) Zig Leszczynski/Animals Animals; (right) Alan H. Blank/Photo Researchers, Inc.; 10–11 Howard Hall; 12 Kim Taylor/Bruce Coleman Inc.

Section I: p. 15 Luciano Bolzoni/Bruce Coleman Inc.; 16–17 David Muench; 18 K.C. DenDooven/K.C. Publications, Inc.; 19 J.C. Stevenson/Earth Scenes; 20 David Muench; 21 Bonnie Dalzell, Lynne Komai/Watermark Design; 22 (top) Kjell B. Sandved; (bottom) Dennis Serrette/Collections M.N.H.N. de Paris, courtesy DISCOVER Magazine; 23 (top) William Kier; (bottom) Bonnie Dalzell; 24–25 (top & bottom) Charles H. Phillips; 26–27 Nicholas de Vore III/Bruce Coleman Inc.; 27 (top) Allan Power/Bruce Coleman Inc.; (bottom) C. Allan Morgan; 28 Carol Hughes/Bruce Coleman Inc.; 29 (left) Jean-Paul Ferrero/Ardea, London; (right) Jack Donnelly/Woods Hole Oceanographic Institution; (bottom) Gary Ladd; 30 (top) Co Rentmeester/LIFE Magazine © 1970 Time Inc.; (bottom) John Shaw/Bruce Coleman Inc.; 31 M.P. Kahl; 32 Lynne Komai/Watermark Design; 33 Warren & Genny Garst/Tom Stack & Assocs.; 34 George Holton/Photo Researchers, Inc.; 35 Christopher Ralling; 36 Courtesy of Down House, The Royal College of Surgeons of England; 38–39 Philadelphia Museum of Art, bequest of Lisa Norris Elkins, (Mrs. William M. Elkins); 40–41 Jack Unruh; 42 (top) David Doubilet; (bottom) WWF/Udo Hirsch/Bruce Coleman Ltd.; 43 (top) Kjell B. Sandved; (bottom) John Running/Black Star; 44 Mike Busselle/BPCC/Aldus Archive; 45 Mark Kauffman/LIFE Magazine © 1958 Time Inc.; 46 By 'Goedecker'/John Freeman & Co. Ltd.; 46–47 Mark Kauffman/LIFE Magazine © Time Inc.; 48 Smithsonian Institution Libraries, photo by Charles H. Phillips; 49 By 'Ape' *Vanity Fair* 1869 & 1871, photos by Charles H. Phillips; 50 V.P. Weinland/Photo Researchers, Inc.; 50–51 S.R. Morris/Oxford Scientific Films; 51 Kjell B. Sandved; 52 Courtesy of Down House, The Royal College of Surgeons of England; 53 Mark Kauffman/LIFE Magazine © 1958 Time Inc.; 54, 55 (top) Peter Kain © Richard Leakey; 55 (bottom) Peter Beard; 56–57 Clem Haagner/Bruce Coleman Inc.; 57 (top) Robert W. Hernandez/Photo Researchers, Inc.; (bottom) Jeff Foott/Bruce Coleman Inc.; 58 Painting by H. Douglass Pratt, Bishop Museum, Honolulu; 59 Bonnie Dalzell; 61 Lisa Biganzoli © National Geographic Society; 62 (top) Jane Burton/Bruce Coleman Inc.; (bottom) © Walt Disney Productions; 63 (top) Animals Animals/Oxford Scientific Films; (bottom) Soames Summerhays/Photo Researchers, Inc.; 64–

65 Jack Unruh; 66 (top left) Douglas Faulkner/Photo Researchers, Inc.; (top right) Howard Hall; (bottom) J.A.L. Cooke/Oxford Scientific Films; 67 (top) Michael Philip Manheim/Photo Researchers, Inc.; (bottom) Tom Stack/Tom Stack & Assocs.; 68 Lynne Komai/Watermark Design 70 From *Horses:* by George Gaylord Simpson, © 1951 Oxford University Press, Inc., renewed 1979 by George Gaylord Simpson, reprinted by permission of the publisher; 71 L. West/Bruce Coleman Inc.; 72 Francisco Erize/Bruce Coleman Inc.; 73 (top) U.S. Navy Photo; (bottom) Gregory S. Paul; 74 (center) U.P.I.; (bottom) From *Die Entstehung der Kontinente und Ozeane:* by Alfred Wegener © 1920 Friedr. Vieweg & Sohn; 75 (top) The John Carter Brown Library, Brown University; (bottom) From *The Scientific Results from the Voyage of the Challenger, Vol. 1 1873–1876:* photo by Charles H. Phillips; 76 (left) Dr. Harold Simon/Tom Stack & Assocs.; (right) Georg Gerster/Photo Researchers, Inc.; 76–77 Jaime Quintero; 78 (top) Courtesy of Global Marine Drilling Company; 78–79 Jaime Quintero; 80 (top) David Muench; (bottom) Dewitt Jones/Woodfin Camp, Inc.; 81 Carol Hughes/Bruce Coleman Inc.; 82 Gregory S. Paul; 84 (top) Norman Myers/Bruce Coleman Inc.; (bottom) Jean-Paul Ferrero/Ardea, London; 85 Harald Sund.

Section II: p. 87 Soames Summerhays/Photo Researchers, Inc.; 88–89 Fred Bavendam/Peter Arnold, Inc.; 90 Charles H. Phillips; 91 Byron Crader/Tom Stack & Assocs.; 92–93 Jack Unruh; 95 (top & bottom) Robert W. Madden; (right) Victor Krantz/Smithsonian Institution; 96–97 Jack Unruh, adapted from photos by 96 (bottom) Schroeder/Eastwood, 97 (top left) Fritz Goro/THE EMERGENCE OF MAN—*The Neanderthals,* Time-Life Books © 1973 Time Inc., (top right) Charles H. Phillips, (center right) John Reader; 98 © A.C. Barrington Brown/Weidenfeld & Nicolson Archives; 98–99 Robert Langridge/UCSF, Dan McCoy/Rainbow; 100 David Attenborough; 101 David Doubilet © National Geographic Society; 102–103 Paul Chesley; 104 (top) Bonnie Dalzell; (center) Kim Taylor/Bruce Coleman Ltd.; (bottom & 105) Peter Parks/Oxford Scientific Films; 106 Dr. David Schwimmer/Bruce Coleman Inc.; 107 Smithsonian Institution Archives; 108 (top left) Simon Conway Morris; (bottom left & right) H.B. Whittington; 109 (top) Desmond Collins; (bottom) Jaime Quintero; 110–111 John Gurche; 112 (top) David Attenborough; (bottom) Jane Burton/Bruce Coleman Inc.; 112–113 Peter Parks/Oxford Scientific Films; 113 Kim Taylor/Bruce Coleman Ltd.; 114 (top) Fred Bavendam/Peter Arnold, Inc.; (bottom) Jeff Foott; 114–115 Kjell B. Sandved; 116 (top) James H. Carmichael/Bruce Coleman Inc.; (bottom) From *Kunstformen der Natur:* by Ernst Haeckel, 1904/Smithsonian Institution Libraries, photos by Charles H. Phillips; 117 (top) Douglas Faulkner/Photo Researchers, Inc.; (right) Chip Clark/Smithsonian Institution; 118 Townsend P. Dickinson/Photo Researchers, Inc.; 118–119 Bill Wood/Bruce Coleman Ltd.; 119 David Doubilet; 120 (top) G.I. Bernard/Oxford Scientific Films; (bottom) Tom

McHugh, Steinhart Aquarium/Photo Researchers, Inc.; 121 (top) Bonnie Dalzell; (bottom) Peter Parks/Oxford Scientific Films; 122–123 Chip Clark/Smithsonian Institution; 123 Howard Hall; 124 Leonard von Matt/Photo Researchers, Inc.; 125 Jeff Foott; 126 Jack Dermid/Bruce Coleman Inc.; 127 M.P.L. Fogden/Bruce Coleman Inc.; 128 Chip Clark; 129 (top) Frank M. Carpenter; (bottom) Tom Stack/Tom Stack & Assocs.; 130 Kim Taylor/Bruce Coleman Inc.; 130–131 Harry Ellis/Tom Stack & Assocs.; 131 John Gerlach/Animals Animals; 132 Stephen Dalton/Oxford Scientific Films; 133 Millard H. Sharp/Black Star; 134 W.H. Hodge/Peter Arnold, Inc.; 134–135 L. West/Bruce Coleman, Inc.; 135 W.H. Hodge/Peter Arnold, Inc.; 136 (top) Richard L. Carlton/Photo Researchers, Inc.; (bottom left) Charles Palek/Tom Stack & Assocs.; (bottom right) Bob & Clara Calhoun/Bruce Coleman Inc.; 139 (top) E.R. Degginger/Earth Scenes; (bottom) Leonard Lee Rue III/Photo Researchers, Inc.; (right) Patti Murray/Earth Scenes; 140 (top) Jonathan Blair/Woodfin Camp & Assocs.; (bottom) Zig Leszczynski/Animals Animals; 141 J.A.L. Cooke/Oxford Scientific Films; 142 Chip Clark; 143 Adapted from *The Evolution of Life:* by David John & Richard Moody, publisher U.S., Silver-Burdett, © 1980 Macdonald Educational Ltd.; 144 John Markham/Bruce Coleman Inc.; 145 From *Vertebrate Paleontology:* by Alfred Sherwood Romer, reprinted by permission of The University of Chicago Press, © 1933, 1945 & 1966 The University of Chicago.

Section III: p. 147 Jean-Paul Ferrero/Ardea, London; 148–149 Robert Gillmor/Bruce Coleman Ltd.; 150 British Museum (Natural History); 151 Charles H. Phillips; 152 A. Blank/Bruce Coleman Inc.; 153 Pamela J. Harper; 154–155 Gregory S. Paul; 156 (top) Gregory S. Paul; (bottom) Chip Clark; 157 Roland T. Bird, courtesy of American Museum of Natural History; 158 (top) Chip Clark; (bottom) Jim Dockal/U.S.D.I., National Park Service; 158–159 Jerry Freilich/U.S.D.I., National Park Service; 159 Michael Lawton; 160 (top) Smithsonian Institution; (bottom) Carrie Padgett; 161 Adolf Schaller, painting reproduced by permission, *Astronomy* Magazine; 162 Leo J. Hickey; 163 (top) Edward Davidson/Smithsonian Institution; (bottom) Lynne Komai/Watermark Design; 164 Eleanor M. Kish, courtesy of National Museum of Natural Sciences, National Museums of Canada, photo by Susanne M. Swibold; 165 Chip Clark; 166 Bob & Clara Calhoun/Bruce Coleman Inc.; 167 (top) Godfrey Merlen/Oxford Scientific Films; (bottom) Jen & Des Bartlett/Bruce Coleman Inc.; 168 (top) Kjell B. Sandved; (bottom) Dale & Marian Zimmerman/Bruce Coleman Inc.; 169 (top & right) Zig Leszczynski/Animals Animals; (left) J. Alsop/Bruce Coleman Inc.; 170 E.R. Degginger/Earth Scenes; 171 (left) O.C. Marsh, reproduced from *Vertebrate Paleontology:* by Alfred Sherwood Romer, The University of Chicago Press; (right) Chip Clark; 172–173 John Gurche; 174 (top) John H. Ostrom; (bottom) Neg. 218171, American Museum of National History, reproduced from *Vertebrate Paleontology:* by

255

Alfred Sherwood Romer, The University of Chicago Press; 175 (top left) John H. Ostrom; (top right) Lois & Louis Darling; (bottom) Andreas Feininger/LIFE Magazine © 1951 Time Inc.; 176 Tui de Roy/Bruce Coleman Inc.; 176–177 Stephen Dalton/Photo Researchers, Inc.; 177 Roger Tory Peterson/Photo Researchers, Inc.; 178 Robert W. Hernandez/Photo Researchers, Inc.; 179 (left) M. Philip Kahl; (right) Glenn Van Nimwegen; (bottom) Bruce A. Macdonald/Animals Animals; 180 Peter Ward/Bruce Coleman Inc.; 180–181 Merlin Tuttle; 181 Merlin Tuttle/Photo Researchers, Inc.; 182 M.P. Kahl; 183 James H. Carmichael/Bruce Coleman Inc.; 184 Henry B. Beville; 185 Thomas Nebbia/Woodfin Camp & Assocs.; 186 (top) Fritz Goro/THE EMERGENCE OF MAN—*Life Before Man:* Time-Life Books © 1972 Time Inc.; (bottom) Bonnie Dalzell; 187 Chip Clark/Smithsonian Institution; 188 (top) C.B. Frith/Bruce Coleman Inc.; (center) Al Giddings/Ocean Films, Ltd.; (bottom) Tom McHugh/Photo Researchers, Inc.; 189 (left) Co Rentmeester/LIFE Magazine © Time Inc.; (right) Stan Wayman/Photo Researchers, Inc.; 190 (left) Animals Animals/Oxford Scientific Films; (right) Jean-Paul Ferrero/Ardea, London; 191 (left) Mitch Reardon/Photo Researchers, Inc.; (right) Leonard Lee Rue III/Bruce Coleman Inc.; 192–193 M.P.L. Fogden/Bruce Coleman Inc.; 193 James Joern/Bruce Coleman Inc.; 194 (left) Jack Unruh, adapted from *Biology:* by Donald D. Ritchie & Robert Carola © 1979 Addison-Wesley, Reading, MA, Fig. 15.22, reprinted by permission; (right) David Hiser/Photo Researchers, Inc.; 195 (left) Jack Dermid/Bruce Coleman Inc.; (right) Jack Unruh, adapted from *Biology* 3rd ed.: by Willis H. Johnson, Richard A. Laubengayer, Louis E. DeLanney & Thomas A. Cole © 1966 Holt Rinehart & Winston, Inc., reprinted by permission of CBS College publishing; 196 (left) Richard Dranitzke/Photo Researchers, Inc.; (right) Kim Taylor/Bruce Coleman Inc.; 197 (left) Nina Leen/LIFE Magazine © Time Inc.; (right) Robert P. Carr/Bruce Coleman Inc.; 198 James P. Ferrigno/Smithsonian Institution; 198–199 Raymond L. Nelson/National Audubon Society/Photo Researchers, Inc.; 199 L. West/Bruce Coleman Inc.; 200 (top) Carlo Bavagnoli/LIFE Magazine © Time Inc.; (bottom) J.A.L. Cooke/Oxford Scientific Films; 201 Frank M. Carpenter; 202–203, 204–205, 206–207, 208–209, Murals by Jay H. Matternes, photos by Victor R. Boswell Jr. © National Geographic Society; 210–211, 212–213, Murals by Jay H. Matternes, photos by Chip Clark/Smithsonian Institution.

Section IV: p. 215 B. Crader/Tom Stack & Assocs.; 216–217 J. Messerschmidt/Bruce Coleman Inc.; 218 Tim D. White; 219 From *Missing Links:* by John Reader © 1981; 220 Lynne Komai/Watermark Design; 221 (top left) Nick Nichols/Woodfin Camp & Assocs.; (top right) M.P.L. Fogden/Bruce Coleman Inc.; (bottom) Norman Tomalin/Bruce Coleman Ltd.; 222 (top) Lynne Komai/Watermark Design; (left) Roger Lewin; (right) David L. Brill © National Geographic Society; 223 Drawings by Luba Dmytryk Gudz from *LUCY—The*

Beginnings of Humankind: © 1981 Donald Johanson & Maitland Edey; 224, 225, 226 (left) From: *Missing Links:* by John Reader © 1981; (right), 227 (left) Peter Kain © Richard Leakey; (right) John Reader; 228 Peter Kain © Richard Leakey; 228–229 Lynne Komai/Watermark Design; 229 John Reader; 230 (top & bottom left) Michael Holford; (right) Peter Kain © Richard Leakey; 231 (top & bottom left) Pat Shipman & Richard Potts; (right) Roger Lewin; 232 Simon Trevor/Bruce Coleman Inc.; 233 George Holton/Photo Researchers, Inc.; 234 (top) Sandak Inc.; (bottom & 235) Peter Kain © Richard Leakey; 236 Sepp Seitz/Woodfin Camp, Inc.; 237 Scotty Casteel/Freelance Photographers Guild; 238 (top) Warren & Genny Garst/Tom Stack & Assocs.; (bottom) Fred J. Maroon; 239 (top) Kenneth Pellman/The People's Place; (bottom) Momatiuk-Eastcott/Woodfin Camp & Assocs.; 240 (left) Peter Kain © Richard Leakey; (right) National Gallery of Art, Washington D.C., Andrew W. Mellon Collection; 241 Fred J. Maroon; 242 (top) Michael Holford; (bottom) Founders Society Purchase, Edsel B. Ford Fund, gift of Edsel B. Ford, courtesy of The Detroit Institute of Art; 243 NASA; 244 Michael Holford; 244–245 Fred J. Maroon; 245 Joel Landau/U.P.I.; 246 Kay Chernush; 246–247 John Zimmerman/Alpha; 247 William Strode/Woodfin Camp, Inc.; 248 The Bettman Archive Inc.; 249 NASA; 250–251 Artwork by permission of Grisewood & Dempsey Ltd. London. Extract from *The Story of Evolution:* by Ron Taylor © 1980.

This book was typeset in Life Simoncini by York Custom Graphics, York, Pennsylvania. Color separations were furnished by The Lanman Companies. It is printed on 70 lb. Westvaco Sterling Web Dull, and bound in Holliston Zeppelin cloth by Holladay-Tyler Printing Corporation, Rockville, Maryland.